Prayer as Memory

Princeton Theological Monograph Series

K. C. Hanson, Charles M. Collier, D. Christopher Spinks,
Robin Parry, and Rodney Clapp, Series Editors

Recent volumes in the series:

Nico Vorster
Created in the Image of God:
Understanding God's Relationship with Humanity

Susan Marie Smith
Christian Ritualizing and the Baptismal Process:
Liturgical Explorations toward a Realized Baptismal Ecclesiology

James L. Papandrea
Novatian of Rome and the Culmination of Pre-Nicene Orthodoxy

Aliou Cissé Niang
Text, Image, and Christians in the Graeco-Roman World:
A Festschrift in Honor of David Lee Balch

Sara M. Koenig
Isn't This Bathsheba?: A Study in Characterization

Gale Heide
Timeless Truth in the Hands of History:
A Short History of System in Theology

Koo Dong Yun
The Holy Spirit and Ch'i (Qi):
A Chiological Approach to Pneumatology

Stanley S. MacLean
Resurrection, Apocalypse, and the Kingdom of Christ:
The Eschatology of Thomas F. Torrance

Prayer as Memory

Toward the Comparative Study of Prayer
as Apocalyptic Language and Thought

DAVID REINHART

PICKWICK *Publications* · Eugene, Oregon

PRAYER AS MEMORY
Toward the Comparative Study of Prayer as Apocalyptic Language and Thought

Princeton Theological Monograph Series 186

Copyright © 2012 David Reinhart. All rights reserved. Except for brief quotations in critical publications or reviews, no part of this book may be reproduced in any manner without prior written permission from the publisher. Write: Permissions, Wipf and Stock Publishers, 199 W. 8th Ave., Suite 3, Eugene, OR 97401.

Pickwick Publications
An Imprint of Wipf and Stock Publishers
199 W. 8th Ave., Suite 3
Eugene, OR 97401

www.wipfandstock.com

ISBN 13: 978-1-61097-191-1

Cataloging-in-Publication data:

Reinhart, David.

  Prayer as memory : toward the comparative study of prayer as apocalyptic language and thought / David Reinhart.

  x + 200 pp. ; 23 cm. — Includes bibliographical references and index.

  Princeton Theological Monograph Series 186

  ISBN 13: 978-1-61097-191-1

  1. Prayer. 2. Barth, Karl, 1886–1968. 3. Habermas, Hans Joachim, 1925–. 4. Derrida, Jacques. 5. Ricoeur, Paul. I. Title. II. Series.

BX4827 R315 2012

Manufactured in the U.S.A.

For Family

Contents

Acknowledgments

THERE ARE MANY CONVERSATIONS that a person has with others—gifts throughout a lifetime. Some are short and some long—some are ongoing and some end abruptly—some are full of laughter and some full of tears. But I go away from conversation often thinking about how others teach me a variety of things. And like waves from the ocean our conversations never stop impacting—even in later silence. So most of all I wish to thank Elisa Brandt, whose husband I try to be, for being there in all circumstances. She sees me at my best and at my worst and yet continues to amaze with her seemingly bottomless well of love. I also want to thank my parents, Larry and Loretta Reinhart, educators, whose dedication is my constant example. There are countless friends and colleagues who honor me with their criticisms and advice. Some are memories from childhood and growing-up times. Some are at University of Wisconsin—Whitewater, like Wade and Dick, and many others who give their perspective as well as knowledge. Some of my friends are scattered around the world, like Jens-Christian, Valdas, Luis, best-men who are all teachers as well. I also wish to say thank you to Robin my editor who corresponds always with a smile in his words. To all these people and countless others, for all our conversation—thank you.

"O Lord, remember not only the men and women of good will, but also those of ill will. But do not remember all the suffering they have inflicted on us; remember the fruits we have bought, thanks to this suffering—our comradeship, our loyalty, our humility, our courage, our generosity, the greatness of heart that has grown out of all of this, and when they come to judgment let all the fruits we have born be their forgiveness. Amen."

—Reported prayer by an unknown prisoner in Ravensbrück concentration camp at the end of World War II, written on a scrap of paper and left on the body of a dead child.

Introduction

PRAYER IS AT ONCE THE MOST BASIC FORM OF RELIGIOUS PRACTICE AND also the basic form of religious imagination. If religion itself has a birth date it is the day prayer was first given breath: uttered at the moment human consciousness first imagined an entity, deity, or when consciousness was first produced. Regardless of the specifics of this theoretical *Urspruch*—the original prayer is the origin of religion and also the practice of religion today continues by prayer. So when I think of all the various beliefs about the sacred, including gods, one God, or kami, with different accounts of creation and history, different values, norms, and social agenda, then I recognize that each specific prayer is both an expression and a description of each religious tradition. So not only do all religions practice prayer but also prayer remains a summation of each theological or critical theory of the sacred. Prayer touches on all levels of the myth-ritual-praxis complex often called religion. Prayer is unavoidably theological in the sense that the words, "Oh, God" are unutterable outside some conception of God, be it Hindu Truth, Christian Trinity, Shinto kami, or whatever. Thus prayer is a unique form of discourse that is at once the most basic religious practice and also a summation of one's real theology at the moment.

So questions and reflections regarding prayer bridge two distinct fields or modern disciplines, Religious Studies and Theological Studies. If Religious Studies is primarily the social scientific description of what happens within particular religions, a view as if from nowhere, it is only the start of a description. Legitimacy is lost in Religious Studies when the theorist moves beyond methods of description, or tries to draw universally transferable conclusions. Systematic theology, on the other hand, is an imaginative conceptualization of God or ultimate reality and designed to test the coherence of doctrines. Legitimacy in systematic theology is seen in the light of how universally transferable conclusions relate to normative claims. The structure of these two disciplines, specialized products of post-enlightenment criticism, makes it difficult to mix or even have an exchange. But much of prayer performs upon the overlap of these two fields of study. Consequently I would propose that aspects of prayer are either misunderstood or missed entirely by academic specialists. Yet whether practiced or reflected upon, prayer epitomizes the intersection of these two fields.

This book explores the premise that prayer is not adequately understood as a public discourse today (nor even as a theological practice) until its dynamic connection with memory is described. It is more and more evident that prayer is a form of discourse that demands our critical attention. The world continues to shrink: a pastor of a tiny church in Florida can have an impact on the world political scene like never before. Or when a place of prayer is proposed within blocks of the former World Trade Center, it becomes difficult to assess the proposal in a rational way. Simple prayers that are intended as sincere acts of devotion are sometimes heard as a challenge from another continent or another religion. It becomes more important than ever to understand the sameness of prayers and discuss how particular prayers participate in a shared experience and are not a threat.

I propose that prayer without theological imagination becomes an economization of religion; that is, religion as fetish, or a performance commodity exchanged only under proper rules of procedure. On the other hand, prayer less practiced becomes theologized and thus less relevant to the present. Economized prayer is where good will is purchased in exchange for one's life, or proper living. When the practice of prayer is hostile to theology then it often becomes stifling to free thinking or independent growth, as one sees in brands of sectarianism. And strictly theologized prayer can often put ideas above people. I would say that the former can become a religion of proper behavior while the latter tends to be a religion of abstraction. Neither type is entirely wrong except when they become closed to each other. Then I would call prayer a dysfunctional element within public discourse.

In this book, I try to distinguish the "ineffable" from the naming of an Abrahamic God. By sometimes altering the spelling to G*d, I try to distinguish an unnamable—an ineffability of the divine—from the itterability of a traditional name.

The measure of the functionality of prayer, the discourse with G*d, is often its honest hearing as well as speaking. Since prayer is a discursive relationship between oneself and the sacred object, or truth, or G*d, it is always contextualized within the norms, values, and facts of one's life where nothing is inadmissible or hidden; everything is potentially criticizable. If prayer can be an open conversation where nothing is off limits then it can also be an opening of religion to the extent that it includes hearing as well as speaking. Religion without such prayer closes itself off to others and becomes banal, lacking any freshness. A banal identity and a banal relation to G*d and others is sealed—closed off to the extent questioning of one's ideals and relations are no longer matters for consideration. Henri Nouwen summarizes well the non-banal form of prayer in the following sentences. "When you pray, you discover not only yourself and God, but also your neighbor. For in prayer, you profess not only that people are people and God is God, but also that your neighbor is your sister or brother living along side you."[1] Much depends on the word *profess* here, but it is sufficient to say for now that a profession should be an open declaration which remains questionable. For example, an un-criticizable *profession* of belief would be only a banal assertion.

Prayer functions in everyday life when both behavior and ideas are questionable and open to each other. While the protection of an idea as unquestionable is ideology, and unquestionable behaviors close prayer to others, one cannot be daily fed or informed by such self-contained prayer. Prayer that either is a commodity within an economy of behavior or prayer which is idealized within a utopian system is not finally a functional prayer because it closes some aspect of life off from G*d. Banal or false prayer is a closure of reality to anything more than one already knows—it is the sacrifice of the religious impulse. But when one's behavior is questioned from outside the immediate economy of meaning, such prayer breaks the cycle of parochialism and mutual admiration that so often codifies proper behavior. Likewise when theological concepts—no matter how logical or coherent—are prayerfully applied in everyday living, then their real value is discovered.

If one observes traditionally called "low" and "high" church settings, one can characterize these two tendencies in the prayers of the community. Where "low" church encourages everyone to pray aloud simultaneously, and therefore to participate by one's behavior, often without much reflection, "high" church encourages theological and thought-out words in prayer, to the extent that written prayers are prized over spontaneous prayer, and often one leader is chosen to speak the prayer clearly which

1. Nouwen, *With Open Hands,* 86.

encourages participation to take a more cerebral quality. But for prayer to function as prayer, and not as a way to re-enforce social norms or mores, then both elements must coincide. In prayer, life behaviors are questioned from a non-parochial and a most deep reflective manner; but also, theological concepts are integrated into the everyday and common issues of life. Only when both approaches are included in the study of prayer can an economy of meaning and/or an ideology of faith both be accessible to criticism.

One must pray without knowing how to pray and without ceasing to pray. Prayer then is discourse that is both deconstruction and rationality; it is discourse that operates in the world but is not operatively of the world. It is a practice that has no particular or correct understanding of itself. I would say that prayer is understood as prayer only as falling from the air—like the story of manna—to borrow a metaphor. It cannot be finally distilled or made a commodity to save, buy, or sell. Yet, prayer *feeds* one everyday, it sustains one by being eaten. Prayer can thus be described as a rational discourse insofar as it is spoken from a certain understanding and from a certain belief—but without making this certain understanding the understanding for all time. I would say that responsible prayer is said within a tradition or scheme of belief, but not said within a Tradition. The outcome of prayer remains unforeseeable, indeterminable; in this way prayer is spoken rationally in faith, as primarily risky words that pray for an answer. In sum, prayer is prayer when it ceases to be either a proper practice or an ideal speech.

Prayer then is fundamentally a complete vulnerability to an ultimate or divine reality. The person of prayer bows both head and body, mind and heart. This is why theology without prayer is an ideology, while religious practice without prayer is a closed economy of exchange, even superstition. Both are closures of history and life, which pre-determine outcomes and make prayer less necessary.

So the questions posed in this book can be simply stated. How does prayer function as a social discourse? Does prayer question religious descriptions of salvation? How does prayer become ideological—becoming satisfied that it has the final answer and therefore proselytic toward other religions? To begin answering these questions, this book reflects upon prayer as an action and as a unique form of listening. Prayer is *both pietism and quietism.* These terms are not to be understood in relation to a feeling or affectation but in relation to the orientation of an intersubjective discourse to action and/or listening for meaning. Taking some meaning from the seventeenth-century religious movements within Christianity, my generalized point is to characterize current attitudes toward language and their relation to prayer. *Piety* is the virtue of character that acknowledges a dependence upon appropriate structures and strives toward a more exemplary form of practice, sometimes based in tradition or sometimes a commitment to reason itself. *Quietude* is the virtue of character that is based upon an indescribable or wordless source often by means of mystical meditation. Pietism and quietism are both part of prayer; they make it capable of orienting communication by privileging either the act of speaking or silence in listening to being.

Religion scholars have become more aware of the need for "subject positioning" and of finding ones blind spots, interests, and assumptions. The view that good will triumph proves to be a short step away from identifying oneself as the instrument of memory, progress, and inevitable triumph. We are quick to neatly place ourselves on the side of the tortured rather than remembering the ways that we are more like the torturers. This makes clear the importance of studying prayer as a site of commemoration; it is a discourse of memory that operates out of sight of historians but, for religion scholars, becomes the lens through which everything is seen.

For the religious person, prayer is so authoritative that the prayer is sometimes used as a symbol. It performs symbolically, and not a critical perspective, when it is a means by which shared behaviors and meanings become normalized within a certain group. The norms and mores communicated provide a link between the devotees of the prayer and the original sufferers within the narrative—what some call the *community of suffering*. And what prayer is not fundamentally an expression of some suffering? Aren't prayers necessary because of a separation between what *is* and what *ought to be*? Prayer comes from a rupture between the created and the Creator, the profane and the sacred. It is what Jean-Louis Chrétien calls a "wounded word." But what is done with this wounded word is also to the point. The same prayer remembers differently by a variety of subtleties. If it is possible to develop what Alphonse Dupront calls a "palette of the soul's exigencies" through simple observations, then I find it helpful to ask how the sacral is seen within the cosmogony of the prayer. A sacral vision has as much to do with the context and outcomes as it does with the ideas of the sacred within the text. The ideas may not even be operative in a given moment. Possible questions that result from these observations include the following.

- Does the particular use or re-use of the prayer define or utilize norms and mores? And if so, does this use function to inhibit or close questioning or criticism in any way?

- Does the wound of prayer generally contribute to the act of questioning the sacred?

- Does the prayer's implied cosmogony leave room to consider one's own culpability rather than evade the questions of conscience?

- Is the prayer more an act of talking *about* God rather than talking *to* God?[2]

In the first chapter, I discuss the problem of prayer's transparency. Prayer is perceived as inscrutable by some and as an indispensible meta-narrative by others. A third alternative is the reconsideration of prayer's relation to collective memory. The study of prayer as memory provides a perspective on prayer's social significance that also makes space for the secret aspects of a personal discourse of faith. I suggest that prayer involves not only how to remember but always also how to forget and is thus capable of the pathogenic effects of conscience. This is not a criticism that religious adherents should shirk or toss aside. It relates to the problem of eschatological structuring of discourse and the teleological suspension of the ethical within much of monotheism.

In the second chapter, I introduce a positioning that is observable in prayers. Given that a cosmogony is at least implied in each prayer, then the prayer is speaking within a normative discourse. This becomes an unsolvable problem for any universally critical perspective, and an open

2. Here I am thinking of Elie Wiesel's quotation of Kafka, who says he could not speak about G*d but only "to" G*d. Prayers are more appropriately used as the latter and may be studied to this effect. Ultimately, if one is speaking to G*d then there is always still an opening, something to change judgment, change justice, change everything. Wiesel says that this enables him to be angry with G*d and to even revolt against G*d even as one does with a friend, "I can argue fiercely with a friend, which does not mean that I reject his friendship." Here, questions of theodicy can be discussed with G*d in solidarity or assurance.

question for any faith perspective. So, to open the discourse about prayer I propose a conceptual framework that will enable a comparative study of prayer. The goal of this is to begin to understand prayer as a language of brokenness, suffering, and fragmentation. The categories developed in this chapter are an attempt to discuss the proximity between suffering and prayer. When too close to suffering or even utter brokenness, then prayer is not possible. For most, only the deepest silence seems appropriate. As distance from suffering is created, then a systemization of prayer develops.

In the third chapter, I propose that prayer is an apocalyptical discourse. This begins with Karl Barth's description of apocalyptic and his subsequent use of prayer as a method for theology. Prayer is like an apocalyptical speech-act insofar as this means a given ability of prayer to question both a brokenness of existence and one's sense of something beyond this brokenness; prayer questions all inter-subjective norms from both perspectives of brokenness and its beyond.

Moving from Barth's theological framing of prayer to philosophical theories of language, notably those of Jürgen Habermas and Jacques Derrida, two chapters enter a debate between current philosophical descriptions of discourse. I then discern the issues that arise from the description of prayer's place within these approaches. My argument in these chapters is that prayer and its relation to discourse is not completely or adequately understood either by performative theory nor as deconstruction: but both make important contributions to the understanding of prayer as piety and quietude.

Jürgen Habermas describes three distinct spheres of discourse and questions how self-expressive language relates to language directed to things in the world; how truths relate to rules of seeking the True; how one sphere of questioning can ask about perspectives on self while another asks about social systems. But also how these spheres of discourse need to be left in a creative tension with one another to allow for a norming of cooperation. The theory of communicative action that revolves around these three distinct types of validity claims is narrated in *The Philosophical Discourse of Modernity*. Do these lectures on the unfolding of critical discourse in modernity, amount to a narrative of exemplary existence?

I question Habermas in the light of Ricoeur's description of narrative, so that any historical account of the opening of philosophical discourse is itself questioned with regard to its confusion of faith with history. More explicitly, does Habermas turn away needlessly from an imagination that hinges upon the shared inter-subjective rules of a narrated existence? I will investigate his argument that cultural norms of society are not set aside in discourse where cooperative efforts are desirable. In Ricoeur's terms, sameness (*idem*) and selfhood (*ipse*) are sometimes confused by a modern rationality. Habermas argues that modernity can make these spheres more distinct when it respects the processes by which norms are criticized and accepted in an inter-subjective communication. Thus, he describes this general position as post-metaphysical thinking. I will characterize his attitude as a *piety* of mutual discourse. And I will affirm this point as helpful to a pious prayer in agreement with his views about the damaged life and truth as an unfinished project. However, one finds that piety alone as the basis of action is insufficient to a grounding of an inter-subjective discourse.

One hears Jacques Derrida's criticism that a discourse can sometimes diminish moral autonomy or alterity. He argues that the inter-subjective question of the relation between one-and-the-other and also each tradition's "familial" transcendence is to be left unanswered, like an eschatological reserve or what he calls a "messianicity" within messianism. Derrida raises the issue of how the address of the other, which takes place within structures of language, is able to present transcendence. His call for an opening of metaphysics within language is in opposition to Habermas' post-metaphysical thinking. I will characterize this general position as one of *quietism*, as opposed to piety, where the authenticity of communication is measured in terms of listening to the other, even in tears.

The courage to pray is associated with the failure to remember suffering—to too quickly resort to argumentation rather than standing in solidarity with the suffering. Johann Baptist Metz describes prayer as a questioning of God operative within the narrativity of life that informs and sustains critical and constructive tensions. For example, he views religious orders as a form of social criticism, or, in other words, a place for social-spiritual experimentation that works toward stated ends of rightness, values, and justice. This brings into relief a problematic issue facing any religious community attempting to exercise criticism: that is, the timing of its destructive and constructive modes. When is a religious coordination to be accepting of the world and when does it exclude itself

from the world? Or put another way, what is the relation of a public practice of prayer and a singular performance of prayer that stands alone?
The answer comes in an everyday life that considers how our limited
conceptions of G*d are always already part of memory.

This leads one to a reflection upon the "way prayer happens" in
general. Religion is a practice of prayer and different religions may be
distinguished culturally by their peculiarities of prayer. Thus, prayer is an
essential concern to any internal or external understanding of religion.
In other words, prayer is not arbitrarily separable from either external or
internal, public or private, exoteric or esoteric, perspectives on religion.
Prayer is already an admission of a transcendent unity from within the
damaged life and its fragmentation. More commonly experienced, when
a congregation in worship prays to G*d, it prays both as individuals and
as a community. This amounts to a negotiation of cultural plurality.

A description of prayer's opening allows a consideration of prayer's
constant flexibility between a private and public language. It is my hope
to understand the function of prayer as this flexibility. To understand the
dynamics of prayer and its potential for bringing hope to the hopeless,
power to the powerless, makes it uniquely suited to address suffering
from within. Prayer is the original liberation theology and as such is the
source of all religion.

Throughout, the argument is essentially that even if language is
agonic or always enmeshed within decisions of power, as Derrida and
many others insist, this does not necessarily detract from a pursuit of
non-coercive communication. Rules for verification of knowledge and
coordination of action may be developed by all participants, as Habermas
insists. I propose that the criticism of prayer be developed by considering the effects of an operative concept of G*d upon the distinct pursuits
of knowledge.

I argue that by questioning G*d in prayer, one is able to question
the status of memory more effectively. Prayer can be an interruption of
history and time. This is an apocalyptical discourse that engages one's
piety as well as a capacity for quietude. Insofar as one speaks from a
formal structure inherent to a language of signs and also to the other
beyond each structure's own end this study of prayer is reasonable. Thus
prayer is a discourse about the relation between all the known ends and
the unknown end, between all unjustified deaths and a final day of judgment. The maieutic function of this discourse is to open a space within

language for true listening and exchange—for a language beyond *pietism* or *quietism*.

My concluding proposal is to study the relation of prayer and discourse within an apocalyptical framing of language. In this way prayer can open flat linear accounts of history by questioning them from within, especially with respect to their end. This is prayer that has the character of what Ricoeur calls the pastoral act. "I can be open to the story, the history of others, each of whom is in question as a self. Then the question arises of my participation in the stories and histories of others, which themselves are open/closed stories/histories . . . Is not this kind of mutual exchange and mutual aid in the dialectic of openness and closure the essence of the pastoral act?"[3] I would call this a type collegiality with others inseparable from their histories, surrendering authority by partially acting as a character in a larger plot shared with others but also as a responsible author of one's own story.

Perhaps speaking with G*d cannot be separated from listening to others. When one refuses to listen then prayer becomes a monologue, a speaking *at* G*d, an existential dead end. For example when one says "God bless America," this oft spoken phrase is rarely uttered as a prayer that questions but more like an announcement, a declaration of fealty to a certain America, rather than a questioning that might include other Americas: South, Latin, or the diverse experiences of America. Might one say that it is more like a prayer if it listens carefully to how others experience the word "America" and then questions its meaning as heard by others, even as it is heard by the deity referenced?

---

3. Ricoeur, *Figuring the Sacred*, 313–14.

1

Coming to Prayer

The Problem of Prayer

CREDIT CARD COMPANIES AND OTHER FINANCIAL CORPORATIONS ARE becoming infamous for a practice called "black box accounting." Enron Corporation rose to its height hiding its calculations and then fell disastrously when outside observers finally recognized that everything did not add up. Yet many financial institutions still use these same methods that are not regulated. "Black box" refers to a company's central accounting that is not transparent to external observers. Critics of black box accounting say that if there is no access to these hidden methods and calculations then the public is not treated with fairness. Not only is it difficult to verify or know the truth of the calculations, also there is little way to know whether decisions are arbitrary or consistently applied to all. This lack of transparency gives rise to the name "black box."

Please excuse me for beginning with an obscure analogy, but here it goes. Prayer is the black box of religion. Prayer is foundational to religion. It is at the core of religious experience, thought, and decision-making. Within each prayer there is already a basic algorithm at work that relates the sacred to profane everyday existence. Prayer is like the black box of religion because it is a problem to anyone who wishes from the outside to know or critically evaluate the religious decision. Whether there is any other way to pray is uncertain, maybe all prayer is obfuscation or maybe not. I merely want to point out general problem for now and ask the question, "Can the language of prayer be understandable to others?"

The issue I am raising is the relation between religious experience and it's object. Succinctly stated, what is religious experience an experience of? How can religious experience be subsequently applied in an inter-subjective decision? This is an especially difficult and important question for the Abrahamic religions that affirm a transcendent G*d, all holy and all loving. The experience of G*d within these traditions is traditionally described as "revelation"; an in-coming, a breaking into, an overlapping between the sacred and profane that occurs as that which is complete(d) gift. This providence, from a wholly Other, can only be expressed as a reduction or symbolization of G*d's gift. This is the observation, expressed by Wolfhart Pannenberg, that all that is called revelation is *indirect* revelation; Pannenberg then needs to speak to the breadth of history as a *proleptic* truth. Within this type of monotheism a decision of faith is always unavoidable, or one could say the providence of the place of faith is always either acknowledged or ignored. But regardless of all this providence, there is a persistent problem that is never settled regarding whether and how the invisible may (not) be reduced or symbolized visibly. This can lead to many forms of moralism, for instance among the most militant fundamentalists who set out to destroy all "strange" symbolizations of the sacred.

The problem is illustrated in the broad logic of twentieth century phenomenology of religions. On one hand, transcendental experience is seen as a reflection if not a proof of a larger transcendence. (See, for instance, by Karl Rahner.[1]) On the other hand, this may lead to the further step that if an Other is assumed or even named, then the person who names the Other is more original than G*d; this is an audacious act by any standard.[2] I am asking a similar question as Jan Assmann; whether secondary religions of revelation that yet depend upon an earlier worldview or their primary religions, are either enhancements or corruptions. How would one begin to think about this relation? So while a transcendental approaches to religion begins with the limit of what humanity can know and recognizes a relation to an experience of the limit, the

1. "In the ultimate depths of his being man knows nothing more surely than that his knowledge, that is what is called knowledge in everyday parlance, is only a small island in a vast sea that has not been traveled. It is a floating island, and it might be more familiar to us than the sea, but ultimately it is borne by the sea and only because it is can we be borne by it." Rahner, *Foundations*, 22.

2. This is an early theme in Ricoeur's work that is reinforced by Rudolf Otto who is credited by Ricoeur. "Can a hermeneutic of proclamation extricate itself from a phenomenology of the sacred? . . . The sacred is experienced as awesome, as powerful, as overwhelming . . . The 'numinous' element is not first of all something to do with language, even if it may become so to a certain extent subsequently." Ricoeur, *Figuring the Sacred*, 48.

subsequent critics of this position understand a wholly Other beyond even the limits of human understanding of limits. However, there is a mediating stance between these two. This is represented by a position like that of Maurice Merleau-Ponty who describes human reflection as always already within a given reality. This is a mediating reflection in so far as it acknowledges that any human experience works as if it is horizontal; we come to know ourselves in relation to society, even when humanity can't or doesn't decide upon a vertical transcendence. So *epistemicly* the self is more original than G*d insofar as one begins to know something of the wholly Other or a Holy G*d by knowing human limits. While this does not solve our dilemma about religious phenomenology, it does indicate a dimensionality that is important to the understanding of religious language and experience. It is the recognition that where religion is concerned, map may not be territory but the knower is a maker of language and symbols that are entwined with experience and understanding. Some of these symbols both represent a formative event and provide ground for rich discourse for centuries, uniting many interpretations of a shared past.

This inadequacy of knowledge to figure out and penetrate the inner core of religious experience leads to the theme "manifestation is not revelation" played out in various manners in the thought Emmanuel Levinas, Jacques Derrida, David Tracy, Jean-Luc Marion and a host of critical theorists. These recent approaches probe Enlightenment reason as a metaphysics of presence that privileges verifiable and visible knowledge. All of these ask the same question in different ways, "Was the modern turn to the subject also a turn to the same?"[3] With respect to prayer, how is modernity different from earlier times, the ancients and the middle ages? What place does prayer have within modernity, especially insofar as past and future are marginalized by a concern for the present or the now? This question entails a "floating" or hermeneutical positioning of phenomenology that is neither an approach to nor a stepping back from naming religious experience. Positively stated, Hans-Georg Gadamer defines this kind hermeneutics: "Hermeneutics may be defined as the attempt to overcome the distance in areas where empathy is hard and agreement is not easily reached. There is always a gap that must be bridged."[4] Understanding remains a mutual enterprise, a bridge

---

3. Tracy, "Theology and the Many Faces of Post-modernity."
4. Gadamer, "Hermeneutics of Suspicion," 57.

built from both ends. With regard to religious language this becomes especially difficult. This neutralized phenomenological description of consciousness can eventually decline into a pure form of the positioning a formless self.[5] This purity provokes criticism from a rhetorical perspective.

Rhetorical Criticism

The word rhetorical here is meant to describe an intentional influencing of oneself and others regarding an indeterminate issue or decision. "The rhetorical trope upsets the literal proposition, decenters conceptual argument, and calls into question empirical fact and rational first principle. Argument occurs on either side of a question, stabilizing a position, but only for a moment, until it starts up all over again . . . [W]ord unto world without end."[6]

Rhetorical theology often plays with two options of ethical method, situating itself within the dialectic between a normatively weak contextualism and a context-insensitive universalism. On one hand, ethical contextualists argue that norms arise only *within* cultural boundaries. On the other hand, soft universalists believe some norms transcend cultural boundaries. Regardless of the veracity of the arguments presented by both contexualists and universalists, the social situation remains that neither side is able to advance theological conversation. Mediation between global and localized perspectives or liberal and fundamentalist conceptualities remains unattainable. In addition, the ever-changing gravity and proximity of cultural applications further complicate this situation, which contributes to cynicisms and terrorisms when there may seem to be no valid or legitimate norms that make a difference in the world at large.

In response to these complications, neo-Augustinians sometimes attempt to by-pass this seemingly endless fluctuation of theory, sometimes characterized as "epistemological crisis." This broad range of exemplary argument focuses on the moral imperative at an intersection of tradition, practice, and narrative. Some neo-Augustinians try to es-

5. At best this hermeneutical placement, always between impossible objectivism and a vicious relativism, amounts to what Richard Bernstein calls "perennial impulse of wonder." Bernstein, *The New Constellation*, 28.

6. Gadamer, *Rhetoric and Hermeneutics in Our Time*, xix.

tablish the communitarian parameters of a virtue discourse. Of course, there are various strategies of disengagement from a more public discourse. For example, John Milbank and Elaine Pagels enlist Augustine as the non-liberal, while Oliver O'Donovan and Jean Bethke Elshtain see Augustine as a morally robust liberal. Perhaps on the boundary of neo-Augustinianism, William Connolly and Romand Coles read Augustine as an anti-liberal and John Caputo enlists Augustine as an ancestor of deconstruction. In addition to religious scholars mentioned above, Augustine continues to influence modern theory. Arguably the two most influential political thinkers of the twentieth century, Hannah Arendt and Reinhold Niebuhr, are not adequately understood apart from Augustine. The Bishop of Hippo not only represents the bridging paradigm of the ancients and the Middle Ages; he infuses our time with a conception of memory that is able to move conscientiously, longing for the beautiful and the good. Human nature and its concomitant destiny justifies the tension between the secular and sacred institutions of his day. So although Augustine is most of all a thinker of prayer, it is easy to see his appeal to theorists of late modernity, religious and political.

Much of the wide variety of neo-Augustinianism is a productive and telling movement within current religious and political theory because it indicates some of the limits of modern categories of social theory, especially in relating the past, present, and future. However, I would argue that the complexities of a plural society and the need for values that make a difference in this society are better served by a more participatory criticism. Quickly stated, my point is that an over reliance upon appropriations of an exemplary virtue often results in a false consciousness and reification of metaphysics. This is often indicated by a selective reading of history. The response I propose is a more public historiography that will utilize a hermeneutic phenomenology in tension with an ongoing moral-ethical praxis and discourse, thus opening an exceedingly creative relation of past, present, and future.[7] In simpler

---

7. Breisach, *Historiography*, 410. The author insightfully describes historiography as the various ways the relations of the past, present, and future informs all culture. "Historians must assume an order in which the influence of structures and forces beyond the scope of individuals is at least matched in importance by the actions of responsible individuals who act guided by values and make choices moral in nature. Logic, seems to rule out such a solution, but human life affirms it everyday, and historiography must depict that life and not one of manageable but artificial simplicity." Ibid., 410.

terms, this is a comparative study of prayer; how it works within public spheres of discourse and also how it references the sacred.

Memory

Most people admit that how you remember makes a difference for the future but does how you forget the past make a difference? Is forgetting simply the absence of remembering or are these two distinct modes of memory? While remembering privately and forgetting publicly is dishonest or disingenuous to many, it might also be a form of virtue.

The danger of human memory is its pathologically inclined habits. Sigmund Freud was among the first to study these habits more scientifically. He observed that past traumatic experience inadequately discussed contributes to neurotic behavior. This begs the question of why the mind filters evidence by memory to control action. The psychologically paralyzed or functioning, both coordinate action and inaction by memory.

Likewise it is suggested by sociologists today that societies have a collective memory that can inform cultural wisdom and maturity if cultivated. A reified collective memory becomes excessively assured of itself, contributing to a loss of healthy skepticism and a forgetting of its natural limits. Sometimes a nation embarks on this path intentionally and even with audacity as for example did fascist Italy in the 1920s.[8] This is maybe the most obvious example of a nation choosing to revise its own history for political purposes but there are many more.

A society convinced that it has the right view has conquered the problem of its own history and lives as if it occupies the best place and time to see it all. This seems to me easier now than ever because of technology. Some social critics see today's techno-collectivized memory even more capable of constructing an alluring ideology or, more to point, competing ideologies that assault one another. The issue in our time is not the need for one overarching set of values to unite society, as in Augustine's day, but instead an arbitration and cooperation between a plethora of competing values and ideologies.

In our time Jacques Derrida describes the spiral of violence within the ideological closure of onto-theology, over and over again. Expanding upon the work of Michel Foucault, Derrida describes one example of a closure of reality in the Cartesian impulse to subject knowledge to

8. Olick, *States of Memory*, 43–71.

certainty that metaphysically enthrones the person and thus devises an economy of domination. This "logic" of mastery subverts identity and internalizes aggression, spiraling fear into absolute terror. So Derrida and others can see the furnaces of the Holocaust and other Holocausts as the continuation of a partial nihilism that asserts self by negating the other.

Jürgen Habermas also criticizes modernity for its loss of memory. He advocates a post-metaphysical sociality, in contrast to Derrida's opening of metaphysical closures. Habermas's project is more sociological than literary, developing discourse on a societal level through recognition of public spheres of reason. His goal is to more clearly distinguish three types of statements: personal value, social norms, and fact. His commitment is that modernity can pursue justice by appropriately separating types of validity claims. His unfinished project of modernity pursues a society that provides space for all types of claims, except claims that mistake personal beliefs to be objectively verifiable as facts that are acceptable by the world.

This book thinks about prayer in both metaphysical and social terms; as a discourse of memory. If, as a North American white male, I wish not only to notice the crucified peoples of the world, to see the previously invisible, but to also help remove these others from their crosses, alleviate suffering in some way, then both Derrida and Habermas give help in devising mutual and pedagogical praxis.[9] While Derrida helps recognize an inescapable responsibility through a recognition of death, then Habermas helps a performance of responsibility within the communicative-act. While Derrida helps understand the context of all writing and human reason, its "prior substance" to use Ricoeur's words, Habermas recommences a limited reasoning, a discursive reason that claims the "prior" praxis of morality within acts of communication. Such moral consciousness is necessary for any human society (*sittlichkeit*) and may be the basis for the study of how religious traditions are able to evolve and progress toward post-metaphysical reason. In short, the functions of deconstruction and re-construction of reasoning for the sake of a moral consciousness have epitomized functions of prayer in religious practice.

The work of prayer, its laboring, is a performance that relies heavily on the descriptions of memorial responsibility, seen from differ-

9. Sobrino, *The Principle of Mercy*, 50.

ent angles simultaneously. The work of this book is to point out how prayer can connect and work within the ethical theory of Derrida and Habermas. I will outline how Derrida describes the recognition of death and of the other as a way toward responsibility while Habermas reflects profoundly on what it means not only to respond to the other but also what it means to speak in the first place. As Paul Ricoeur wrote many years ago, there are two distinct perceptions of human reflection that are inseparable if always also irresolvable. "Humanity appears to us to be no less discourse than perspective, no less a demand for totality than a limited nature, no less love than desire . . . Humans are no less destined to unlimited rationality, to totality and beatitude than they are limited to a perspective, consigned to death, and riveted to desire."[10] The argument of this book build here. Prayer's functioning relates to this double perspective that is able to suspend a performance and live inside. A life of prayer is the sustenance of a critical and constructive tension between an opening of metaphysics and a post-metaphysical praxis. For example, religious orders are still today living as intersubjective criticisms of human society; in other words, a place for social-spiritual experimentation where work is redefined in relation to stated ends of rightness, values, and justice. A life of prayer characterizes this ongoing experimentation with inter-subjectivity.

Post-Religious Prayers from Memory

All knowledge is cultivated in an incalculable conversation between past, present, and future. The twin oaks of history and moral imagination grow from the soil of memory, the loam of forgetting as well as remembering. These two protect ambiguities in the shade that truth redeems. If not, nuance withers in the hot sun of certitude. I propose that piety functions best inseparable from quietude; when it leaves an opening for listening to the other without prejudice or labeling.

    This is a version of post-religious prayer. One that uses the language of a religious tradition, lives inside a tradition and is nourished by it, but is capable of suspending and questioning all its claims. This is a form of prayer that questions in a way that humanity has not outgrown. Prayer is able to ask questions like, "When does religion go too far by explaining and justifying suffering?" "Does a religious hope go beyond reasoning

10. Ricoeur, *Fallible Man*, 7.

and privilege a certain reading of the past?" "Is it irrational to think the dead are not finally dead?" "How does soteriology overlap theodicy?" Or, in other words, "Does the study of salvation confuse and corrupt questions of suffering?"

There would be little religion without prayer, while prayer has often survived without religion. One way, maybe the best way, to open up ossified religious belief is to understand how the believer prays. To learn the language of prayer is to learn to speak with the religious. So how does one understand the language of prayer in today's multi-cultural world? Is prayer in any way the same for the Hindu as it is for the Christian or the Muslim?

One can say with more certainty that without adequate understanding of prayer, it is increasingly difficult to address controversies about prayer. The world shrinks everyday as it becomes more interconnected by electronic media and mobile populations. It is so small that a pastor of a tiny Christian church in Florida can have an impact on international politics by saying he is praying about burning a Koran. This happened in the summer of 2010 in response to a proposal to build a place of prayer—not a mosque, as it was reported—within blocks of the former World Trade Center. There was much vitriol about prayer, amounting to an argument about whose prayers were welcome. Prayer in this case was seen more as a spark for violence than a peaceful reflection. No one seemed to ask how their own prayer may be taken as a threat by others who also were praying. This situation, among others, was what prompted this book.

As I see it, prayer is one way, maybe the most used way, to navigate the subtleties of memory while also listening to them. Prayer is learning not only how to remember but always also how to forget. It thus represents the broad life of the mind.

Prayer is too often associated with banal habit; a ritual with no power of explanation. This is often the truth of how people pray while sitting down to eat or before a difficult exam with little conviction or need; we pray because it can't hurt. Some understand prayer as a habit of the savage mind; a vestige of an earlier time that is no longer useful. Both perspectives on prayer avoid an important question posed here. Is prayer necessarily in conflict with modernized approaches to memory? If it is useful to study how religious worldviews are at the bottom of many of the world's conflicts then it is also useful to see that prayer is at the bottom of any religion. Prayer saturates religion. John Dominic Crossan recently called prayer the electricity that powers the religious life.[11]

Prayer can be a shared experience that shapes a common discourse of memory. While prayer engages theological concepts as well as ritual and behavior, none of which are directly translatable, it may still participate in a variegated religious experience that a comparative study of prayer may yet understand. Recognizing that prayer is indebted to separate traditions is a step toward understanding prayer as a form of communication capable of remembering a responsible coordination of action in reason and faith. However prayer constantly forgets as well.

For these reasons prayer involves the pious act of praying as well as the quietude of being still. This prayer has involved memory since before recorded history; it takes place between conscience and community in a way that can be inclusive or exclusive of others. This insider/outsider reflection is continuing across time often without our noticing its most critical function. Because of this conversation within memory that relates the person to community, it is the basis of an imperceptivity of others. It is a place of both memory and counter-memory. Thus prayerful consciousness cultivates, turns around, and opens up our identities, languages, and patterns of knowledge.

Prayer is the recognition of the unfinished work of understanding what is called "G*d," or any conception of the sacred. It is a mode of being encountered; therefore the truth of prayer is not *underneath* or *behind* it, but truth is what happens *in the encounter*. Are norms questioned and tried on for size? Are presuppositions turned around and upside down? It engages what Miranda Fricker recently described as "testimonial injustice." Such injustice is committed when an interpretation of the speaker is governed by norms that operate to either give too much credit or too little.[12]

I will suggest that prayer functions best by raising human consciousness of a more pervasive questioning, tapping a dissatisfaction with three spheres of memory: conscience, knowledge, and representation.

One may ask what the history of the world would be without the language of prayer. This question spurs a critical study of prayer, how it contributes to peace and justice but also how prayer has entrenched positions that justify violence. The questioning of prayer asks not only

11. Crossan, *The Greatest Prayer*, 10–13.
12. Fricker, *Epistemic Injustice*, 17.

how prayer contributes to a consciousness of exchange within memory but it can also shut it down. Political pathologies can be born in prayer that spiral from an apocalyptic desire into violent action and implementation. Tweaking a famous phrase, prayer without memory is blind but memory without prayer is certainly not lame.

The study of prayer is a critical work that relates to cultural memory, a form of *anamnestic reason*. Toward a description of a functioning of cultural memory, the chapters each describe prayer within one of the levels of memory. Within each there are forms of pathological reasoning or problems of ideology. So on one level this book describes prayer's general function as the questioning of cultural memory, dissatisfied with forms of conscience that appear limited to knowledge. The purpose here is to show how prayer works as a critical exchange of reasons within a given narrative. The second level is to suggest a framework appropriate for the constantly dissatisfied prayer given the absence of justice in the world. To bring these two levels into a relation—as memory suspended yet ongoing in history—I will suggest a new definition of the apocalyptical imagination, one that sees that consciousness is irreducible to any single human nature.

Conscience

In 1968 *Science* magazine published an article by a biologist named Garrett Hardin. The article is a retelling of an ancient parable renamed, *The Tragedy of the Freedom of the Commons*. For decades this essay has been at the center of public discussions on environmental ethics and a search for sustainable practices.

It is a simple description of a community of farmers, each owns a herd of cattle. Each farmland borders around a shared plot of land known as the commons. This shared or common pasture is used by each farmer for his or her respective herd. This is a successful arrangement to start with but each herd grows and doom becomes inevitable, much like a Greek tragedy. Because each herdsman receives the full profit of each animal that they send to market, while also they share the cost of raising each animal by relying more on the common pasture, then enlightened self-interest will inevitably lead to overgrazing of the commons sooner or later.

Students quickly grasp the analogy between Hardin's parable and our planet, which has limited natural resources for generating production and private profit. But there is another part of Hardin's description that often provokes strong disagreement among students during the discussions. Hardin adds to the ancient parable by discussing the pathogenic effects of conscience. If the community appeals to an individual farmer's conscience to limit their pursuit of legitimate self-interest for the sake of the community then this has unhealthy effects. This is described in the article as a conscience caught in a *double-bind*.

> The long-term disadvantage of an appeal to conscience should be enough to condemn it; but has serious short-term disadvantages as well. If we ask a man who is exploiting a commons to desist "in the name of conscience," what are we saying to him? What does he hear?—not only at the moment but also in the wee small hours of the night when, half asleep, he remembers not merely the words we used but also the nonverbal communication cues we gave him unawares? Sooner or later, consciously or subconsciously, he senses that he has received two communications, and that they are contradictory: (i) (intended communication) "If you don't do as we ask, we will openly condemn you for not acting like a responsible citizen"; (ii) (the unintended communication) "If you do behave as we ask, we will secretly condemn you for a simpleton who can be shamed into standing aside while the rest of us exploit the commons."[13]

This double-bind is a form of social control without a visible external coercion. It is disguised as a moral appeal but in truth overpowers the individual's freedom to pursue self-interests and forces a suppression of desires. Hardin taps into psychoanalytic theory coming from Freud down to Bateson, whom he mentions in the article. Bateson theorized that parents who give problems to children and then usurp the freedom to confront their problems, create no-win scenarios that children are taught to internalize and suppress. Bateson thought this created a propensity toward schizophrenia. Similarly Gilles Deleuze writes in the same year as Hardin, 1968, "Conscience, however, suffers from the following ambiguity; it can be conceived only by supposing a moral law to be external, superior, and indifferent to natural law; but the application of the moral law can be conceived only by restoring to conscience itself

---

13. Hardin, "Tragedy of the Commons," 1246.

the image and the model of the law of nature."[14] Similarly, René Girard later described religious traditions that establish moral exemplars that are unattainable perfections thus creating the desire to be as good as the exemplar was and at the same time putting true moral goodness out of reach.[15]

C. S. Lewis had already observed that the meaning of the word "conscience" has changed over the past 300 years, "whereby con-science, so to speak, passed from the witness-box to the bench and even to the legislator's throne."[16] Here is some recognition that conscience is insepa-rable from interpretation. As Plato saw it, there may be no "mythless" morality and no moral without "myth."[17]

So the idea that conscience is politics disguised as morality is also to be taken as true in this study. It may often be the case that the conscience of a thinker not only reduces the range of legitimate interests but also is a source of pathology, a binding of freedom that is truly an illness to existence and a problem for faith. The concepts of super-ego and nausea certainly find there way into Hardin's description of the tragedy of the commons, which is an attempt to develop conceptions of power and politics at work in the "state of nature," like Thomas Hobbes.

It is interesting to note that Hobbes argued in favor of appeals to conscience in decision-making. He is in favor of appeals to conscience in the case of a jury trial where the issues of human rights were important. Here any decision by a juror made on the basis of conscience should be immune from punishment.[18] Hobbes writes to defend a juror who will not find someone guilty, not because they did not commit the act nor because the law does not apply but because the juror's conscience sim-ply does not permit a guilty verdict. My point is not to decide between Hardin and Hobbes here but awaken recognition of different perspec-tives on the relation between political power and human conscience.

Hardin's disparagement of the double-bind implies that conscience is judge rather than juror, pronouncing final judgment more than inter-preting and voting. It may make a difference as to what kind of conscience is being appealed to and under what circumstances. Is it not one of the

14. Gilles Deleuze, *Repetition and Difference*, 4–5.

15. Renee Girard, *Violence and the Sacred*, 156–57.

16. C. S. Lewis, *Studies in Words*, 191.

17. Schweiker, *Theological Ethics and Global Dynamics*, 15.

18. Hobbes, *Leviathan*, 26, 184.

benefits of a democratic society that appeals to conscience are plural and thus liberated? Hardin's pathogenic effects of conscience might be problematic only in a hegemonic society that pressures or overpowers the society. In this case, one could imagine an unhealthy burdening of the individual to conform. In this scenario, a questioning conscience that is empowered to critique the laws of the land no matter what, is the best hope to pursue a more just arrangement that is sustainable. Questions that include, "Am I living a life of integrity that is accountable?" but also, just as important, "What actually is a good conscience and what are its limits?" "When am I wrong to expect others to adopt my interpretation of a life of integrity and when must I say something to keep from losing integrity?"

For now I am in agreement with Hardin's statements that obedience to an external law is unhealthy if it creates political hypocrisy. Experience shows that brow beating evangelists as well as secularized moralists alike can travel a conscientious path to ideology and totalitarian politics. Karl Marx need only read Shakespeare to write, "The path to hell is paved with good intentions." I do not argue for an exoneration of conscience nor a judgment upon it. If a society strives to separate religious and political institutions, even if complications will always arise (as individuals are not always capable of achieving this separation) then appeals to conscience may not be as problematic.

Normative Traditions and Discourse

Some of the issues relating to conscience also relate to norms that involve the organization of a society, often according to values and perceived social purposes. There are many streams of discourse that feed a civil society to be healthy enough to celebrate diversity. It is also possible for one hegemonic tradition to damn its others, shifting a society away from values of freedom and tolerance. One does not need to go beyond the stories we tell children to see how socialization through narrative takes place. However it is a tricky thing to identify how these stories and normative identities inter-relate.

In 1840 Alexis de Tocqueville famously published his observations of American society and its new experiment with democracy. He famously made many correct predictions that included the civil war over slavery, and the eventual rise of America and Russia as the world's two

super-powers. However, his observations concerning the social norms
he observed proved to be more tricky. Tocqueville lamented the state
of the arts and literature. Also he wrote that Americans were indifferent to their natural surroundings. "Europeans talk a great deal about the
wilds of America, the Americans themselves never think about them
. . . [T]hey may be said not to perceive the mighty forests that surround
them until they fall beneath the hatchet."[19] It's almost laughable that
Ralph Waldo Emerson had already written his essay *Nature* in 1836,
which later became the basis for an distinctly American philosophy of
nature called transcendentalism. These values and thoughts would inspire Henry David Thoreau, John Muir, and a host of others around the
globe. We can ask today if Tocqueville's description of American indifference to nature was correct but this is difficult to answer with finality,
even today. Debates between naturalism, born in America, and exploiters
of nature still rage through this society today. Tocqueville's description
of American norms is still accurate on one level while also inaccurate
and this is often the case of any description of social norms that are often
in a process of dynamic tension. In this confusion prayer is often used
to justify a political viewpoint even if it too quickly clarifies confusions
about normative perspectives.

Some of these prayers are short and not noticed as a prayer. "God
bless America." By itself, this may be an uncomplicated and straightforward desire. A person calls for a blessing from G*d upon their land.
Taken from an old popular song, these words are today frequently used
at the end of political speeches. Repeatedly these same three words are
pasted across storefront windows and painted on highway billboards;
T-shirts, glassware, and bumper-stickers repeat the words, "G*d bless
America," and this statement is for some an expression of nationalist
pride and patriotism. They are not repeated as tribute to the song and its
composer, Irving Berlin, but *as political speech*. Their power is because
they are addressed to G*d. They are words that convey a worldview—a
world under G*d and a world that features a particular place. It is no
wonder that these words unite and inspire many people who find G*d
and America related; thus this prayer also has political consequences.
Nevertheless the utterance speaks to or about G*d, and as such the utterance is a prayer and its validity or truth is questionable in terms of a

19. Tocqueville, *Democracy in America*, 181.

prayer. However, if, "Prayer is turning to G*d," then how does one ever speak of prayer's validity one way or the other?[20]

How one hears a prayer can depend on one's narrative identity; the stories by which one understands oneself. For example, people who are socialized within modernity and are religious "within the limits of reason" will probably roll their eyes when they hear a candidate repeat this motto at the end of a speech, perhaps dismissing it as pandering. There is no doubt that prayers uttered in public as political rhetoric offend a democratic sensibility to not mix religion and politics. The prayers of a politician remind one of an imperial past that claimed a divine right and thus an unquestionable power. American independence is born in direct opposition to royal declarations and yet this opposition is also its lineage. This plural society that is designed to equally protect many religions at once has a hard time invoking a particular G*d in its schoolrooms without appearing to favor one religion over another, let alone when a president does this.

What some call the culture wars is a conflict of narrative identities. Although narrative identities are not stable or seamless and are often shifting the boundaries of perspective and truth, I suggest that prayer is one way in which narrative identity is stated and questioned. Thus a question is posed about the critical discernment of the use of prayer in public discourse. The function of prayer is pressed upon me whenever there is open conflict between some who dismiss any or all religion and others who hunger for a renewal of a traditional piety.

When historical narrative refrains from both rigid universalism and soupy relativism and observes and narrates events in all their complicated intricacy, then it enables a critical capacity of discourse. However, from the perspective of historiography or historicism there is a problematic character of religious narrative that identifies some events as either good or evil, as if time were already understood primarily from the vantage point of eternity. Religion and history are often at cross-purposes insofar as narrative becomes a questioning of social identity. The telling of history proceeds from a suspension of belief by doubt, important in testing and fairly questioning various past accounts of history. Religious narrative proceeds from a suspension of doubt in belief so as to tell the purpose of history.

---

20. Ebeling, *The Lord's Prayer*, 28.

A relation between religious belief and the fair questioning of historical narratives entails the suspension of faith in either piety or quietude. One finds that doubt is not exclusive of faith but often its possibility, when understood in narrative theology.[21] This is how narrative is distinguished from a theology of history. The latter is understood as an attempt to write a completed story of oneself in the world rather than the recognition that I am both an author and a character in the telling of history. Ricoeur shows that there are many aporias that relate to the nature of historical time, and thus he discusses the incommensurability of its phenomenology and cosmology. In short, the physical definition of time by itself is incapable of accounting for the psychological conditions for the apprehension of time.[22] Time is not adequately characterized as eternal nor as movement from past to future. This would be as if a metaphysical speculation could cover over the fissure between thought, language, and acts of speech. Narrative, in contrast, often functions as a bridge between phenomenological approaches to time and cosmological time but one that is capable of more transparency. This is how humans work to find meaning within this aporia, by allowing for "the criss-crossing processes of a fictionalization of history and a historization of fiction."[23] In this way narrative is the source of shared identities that shape and orient the way we relate to one another in even the worst times.

Religious narratives represent an advance beyond pure speculative theology because a narrative theology affirms all conceptual discourse within traditional horizons of meaning or narrative. Instead of an orientation of morality that retains only atemporal teachings, narrative theology "has to disentangle the intelligibility immanent in recounted stories from our own individual and communal histories and stories."[24] Therefore, another goal of the use of narrative is a socialization of individuals within a larger system without losing autonomy to an abstract vision. This suspension within the narrative is distinguishable from other existential forms of thought that may be indifferent to historical contexts. While the latter pays attention only to "the irruption of the word in the instant of a decision of faith," narrative theology takes into account

---

21. Hauerwas and Jones, eds. *Why Narrative? Readings in Narrative Theology.*
22. Ricoeur, *Time and Narrative*, 244.
23. Ibid., 246.
24. Ricoeur, *Figuring the Sacred*, 236.

"the long duration of a history of several millennia."[25] The performance of traditional stories is also capable of addressing the confusion of "the narrative dimension of the biblical faith *and* a more or less sophisticated theology of history."[26] Too often it is the case that naïve understandings of a religious narrative regain a following; its rhetoric unifies a semblance of community. However a naïve understanding does not also address the history that deals with the brokenness of such unity; it then levels off the varieties of discourse through an imposed order. A flat linear use of narrative amounts to a world history that cuts off questions.

When narratives learn to include and encourage questioning, then conceptual arguments can be placed within traditional horizons of meaning. This allows for autonomy and diversity even insofar as encouraging the audacious questioning of a G*d; that for some is associated with continuity and coherence, while others are skeptical of a metaphysical G*d-talk.[27]

Given this cosmopolitan project and the problem of narrative theology, prayer is also a questioning of the status of memory as well as the possibility of G*d-talk. Is it not in prayer that one not only reads the religious text but also allows oneself to be read by the text? I am sometimes corrected by the text in an exchange that can open reality to a non-determination of ends. Prayers that are praise, lament, or meditation are ultimately engaged in the courageous failure of memory. In fact, one possible, if perhaps mundane, definition of prayer is *speech to one perceived to have the advantage of knowing us better than we know ourselves*. Yet one courageously seeks an exchange here as well. This relates on a more theological level to prayer that is speech out of brokenness directed to something beyond. In this case too an exchange is sought that will be redemptive.

This relates to my calling prayer an apocalyptical discourse, almost an oxymoron. I mean to say that when prayer is most essentially a questioning (*investigare*) of that which is called "G*d" then it is able to address suffering within time. Here apocalyptical does not mean necessarily the scriptural genre associated with the Second Temple period or

---

25. Ibid., 237.

26. Ibid.

27. I don't think one needs to have an answer to the question of G*d in order to pray, but one probably needs to have the question of G*d in mind.

the eschatological scheme of the monotheistic faiths.[28] *Apocalyptical* is defined by me as more of an everyday brokenness of life, one that does not know the nature of the other nor the future but can nevertheless act courageously to seek the truth.

The consequence of this understanding of prayer is twofold and eventually laid out through the development of all the chapters. First, this means that prayer is a discourse with two foci—suffering and redemption—and prayer's purpose is first to address the suffering. Second, this indicates possible problems of prayer. When one of these two elements is forgotten or covered over then prayer has a propensity to reinforce ideology. This is why the reader will see that I criticize apocalypticism and distinguish it from an apocalyptical experience of language in prayer.

Jean-Louis Chrétien also describes prayer in apocalyptical terms that may or may not be recognized by Isaiah, Daniel, or Job. Chrétien poetically calls prayer "a wounded word."

> Why call it the "wounded word"? It always has its origin in the wound of joy or distress, it always is a tearing that brings it about that the lips open. And it does so as it is still otherwise wounded. Wounded by this hearing and this call that have always already preceded it, and that unveil itself, in truth always in suffering, always agonic, struggling like Jacob all night in the dust to wrest G*d's blessing from him, and in keeping the sign of a swaying and limping by which speech is all the more confident as it is less assured of its progress.[29]

---

28. John J. Collins defines apocalyptic as "a genre of revelatory literature with a narrative framework, in which a revelation is mediated by an otherworldly being to a human recipient, disclosing a transcendent reality which is both temporal, insofar as it envisages eschatological salvation, and spatial insofar as it involves another, supernatural world." Collins, *The Apocalyptic Imagination*, 5. Hans Schwarz discusses apocalypticism as a development of eschatology, "The whole conception of the coming events of the end is no longer confined within nationalistic or this-worldly expectations. It is supramundane, and the kingdom is viewed as a kingdom of heaven . . . From their vantage point the apocalypticists assumed they could see the past, present, and future in one continuous progression preordained by G*d. In this age all evil tendencies will grow until they culminate in the dominion of the political powers of this world. Then the end of this age will be near." Schwarz, *Eschatology*, 53. Schwarz also observes that Jürgen Moltmann sees apocalyptic as an important contribution to all theology. "Without apocalyptic a theological eschatology remains bogged down in the ethnic history of man or the existential history of the individual." Moltmann, *Theology of Hope*, 137–38.

29. Jean-Louis Chrétien, "The Wounded Word: Phenomenology of Prayer," 174–75.

As much as I can agree profoundly here insofar as each word is wounded by an agonic origin, always a limping speech and not whole, to what extent this is always true of prayer remains an open question. In the next paragraph Chrétien alludes, from my perspective unfortunately, to the Christian Trinity as the metaphor of authentic prayer: "the prayer that would go from G*d to G*d, in a voice, and therefore in a human body, the prayer by which G*d would invoke himself."[30] It seems to me that a phenomenology of prayer is not really a phenomenology if it relies upon a certain form of transcendentalism. Also, it seems the problem of this transcendentalism is that it affirms what was just stated as not affirmable. It strikes me as premature to describe prayer in such exclusively Christian terms. Are we ready to make anonymous Christians of all other religions because they pray? Or judge them to not be people of prayer at all?

Chrétien is on to something here. Apocalyptical is an accurate and helpful category for thinking prayer's wounding of language. However, the distinction between the literary genre and an apocalyptical experience of language needs to be explored further if one is going to describe the "wounds" of prayer. For example, if a working definition of apocalyptic is the "end of time" and this entails the destruction of all worldviews or any human constructions then how is any description possible? Neither the genre nor the eschatological category are entirely fruitful for considering prayer as a speech-act. While the literary genre of apocalyptic puts the world at hand into a new perspective by way of a doctrine of two ages (one that is often revolutionary because interests are redefined in a revealing light or secretive knowledge),[31] an apocalyptic eschatology discusses the wisdom that is realized by an immanent expectation of the end of time that functions as a "theological evaluation of history in light of the expected end."[32] An important aspect of both positions is an interruption that transforms the present community discourse. I am asking

---

30. Ibid., 175.

31. Studies of the literary genre and its contribution to the unfolding of the biblical cannon abound. "Affliction and devastation lay ahead that would outstrip in magnitude and horror anything previously experienced by the people . . . In fact, only after a final climax of devastation, an expression of negation so absolute that only mythical images like the chaos monster (38:4) and the drinking of blood and the eating of flesh in the frenzied excitement of the victory banquet (39:17–20), could salvation be awaited." Hanson, *The People Called: The Growth of Community in the Bible*, 269–70.

32. Schwarz, *Eschatology*, 383.

then if a discourse of prayer is how this interruption or apocalypse functions in relation to knowledge or history.

My set of questions has been considered before in twentieth-century theology, impacted as it was by mid-century existentialism. For example, when Ernst Käsemann stated that apocalyptic is the mother of theology, he touched off a debate with Rudolf Bultmann, Gerhard Ebeling, and others about the nature of an apocalyptic experience and its revelational content.[33] While both sides might agree that apocalyptic as a category raises the question of the kingdom of G*d in the words of Jesus, the issue became whether apocalyptic understanding was up to the task or sufficient to ask about the content of salvation from G*d. So Bultmann asks, "But must we stop at this merely negative definition? What should we understand positively by the Kingdom of G*d? What sort of *events* are meant when its coming is announced?"[34]

Bultmann argues that Jesus rejects the content of apocalyptic speculation while accepting its perspective of an immanent expectation of G*d's kingdom. I wonder if both points of view have an important insight. Final salvation from G*d then has a positive content. If one believes Jesus is the revealed Truth of G*d then certainly there is something to say about this content. However, a posited final salvation also implies an ontological problem or a metaphysical grounding of reason. Not only, why is there something instead of nothing? but also, how does one speak of an ultimate truth at all?

Like Bultmann and other mid-century theologians faced with the remembering of the Holocaust and the deaths of their friends, I am also asking how one correlates the questions of broken existence with a revealed word? However, rather than choosing between philosophical categories or statements of faith in which to frame this correlation, I am proceeding from the space of everyday prayer. How do people everyday relate their questions with answers (perceived to be) from G*d in prayer? So I work here from a theology of religions perspective; not excluding but not primarily from a Christian theological perspective.

The question that I ask about prayer is how it poses questions and also gives credence to positive descriptions of salvation without becoming ideological; without the pray-er becoming too satisfied that s/he has

33. For a summary of the scholarship on the nature or genre of apocalyptic see; Collins, *The Apocalyptic Imagination*.

34. Bultmann, *Jesus and the Word*, 42.

the final answer for all. I am arguing that the fundamental issue of prayer is suffering, or how we can addresses suffering and violence without contributing more to it. This argument is deductive in the weak sense of the term. It is not intended to demonstrate a hard universal standard for prayer by which some persons are said to pray correctly as opposed to others who do not. My intention is the reverse; to address how prayer happens at all and how it can still contribute to public discourse today.

One last explanation here: my use of the terms "pietism" and "quietism" in this book are not intended to be understood in relation to a feeling or affectation but rather to the orientation of an intersubjective discourse; to action and/or listening for meaning. Although at this point I do not completely divorce my meaning from the seventeenth century religious movements within Christianity, my point is to characterize *current* attitudes toward language and their relation to prayer. *Piety* is the virtue of character that acknowledges a dependence upon appropriate structures and strives toward a more exemplary form of practice, sometimes based in a traditionalism or sometimes possibly by a faith in reason itself.[35] *Quietude* is the virtue of character that is based upon an indescribable or wordless source often via mystical meditation. Pietism and quietism orient communication so as to privilege either the act of speaking or silence in listening to being. The question then is, "How can discourse distinguish when and how one may move between these two modes, sometimes speaking in piety and sometimes listening in utter quietude?"

---

35. In his 2005 book *Democracy and Tradition*, Jeffrey Stout describes traditionalists as attempting to restore piety to public life. He includes Stanley Hauerwas and John Milbank. Their reconception of a social practice is ascertainable only from within the church.

2

Perspectives of Prayer

Questioning Prayer

IS IT POSSIBLE OR EVEN DESIRABLE TO ANALYZE PRAYERS FOR THEIR ethical content? If it is not, then how does one respond to anyone that questions the ethics of prayer? Or perhaps the most ethical response is not to respond or question at all and thereby keep private or hidden one's most sincere motivations from external corruptions. If that is so, then how does one know that?

It may be that no one is able to say that one prayer is better than another partly because no one can fathom the mystery behind the words. If analysis is simply taking something apart and looking at how it works then perhaps prayer is inaccessible to that sort of description, which may be more appropriate to inorganic or empirical objects of study. Prayers are like many uses of language, insofar as prayer performs something, it lives in the tension between past and future; the past is where our words are born and the future is where they are interpreted over and over again. Any analysis of an event of prayer will say as much, maybe more about the interpreter and their time as it does about the original prayer. So before beginning an analysis of prayer, this chapter will propose a framework or perspective on prayer that is a helpful starting place for analytical and comparative study of prayer as a discourse of memory.

Beside the problem of language as an event, a study of prayer is further complicated when one carefully and responsibly considers the world religions and is struck by the complexity, ubiquity, and the variety of prayers. For example, anyone attending a Christian worship service is likely to witness a variety of prayers that include praise, thanksgiving, intercession, pastoral, benediction, lamentation, liturgical or doxological prayer, complaint, repentance, and maybe silent prayer. These forms of prayer, or genres, are multiplied when elements of each can be combined. It is common that a prayer that begins as praise can then shift into a combination of others as well. Lamentation can still shift back to praise. This variety of prayer is known by most Christian and Jewish persons. The variety of forms are multiplied if one considers all religious traditions.

Another example of surprising complexity is Buddhist meditation. One could reasonably expect that the Buddhist tradition might be fairly straightforward with respect to meditative practices. One sits in silence to focus, right? Simple. The four noble truths are fairly simple—a winnowing of pretension and justification—so one is surprised to find that meditation is not practiced similarly across the Buddhist world. Meditation in the Mahayana and Vajrayana traditions is more likely to focus on visualization, while Theraveda meditation will more likely use controlled breathing in its mindfulness training. The use of sand painting, prayer wheels, and spiritualist rituals are more likely to accompany meditative devotions in the Tantric tradition. While meditation in Buddhism is consistently a practice of mindfulness, the forms of meditation can be practiced differently. Further, when meditation combines Buddhism with other cultural and religious identities then meditation can change to become a Zen garden or a Japanese rock garden. Some Chinese meditation employs two iron balls (Qigong balls) that can be rolled together in the palm of the hand to release tension and focus the mind. More advanced practitioners can skillfully manipulate three or four metal balls between the thumb and fingers.

This variety of forms is even more complicated by different approaches to prayer with regard to its general aim and effect. In striving to develop a critical theory about prayer, it is crucial to recognize a range of approaches to prayer. It may be that prayer is pathogenic. Sigmund Freud famously saw prayer as an obsessive attempt to assuage a primal guilt for ancestral murder. Auguste Comte predicted the extinction of religion but still recommended two hours of prayer each day for the health of the mind. Søren Kierkegaard saw that the truth of prayer lay in it significance for the person praying as they become a better hearer. The American pragmatist philosopher William James saw prayer as having the power to liberate, a force for positive change in humanity. Ludwig Feuerbach saw in prayer the human capacity to project the most desirable attributes onto a God figure and to strive after them to make the future better.

Others like George Frazer tried to develop a critical approach to prayer, distinguishing between magical and priestly forms. Karl Barth approached prayer as a disturbance from G*d and as such a gift to humanity with the propensity for egocentric thought. Abraham Heschel approached prayer as simply talking with G*d. These many theories and views about prayer are almost as varied as the practiced forms of prayer.

In *method*, some have approached prayer from the human side while others have discussed it as originating from the divine or outside humanity. Despite these differences, the varieties of prayer do have something in common. Prayer is indisputably a human occurrence, an event of conscience. The *substantive* disagreements are about whether, for instance, this prayer-event is a kind of psychosis, contributing to a loss of touch with reality, or a responsible and healthy practice that enables most to deepen their experience. Prayer may be as natural as when a child cries out when they are lost, yelling to be found, or it may also be what some call super-natural, like a calling for the redemption of creation that comes from an unknown. This book proposes to suspend the question of each particular prayer's ultimate claims and to pursue an analysis of the prayer-event; questioning the outcomes of prayer as a discourse of memory essential to the dynamics of conscience and the life of the mind.

The importance of this analysis is heightened by the recognition that religious language is most widely experienced as prayer, practiced by billions of persons every day; it is also the most pervasive form of theological reflection. The primary question of prayer is what would be lost if prayers ceased on this planet? The other side is what could be gained if prayer ceased? So this description of prayer proceeds by also considering its disappearance from the life of the mind or modern evaluations of conscience.

A history of prayer has recently been written by Philip and Carol Zeleski, who describe the varieties of prayer through the ages and in many religions. Here, the Zeleski's call prayer the "crown of mystery." In this stunning book they tell the history of prayer that spans millennia and covers the globe. The story of one person of prayer, the English mystic George Herbert, opens and closes this history. They save a particular story about Herbert for the last chapter, leaving it to the reader to decide if this brings perspective to the history of prayer. They tell how Herbert was dressed for a fine dinner and travelling on the road when he crossed paths with a "poor man and a poorer horse." The horse and its owner were both stuck in the mud, Herbert stopped to help push the horse out. He arrived at the dinner party covered with mud and a friend asked why he would stop to help a horse and dirty himself so much? Herbert replied "[t]hat the thought of what he had done would prove Musick to him at midnight; and that the omission of it would have up-braided and made discord in his Conscience, whensoever he would pass by that place; for if I am bound to pray for all that be in distress, I am sure that I am bound so far as it is in my power to practice what I pray for."[1] For the Zeleski's this story explains something about why prayer spans thousands of years and many world religions. They call Herbert a "meta-physical poet" who knew "prayer is the zenith of civilization and the high road to God." Could one say that the placing of prayer as the crown of mystery combines a metaphysical belief with an ethical prescription like a magical incantation conjures a rabbit? Herbert's anticipated discord of conscience is an unmediated resonance. One can fairly say that he culti-vates and also is cultivated by a musician's ear for acts of justice that assist the stranger on the road or even a poor horse stuck in the mud.

Right away there are different elements to observe in this crowning example of Herbert and the horse. First, there is an undoubted ethical call to do good where one can, not to save the whole world but to do what is in one's power each day. In the event of seeing the stuck horse, the decision is made in consultation within Herbert's practiced memory that is heard either as "Musick" or discord. He immediately knows that this memory will be tied to this place in the road, as it is so often in religious experience. The present is also marked by knowing that one will remem-ber one's choice and action, there is immediate recognition of how the present will be possible harmonization or remembered as discord.

However, there is a second story of prayer, which is almost opposite from Herbert's, that is neglected in the Zeleski history. Robert McAffee Brown writes about his visit to Auschwitz in 1988 on a Sunday morning in January. The group ended its tour standing in front of the crematoria.

> A rabbi led some prayers. A Polish priest read Scripture, the *De profundis* ("Out of the depths") from Psalm 130. The Jews present began to recite the Kaddish, the prayer for the dead. And then it

1. Zaleski and Zaleski, *Prayer*, 35–36, 349.

happened . . . Interrupting the Kaddish and continuing in clamorous competition with its high solemnity as though wishing to shut it out, the church bells from just outside the camp began to peal, celebrating the consecration of the host at the Mass in the parish church. My mind involuntarily and instantaneously took a leap back forty-five years. I reflected that at that time real guards would have been in the room in which we are now standing, thrusting real corpses into real ovens heated to temperatures extreme enough to dispose of corpses quickly, and that the same guards who were burning those same bodies would have gone out of that same camp, walked a few hundred yards to that same church, been absolved from their sins, received communion, and returned that afternoon or the next morning to continue the same grisly occupation, quite unaware of any contradiction between receiving the body and blood of the Jew Jesus, and destroying the body and blood of millions of other Jews.[2]

The title of the essay fittingly asks the reader, "Memory redeemed?" Does the present performance of Kaddish, the prayer for the dead, in any way redeem the past horrors? Can prayers for the dead in any way open the possibility of a redemption or is this too little too late? The reader can respond yes or no.

Comparing this story alongside the George Herbert story, one can quickly see some shared perspective on prayer and also illustrate an issue with the Zaleski mystical perspective on the history of prayer. I recognize some of the same elements of prayer in both accounts. Brown's visit to the crematorium and Herbert's experience with helping the man and horse out of the mud, both hear in prayer a recognizable ethical call and they both connect their memory of that call to a particular place. By an ethical call one means *a universal ought*, a responsibility to life. However, in Brown's experience at Auschwitz the narrative is of a *failing* of prayers to make a difference, overcoming differences for the sake of peace. The assurance of prayer that Herbert personifies is shaken by the competing prayers in Brown's visit.

One is reminded again that some of the magic of prayer remains dependent on a future judgment; not measured as the zenith of a triumphant and enlightened society but as the same society's failure. From this angle, prayer is a call to uncertainty and thus a call to question all ideas of the divine. Does some prayer, because of its power and magic, end

2. McAfee Brown, "Memory Redeemed?" 200.

by *assuaging* conscience and thereby muffle the cries of the murdered? From Brown's perspective, Herbert's confidence in his own experience of conscience is elusive at best, maybe lost forever as a quaint naïveté.

The cacophony of prayers at Auschwitz in 1988 reflects the recognition of a loss of religious centering but not necessarily of all religious questioning. Prayer is not the zenith of civilization, nor any high road to G*d, but it is the disappearance of pretension, the demise of closure with respect to theodicy. Undoubtedly Brown's experience of prayer is characterized as a disturbance at the continuing failure of prayer.

Because prayer can be spoken or silent, private or communal, and may include meditation, fasting, or ritual action, I will not start with a specific definition of prayer and make the mistake of also defining what prayer is not, delegitimizing possible forms. Many things, maybe all things, can be a form of prayer insofar as they may be an attempt to speak to G*d or with a mindfulness. Sand and rocks—which are only sand and rocks—become a window to the soul when placed in a Zen garden. Words are only words until preceded by "Our Father." The difference between the mundane and profound is most thin and most important in prayer. Perhaps for this reason prayer is both fragile and hearty as a linguistic practice; it is in this sense mystical. So in replacement of a definition or theoretical approach to prayer, some broad brush-strokes that paint prayer in the most inclusive outlines possible may be better.

For us to understand prayer as an event of discourse it is useful to know how the possibility of prayer's *mystical centeredness* can be helpful but still not a guarantee of an ethical coordination with others. The development of a critical approach to prayer needs to be able to discuss how sometimes evil is intensified or radicalized by prayers. It will be ready to contend that the practices that pose to be prayer are often dysfunctional and sometimes demonic. But before a theory of how prayer works can be attempted, it is important to describe the basic elements of prayer with a phenomenological simplicity. From this description one may discern an early critieriology of prayer that is based in a generalized experience of abject brokenness, as in McAffee's experience at the crematorium. For anyone living through that type of event, it is an apocalypse, revealing a new world and a new view on the human condition, and thus it is the cultivation of conscience. If so, the hypothesis is proposed that sometimes there may be too much proximity to this experience, or not enough. I propose that one key to prayer is getting close enough to "one's end" without being swallowed by it; to discover one's self and also one's neighbor in an apocalyptic(al) context. This proposal relates to the eschatological structure that is observed in the three major monotheistic faiths that all have apocalyptic tendencies. As such prayer may be an opening of discourse within the eschatological structure of faith. This book explores the possibility that prayer is able to open other religious worldviews and other notions of the Other and thereby contribute to a discourse of memory and its ethical concerns.

A Short Description of Prayer's Genesis

If religion has a birthday, an origin, it is the day prayer first finds breath. This day there is no "right way to pray" already prescribed; no orthodoxy nor orthopraxis to praying; no tradition of prayers. Who was the first person to pray? Where did this person get the preposterous idea to pray?

There are that day, nonetheless, two elements that coincide when prayer occurs; two elements that are indispensable for prayer to happen. The first element of prayer is a *need* to pray; a need to express. When one first feels helpless or broken, this is one condition of prayer. However, brokenness alone is insufficient for prayer. The second element of prayer is just as necessary: a coming into consciousness or a *new* consciousness of something beyond brokenness, whether it is a creator deity or a reality beyond knowledge. Simply stated, the first prayer is possible only when these two conditions first coincided: *brokenness of life* and *something beyond brokenness*.

The first prayer is distinguished from other language by a consciousness of these simultaneous elements. Prayer is not entirely an aesthetic expression that is marked by an individual's valuative claims, neither is it an objective assertion that is marked by a factual claim. Rather, prayer is marked by a coincidence of two simultaneous and perhaps even opposite claims, one about brokenness and the other about something beyond brokenness. Given this description, the validity of a prayer may be assessed in relation to the inherent claims in each prayer about the coincidence of these elements of prayer. Such prayer is assessed not just as an expression of brokenness, and not just as a consciousness of the Other, or even some sacred other, but as the coincidence and possibility of exchange between these two. Prayer is fundamentally two questions, one directed toward human suffering and another question directed toward that which is beyond. One side without the other might be simply existentialism or transcendentalism, but when these two questions occur simultaneously, or in some proximity, then there is prayer.

A hypothesis can begin to take shape. When one considers all the various beliefs, different accounts of creation and history, different religious values and social agenda, experiences and traditions, one finds that each prayer is both an expression and a description of each religion from which it comes. Each prayer performs as a summation of "theology"; in other words, a reflection upon that religion. Prayer is unavoidably theological in the sense that the words, "Oh, God" are unutterable outside some concept of G*d or the sacred, be it Hindu Truth, Christian Trinity, Shinto kami, or some sacredity. Besides a conception of G*d or sense of the sacred, each prayer is a religious expression of one's real belief and thus part of the praxis of religious discourse, a constant combination of theory and practice appropriate enough to each religion. If prayer ceases to engage a concept of G*d or ceases to act in response to this concept, then it would cease to be prayed and become plain utterance or description. On the other hand, prayer as a discourse that has G*d as its focus alone also becomes problematic when such concepts are not criticizable or questionable. All conceptions of G*d must be criticizable in prayer that engages in a social discourse. This study will investigate if a concept of G*d is criticizable in prayer insofar as the condition of suffering is further addressed as a consequence. One may ask about prayer, "Does it help?"

For now the general supposition is that prayer acts as a discourse within the norms, values, and facts of life. If that is so then the corollary is that when prayer ceases to reference the sacred and is subsumed within an economy of meaning, a culture, then it functions in an ideological way and is unable to question the ultimate power represented in the system. Then what passes for prayer is a process by which experience is filtered in order to fit a prescribed perspective. Then prayer functions in service to culture, sometimes as a protection against truth that may be critical of cultural practices, as Durkheim first observed. Prayer's identity then functions more as a reinforcement of moral subjectivism or cynicism than as a moral discourse. Prayer is utilized as the marshaling of power for the performance of one's duties or for protection against others. Such a captive prayer is banal and disengaged from human suffering and inordinately obsessed with its own. Critical powers of prayer are then limited more and more to the extent they serve a determined interest. In many cases a different reality, a new life, is less and less the point of prayer.

If these suppositions ring true to us then it is not only possible to understand how prayer may be a kind of social discourse within culture, but also important to investigate when prayers have functioned to question human perspectives and when they have ceased to question. Important thought needs to be done on the form of prayer itself, so that one is not left with an artificial decision on the authenticity of all prayer but is able instead to engage discursively from within prayer's perspectives.

This description of prayer contrasts with the banal, the dreary and predictable, absent of meaning. Prayer is meaning that comes by way of a coincidence of two elements that make possible the transformation of any person, system, or community. In the least, change enough where it is possible for outsiders to become insiders or where practical concerns are no longer determining concerns; this is a kind of originary position of prayer. For now it must be sufficient to summarize by quoting Henri Nouwen, who devoted his life to the study of prayer and spirituality. "When you pray, you discover not only yourself and God, but also your neighbor. For in prayer, you profess not only that people are people and God is God, but also that your neighbor is your sister or brother living along side you.[3] I think much may depend on the word *profess* here, but for now *profession* should be an open declaration that remains questionable, an identity that is unfinished in prayer. My only reservation with Nouwen's understanding is that an uncriticizable *profession of belief*, understood as finished and perfected, would be a banal assertion of a closed economy of meaning, a "done deal" between God and humanity with nothing more to say except more of the same. When professions of belief are no longer open to criticism, when they become culturally or metaphysically unquestionable, then communities are closed off from one another. Much has been recently written about this type of religious violence but it is my contention that prayer is not always so violent. Instead, a questioning prayer, a prayer that inquires, performed within a community based in a religious culture or even some metaphysical closure, such prayer may be the best hope of an opening. In closed social systems it may be prayer that remains the last possibility of change.

3. Nouwen, *With Open Hands*, 50.

When it seems nobody else is questioning the powers that be, prayers are asking the ultimate questions of why and still more questions about reasoning that is recognized as lacking humility, honor, truth, or love. Thus the social permissibility of questioning while in prayer is important to opening the most extreme ideological forms.

The unfinished nature of any profession of belief in a prayer makes prayer dangerous because identities that are being discovered, either in relation to G*d or one's needs, are particularly vulnerable to a cultural amnesia. It is often the case that one's sense of time and history is hijacked by an unquestionable commitment to a certain concept of G*d or a particular set of rational interests. As Theodor Adorno said, "All reification is forgetting." And Johann Baptist Metz discusses how a performance of prayer might discourage such hidden amnesia that leads to ideology and fanatical intolerance. His description of prayer shows how communicative reason is grounded in *anamnestic reason*, or how the way in which we communicate is related to how we remember.[4] This builds upon theory that refuses to predicate memory without recognition that all such predication itself is a remembrance and a forgetting. However, this is not just a theory for Metz but a description of continuing function.

Everyday prayer brings redemption and suffering into relation. So he succinctly describes how salvation can happen when one remembers and tells G*d: "My thesis is that a soteriology must neither condition nor suspend the event of redemption nor can it ignore or dialectically bypass the non-identity of the history of suffering. A purely argumentative soteriology cannot avoid these dangers. It must be made explicit in narrative. It is a fundamentally memorative and narrative soteriology."[5] This description serves as a short description of prayer's profession.[6] Metz denies any final economy of meaning that neglects or forgets a questioning of G*d [*rückfrage an Gott*]. His point is that G*d must not be separated from religion because this amounts to a cessation of questioning and the beginning of an endless banality of time. Religion that limits or legitimates only certain questions is reduced to the "praxis of

---

4. Metz, "Suffering Unto God," 615.

5. Metz, *History and Society*, 133.

6. Metz observes in a footnote here "It is not simply by chance that, for instance, some of the pertinent passages in von Balthasar and Moltmann cut short the argumentative process and become an encoded form of narrative theology." Metz, *History and Society*, 135.

contingency management" as Metz quotes Hermann Lübbe.[7] It is risk and danger that G*d contributes to any prayer. For only in this way can the future be different than a repetition of the past or present. Most succinctly stated, Metz is saying, no G*d, no interruption; no interruption then only more of the same.

An apocalyptic consciousness is important because it gives expression to the concept of time in a religious discourse. Without an apocalyptic consciousness, discourse is unable to include the full potential of a religion insofar as a new world is unimaginable and prayer is discounted within modern times. This will be explored later in the book by an analysis of two opposing but current philosophers of modern discourse, Jürgen Habermas and Jacques Derrida. For now it will suffice to state that a memory that includes an apocalyptical vision presents a view of a new time typified by a present healing of suffering. Such healing is not reasoned out gradually or adapted to evolutionary understandings of time, rather it happens when an immanent expectation becomes real and calls the future into a pervasive questioning for the sake of a universal community.[8]

The next immediate section will offer a description of an apocalyptical consciousness and inquire into how it may relate to prayer. If prayer is understood as the coincidence of brokenness and that which is beyond then it makes sense to investigate a relationship between prayer's transformative praxis and apocalyptic conceptions of time, in an effort to apply this criteriology.

Prayer and the Meaning of Apocalyptic(al)

Studies of *apocalyptic* are varied in scope and method. Sometimes the object of study is a community like Qumran, sometimes a literary genre, and sometimes a historical or mytho-poetic worldview. So I would like next to propose a clarification of the term apocalyptic, especially as it relates to a response to suffering in prayer.

Beginning with the ancient Persians, an apocalyptic writing is used to abolish past systems of rule and present new ones. The imperial apocalyptic account of its own triumph connects meaning and memory; it attempts to explain the legitimacy of the present monarchy by seeing it as

7. Metz, "Suffering Unto God," 613.

8. Metz, *Faith in History and Society*, 177.

a result of a violent overthrow of the past order by the present one. This framing of legitimacy helps explain suffering and violence as a necessary condition for justice to be done.

Imperial claims to legitimacy are evident in the authorized narrative of King Darius, who legitimates his violent usurping of the throne by claiming his purpose to be G*d's own. His defeated opponents are "followers of the lie" and Darius' victory is the beginning of a good and new age.

> Writing shortly, but securely, after the fact—when Bardiya was dead, the rebellions crushed, and tributes reimposed—Darius offered a very different picture, exercising the victor's control over the historic record to brand the rebels followers of the Lie. At Bistun and Susa, we can observe him shifting from an emergency campaign of military pacification to a long-term project of ideological control . . . [W]ith his accession God's plan for history had been fulfilled, and that further change was as unthinkable as it would be undesirable.[9]

Later, a different victorious king, Cyrus, follows this same apocalyptic strategy of claiming to be G*d's anointed by bringing a past age to its righteous judgment and destruction. This Imperial strategy of ideological control is implemented by reference to an apocalyptic victory, a violent ending of the previous age that begins a new order. Thus, the present rule is legitimate by virtue of its institution by G*d. When the Babylonian Jews are released by Cyrus, they adopt some of the same strategy of connecting its own rebirth and legitimacy to G*d's anointing of Cyrus. The apocalyptic strategy of imperial legitimacy finds its way into ancient Jewish texts like Daniel, Job, and others. But whereas the earthly kings write of past deeds in the first person, Jewish apocalyptical texts speak in the third person, and of a *future* time when all present injustice will be done away. The legitimacy of *all* kings is put into question by apocalyptic(al) texts that locate the definitive conflict in the future rather than the past. The released exiles subvert the imperial apocalypticism by using apocalyptic(al) literature as a response to ideologies of legitimacy and control by force. Even victorious kings are questioned from a post-exilic apocalyptical perspective. All claims of legitimacy are questioned by the consideration of the presence of suffering yet to be resolved. For example, Job even questions G*d's monarchal legitimacy

9. Lincoln, "Apocalyptic Temporality and Politics in the Ancient World," 466.

that still allows rain to fall on the just and the unjust, while a final resolution is yet to come.

The distinction between imperial apocalyptic of Darius and the Jewish apocalyptic(al) literature is largely due to an unwillingness to explain suffering as Job's friends do, especially in order to legitimize kingly authority beyond question. Even G*d's kingship is called into question. But is this unwillingness to submit enabled by prayer or is this type of prayer possible because of an unwillingness to explain suffering? Is it correct to perceive here a stubborn audacity to refuse the mantle of unbrokeness for oneself? Does all prayer necessarily disallow an imperial use of apocalyptic, like that of Darius? Certainly kings like Darius can also pray, but their prayers are to a G*d who blesses the cause of the present kingdom and perform a function of conferring legitimacy on the present order. Prayer for the Jewish apocalyptic writers, even after their homecoming, prohibited a closure of the question of suffering. For now it may suffice to say that there is not necessarily a causal relation between prayer and the non-acceptance of suffering in the present. I will postpone considering how the form of prayer with regard to suffering is different depending upon one's perspective on the end, or in this case on the apocalypse.

Given these historical distinctions between imperial apocalyptic and Jewish apocalyptical prayer, it is possible to distinguish between perspectives of apocalypse, apocalyptical, and apocalypticism. The noun, genre, and doctrine are almost interchangeable in recent books on apocalyptic eschatology by Hans Schwarz, Catherine Keller, and Jürgen Moltmann.[10] This is partly because any apocalypse itself is simply beyond words; book descriptions are always inadequate. Language relies upon some continuity and at least some shared understanding, while an apocalypse is characterized by the destruction of continuity and shared

---

10. Catherine Keller most accurately identifies this problem and explicitly names how she intentionally uses apocalypse ambiguously. "We are in apocalypse: we are in it as a script that we enact habitually when we find ourselves at an edge, and we are in it as recipients of the history of social and environmental effects of that script. In other words, apocalypse is both a state of affairs and an interpretation of that state of affairs, which latter is at times compelling because this vision and habit has been predicting and/or shaping such a state of affairs all along. I find I have no choice but to use the term therefore with a systematic ambiguity: sometimes to focus the script by which reality is being managed, imagined, and narrated, sometimes to stress the blunt horror of the end of the world—genocide, ecocide, some cultural or local omnicide—and sometimes then to stress also the wild hope for a world to come." Keller, *Apocalypse Now and Then*, 13.

understanding. Yet, apocalyptic experiences are nonetheless part of human consciousness, so it is appropriate to ask what is this consciousness or experience an experience *of*? What is an apocalypse? Can one say that the immediate *experience of apocalypse* is simply a violent or abrupt end of a/the world? So if it may be seen from outside the apocalypse as personal or social and thus explainable in psychological or historical terms then one might say an apocalypse is an experience of an end. To the person inside the apocalypse other perspectives on experience have no meaning. Thus an apocalypse cannot adequately be described; it is neither an end of experience nor an experience of an end.

One fictional illustration is found in Toni Morrison's novel, *Beloved*. Sethe is a loving and self-sacrificing mother who kills her child instead of letting Schoolteacher, her former *over-seer* from Kentucky, take her child back into horrific and dehumanizing slavery in accord with the Fugitive Slave Act of 1855. Years later, she tries to explain what happened "when the four horsemen came" for her daughter, but she is always unable to find the words to explain her action, even to her most trusted friend Paul D. Morrison writes, "If she was thinking anything at all, it was No. Nono. Nonono. Simple."[11] Her apocalypse is an event beyond words, where no word or thought is worthy to do it justice. The event continues to traumatize and give Sethe a kind of amnesia because she has no map or economy of memory which is sufficient to adequately address its meaning, nor even her own sense of self. The day of the four horsemen sucks meaning dry, and voids all explanation. Sethe thus evades other relations even as she evades any sense of a reality beyond this apocalypse. The reader comes to discover that an inability to escape from such an apocalypse leaves Sethe in a perpetual state of fragmentation.

Once there is a word, even a word of prayer, that signifies the simple apocalypse then one passes into the signage of the *apocalyptical*. Even the words, "No. Nono. Nonono" begin a new and unique sign. Here one gropes for a sense of some perspective on apocalypse. These signs are left uncovered in their aporetic meaning and they question all metaphysical and eschatological questions. The apocalyptical permits no final explanations except as prayers of utter faith. Suffering remains a passion of memory because no knowledge is sufficient to even name it, let alone cease it. The apocalyptical then is a resonance of apocalypse, a suspension of meaning itself, neither pre-deciding continuity nor discontinuity

11. Morrison, *Beloved*, 163.

between coherence or correspondences of truth, but letting each speak for themselves. Particularity and indeterminacy is the nature of conceptuality here.

The third form, *apocalypticism*, is described as a genre of eschatology.[12] Catherine Keller succinctly identifies Martin Buber's division between prophetic and apocalyptic forms of eschatology, which influences current studies including Paul Hanson and Elizabeth Shüssler Fiorenza.[13] Keller describes how apocalyptic understandings function in ontic terms over against the imperial cults. However, new ontic understandings are the beginning of new imperialisms.[14] I am in much agreement that apocalypticism, over time and history, is a formula that conditions more imperialism. Interestingly Keller and Schwarz both accuse apocalypticism of fueling either passive expectation or doomed rebellion.[15] I will say for now that the validity of an apocalyptical perspective is lost when a formulaic apocalypticism is ontologized and then overlaid onto decidable time sequences. This negative history is no less closed than any myth that is susceptible to a rhetoric of instrumental reason. Apocalypticism closes

12. Bernard McGinn broadly describes apocalypticism "as the belief that God has revealed the imminent end of the ongoing struggle between good and evil in history." McGinn, *Encyclopedia of Apocalypticism Vol.II*, ix.

13. Keller, *Apocalypse Now and Then*, 21–22.

14. Keller beautifully implements her "trickster's" typology of apocalypse, anti-apocalypse, neo-apocalypse, and counter-apocalypse. The later combines the best elements of the former types. "Counter- as prefix at once opposes the encounters; it knowingly performs an analog to that which it challenges. The counter-apocalypse recognizes itself as a kind of apocalypse; but then it will try to interrupt the habit. It suggests an apo/calypse: a broken, distorted text, turned to abusive purposes, only revelatory as it enters a mode of repentance for Constantinian Christendom and its colonial aftermath. If counter-apocalypse reveals anything, it does so in ironic mimesis of the portentous tones of the original, with which it dances as it wrestles." Keller, *Apocalypse Now and Then*, 19.

15. Ibid. Hans Schwarz outlines the issues between two extremes of apocalypticism and attempts to offer a mediating perspective. "This means that apocalypticists are on both sides of the fence: those who passively await the coming of the kingdom and other who join the rebellious forces." Schwarz, *Eschatology*, 66. In the concluding chapter he writes, "If there is a meaningful future at all, it must come not by our own strength but by a provision *from above*. Thus we find it impossible to dispense with the eschatological expectations of the Christian faith and still maintain a meaningful hope in the future . . . This means that we have to avoid two extremes. We cannot on the one hand, concentrate so much on the hereafter and the transitoriness of earthly things that we undervalue the importance of this life; nor can we, on the other hand, ignore the terminal character of death so much that we canonize the goods of this world and distract believers from the pursuit of holiness." Ibid., 369–70.

the framing of narrative and rigidifies an onto-theology of good and evil, when shared by many in a society this could empower a rhetoric of oversimplification of good and evil. This is ironic given that apocalyptic narratives are originally intended as an opening up of reality, a revelation of a new narrative of hope. However, it should also be remembered that apocalypticism is admirable as an attempt to bridge from a broken existence to a future promise.

These distinctions are more explicit when apocalyptic(al) prayers are suspended between a broken past and a hopeful future, without becoming fatalist or formulaic. An apocalyptic(al) prayer may even open an ontologized narrative of history to a reconsideration. When prayer opens and informs history and narrative, then a more exposed and vulnerable self results but also potentially more vigorous and responsible. An apocalyptic(al) prayer is intended as a possibility of a new insight from the questioning of utter suffering without an explanation or systemization of that suffering.[16] The outlines and dynamics of this discourse will be further elaborated through the course of this project. Most succinctly stated, the appropriate critical perspective of prayer is an apocalyptical approach because it suspends language and meaning between a full appreciation of brokenness and that which may be beyond brokenness. As validity is understood in terms of its questioning of supposed facts in the world, and aesthetic truth is understood in terms of supposed private feeling or a valuative perspective on the world, then prayer questions apocalyptical statements or in other words *all things hoped for.*

While eschatology traditionally studies what is anticipated at the end of history, an apocalyptic(al) discourse of prayer questions the end of meanings. At best eschatology is a reflection on a meta-narrative temporally marked by an alterity that provides for discourse, but at worst eschatology is an ontologized process of opaque rationalizations that become a means to legitimize historical conflicts with other communities not ordered by the same process. This later economy of meaning inevitably spirals toward swallowing or delegitimizing the communal other.

Martin S. Jaffee describes "elective monotheistic eschatology" as a positing of a revealed knowledge to a specific community that "is itself the warrant for ontological hatred of the very existence of the Other."[17] Jaffee describes how an eschatology is a self-disclosure of G*d that en-

---

16. Gibbs, *Suffering Religion.*

17. Jaffee, "One God, One Revelation, One People," 774.

ables human action to be understood within an onto-social structure that is discursively elaborated and implemented from within. "Each form of elective monotheism is a distinct *parole*, a historical mobilization of the discursive structure of elective monotheism in a unique symbolic vocabulary, whose distinctive parameters and possibilities of expression are worked out in the context of historical tradition."[18] Then Jaffee goes on to describe how each form of monotheism necessarily uses eschatology to explain and apply the limited nature of the community that is nevertheless established by a universal G*d. The future eschaton is the time when selfhood, community, and the other are at last bound together in a final unity with G*d. Thus, the gap between past revelation to a particular group and the limited nature of that group from the perspective of the world is rationalized by a philosophy of history characterized by violent struggle and conflict. "History is the time of struggle with the communal Other; the eschaton is the moment at which, if at all, that Other is identified with the Self and bound up in a universalist moral community."[19]

Likewise, Catherine Keller finds the warrant for deep hatred of the other in a metaphysics of apocalypse and opts instead for a "cosmology of counter-apocalypse" that she believes will affirm a goodness in an unfinished and perpetual creation.[20] So in the face of apocalypse, Keller seems to favor a more optimistic form of pietism as opposed to Jaffee's scholarly quietism in tune with a morality that waits.[21] This difference between these two is explainable by a (non)confidence in human nature, or more specifically in a courageous use of language. Both describe the embedded problem of the end as a *closed* narrative and thus describe problematic aspects of eschatology, which Schwarz attempts to straddle, but there is contradiction between their respective prescriptions for religion. While both want to avoid a conflation of narratives of history and ontologies of time because of the legitimation of violence toward the communal other, they disagree as to where the resources for nonviolence may be found. Both want true community based in truth, but

18. Ibid., 762.
19. Ibid., 774.
20. Keller, *Apocalypse Now and Then*, 172.
21. Keller is quick to distance a "counter-apocalyptic hope" from optimism in humanity. In contrast Jaffee writes with lament, "The universalist moral implications of elective monotheism, which emerge in the calm interior of the theologian's study, have not much to do with the way in which monotheism is embodied in living sociohistorical systems of religion." Jaffee, "One God, One Revelation, One People," 774.

the relation between history and the end of history seems jumbled when we consider their positions side by side. It is this quandary which I am suggesting prayer is suited to address as an apocalyptical discourse; as a relation of *langue* and *parole*, between the idea behind each word and its particular redemption or veracity. When this question is addressed then the nature of community may be peaceful and just if or when the communal other is addressable in good faith. A discursive relation to the other may be opened from within a religious system that is neither determined by history or its end. The ambiguous tensions of community may then contribute to a pursuit of truth and fairness rather than a spiraling of violence. The description of prayer that first comes about by the coincidence of two elements, brokenness and beyond brokenness, suggests how prayer may open a situation of ontological hatred and spiraling violence.

It is my position that prayer is an appropriate questioning of all visions: moral, eschatological, or apocalyptical. Prayer is uniquely situated to provide a critical opening of the closure of eschatology described by Jaffee and Keller. More specifically, the substance of my argument is that an apocalyptic(al) prayer—described here as a morally suspended narrative that decidedly offers itself to discourse—is a crucial step in opening memory to previous impossibilities. This practice of prayer refuses any covering up of guilt and is a dynamic discourse of cultural memory, neither indebted to a particular tradition nor tied to a universal syncretism. Such a prayer avoids forms of banality or ideology and is itself a criterion both inside and outside religious practices, as this project will elaborate. Thus, prayer may be a discursive participation in a widening of the family of religious persuasions, a practice celebrating each one's differences as a beginning of a new day.

An allegory could compare prayer to the bread found in a wilderness by the wandering Israelites. As morning by morning it is gathered fresh, even before it is called manna, the apocalyptical is a positive act *insofar as it sustains today* novelty itself, newness, and as such a renewal of remembrance. The point is that each act of memory, each calling, is unavoidably embraced by an unknowable apocalypse, an unbridgeable gap between now and the end. The apocalyptical then is memory not enslaved but not in possession of itself either. The apocalyptical does not reveal a secretive knowledge, often outlawed in modern times as gnosis, but is more the ongoing public performance of vulnerability or exposure even of one's own secrets. Such a memory could not only question escha-tology but also question why one asks such questions at all; it might also then listen as well.

Language, as an act of memory, never lingers long in this bottomless sphere of vulnerability. It seems there are pragmatic reasons and attain-able forms of justice when foundational answers are quickly accepted, and then the pragmatic reasons are soon forgotten and the foundations are codified, systematized, and rigidified. The pragmatic performance of foundations soon becomes a conspiratorial reduction of questioning to proper questioning. Even prayer, or what conspiratorially often passes for prayer, then subsumes itself in service to eschatologies, arbiters of truth, and economies of meaning, and all reinforcing apocalypticism. Prayer can become an artificial comfort; a ritual of empty consolation. Such prayer is like travelling on a highway with high walls on both sides, designed to by-pass unpleasant neighborhoods in order to deliver one-self quickly to a pre-decided destination.

The virtue of prayer may be its courageous performance, standing within a broken community, a broken place, a broken time; it is speech out of utter brokenness. An apocalyptical prayer is a remembrance of where one is; it is thus both a recognition and an act of responsibility. Perhaps the potential of prayerful suspension is that it may put one in-touch with an Other. In other words, the function of apocalyptical reflections may be to freshly begin remembrances of catastrophe or the unexplainable, an encountering of history as a risky venture. I contend that without apocalyptical prayer, explanation becomes self-satisfied and history becomes consoling myth, and canons harden. It refuses any final consolation or finalized eschatology. It refuses any escape from human history as anything more than brokenness, even our own. Thus, apoca-lyptical prayer may be understood as a humbling and fragmented partic-ipation in history as itself an apocalypse. This is similar to what Jacques Derrida refers to when using the word *différance*, as both differing and deferring.[22] But simultaneously it touches on what Jürgen Habermas calls communicative freedom, as it is never outlawed but is inherent to the life-world and then, in turn, is lost when opened to criticism.

I will discuss later, prayer's contribution to the issues at the inter-section of the theories of Derrida and Habermas. For now, I want to push aside this discussion to recollect in the next section a theological

22. Derrida, *Margins of Philosophy*, 21.

description of prayer that associates it with an apocalyptical light. This may enable better questions to be posed to Derrida and Habermas. Such a relevant description of prayer is found in Karl Barth's *Römerbrief*, written in eschatological terms and affected by the cultural apocalypse of 1918 Germany. Throughout his career Barth writes first of all as a person of prayer, which he first describes by recognizing Paul's letter to the Romans as a prayer. Karl Barth's career is best interpreted as a reflection on prayer. Although much is written about a shift from eschatology to Christology, from the earlier to later periods of his work, the underlying trope of prayer found in his Romans commentary is consistently at the center of his work until the end of his life.

3

Prayer and Karl Barth's Apocalyptic Discourse

GIVEN THE THREE CATEGORIES DEVELOPED IN CHAPTER 2, APOCAlypse, apocalypticism, and a middle category of apocalyptical prayer, this chapter begins to apply these categories to the comparative study of prayer. How is the study of a Christian theologian like Karl Barth helpful to the task of building a comparative framework for the comparative study of prayer? Barth explicitly links apocalyptical thought to the performance of prayer. Although Barth is overtly committed to the explication of Christian theology, he uses the existential philosophy of his day to describe an experience of the apocalyptic. From a detailed study of Barth's method of prayer, it is possible to see critical issues that develop in the lifetime work of Barth and also, for our more broadly construed program, the comparative study of prayer.

Prayer is the central trope throughout the works of Karl Barth. An appreciation of prayer provides us with the common method of his thought, linking his early, middle, and late periods. His positioning of prayer within apocalyptic thought is seen clearly in *Römerbrief* and it continues through his *Dogmatics*. He takes the reader through a lifetime journey of prayer involved in the critical study of a religion that is conceived as a discourse of memory, that is aware of both therapeutic concerns and problems of historiography. One will immediately see that early on Barth agrees that apocalyptical prayer represents a Christian opening of metaphysical views. Could Barth also accept that prayer is an everyday questioning of other religious traditions that are engaged in a discourse of collective memory? This is a question to keep in mind.

For now lets begin with a description of Barth's prayer as an apocalyptical disturbance, a word spoken to brokenness. This apocalyptical perspective of prayer that is key not only for understanding his scriptural studies but also for his relation to ethical or public discourses. His understanding of prayer is the categorical lens through which a vision of human community is made possible. However, issues arise about how prayer that is apocalyptic in perspective might also inform or allow for cooperative action. Does Barth later place a premium on an absolute quietude of prayer, performed in the scholar's study, listening to the activist's distant world of violent confrontation? What type of political community or *parole*, or political church, arises after an apocalyptic prayer that questions all human social structures? How then is suffering addressed?

Paul's Letter as an Apocalyptic Prayer

Karl Barth reads Paul's letter to the Romans as one continual prayer. He writes that the origin of this prayer as the great disturbance, a breaking into being that opens the possibility of a radically new future. Thus, Barth not only identifies the letter to the Romans as a prayer, this is also the key to his interpretation when he writes, "Are these words aught else but one precise prayer? Yet, even while writing these words he [Paul] knew that he did not know what he should pray for as he ought."[1] Barth's insight is that prayer provides a window upon the topic of salvation by indirectly describing an experience of the end of existence. As such, the letter is written in solidarity with fellow Christians, even though they have not seen each other and may never see each other. This invisible solidarity is a prayer manifest as a letter.

Barth tells us that Paul is "clear sighted" like Job and Dostoevsky. All three acknowledged "our concrete status in the world of time and of men and of things, lies under the shadow of death."[2] This experience beyond experience enables Paul to write about being known by a free G*d while also always keeping in mind the human inability to know the true G*d. This concrete experience of Otherness is intended to move beyond what Ludwig Feuerbach calls species-being, the projection of what is desirable for the species in the future to achieve. Feuerbach sees this as the identifier of true self-consciousness, what separates humans from the brutes: "Man is himself at once an I and Thou; he can put himself in the place of another. He can do so because for him his species [*Gattung*], his essence [*Wesen*], and not only his individuality, is an object of thought."[3]

1. Barth, *The Epistle to the Romans*, 316.
2. Ibid., 238.
3. Feuerbach, *Essence of Christianity*, 29.

Humanity progresses, overcomes alienation, by way of a projection of the future of the species. For example, to say "G*d is love" is to really mean the best ultimate future of humanity is one that actualizes love. Barth makes the point again and again that prayer is uttered by those who recognize that any identification of humanity with G*d is impossible. All human ethics are prone to this *disturbance* from the perspective of a theocentric prayer.[4] This perspective enables a contemplation of salvation but is not the anthropocentric "liberal" theology of enlightenment. This is preferable because anthropocentric perspectives deny G*d's unilateral grasp on creation, they find only the no-God of religion, which falls short of an authentic consideration of G*d's alterity. Paul's performance of letter writing is an act of true prayer because of his humble appreciation and even apprehension of a theocentric reality, while also recognizing the impossibility of this from any human perspective. So the letter has an *apocalyptic* function because it questions all human perspective against an impossible human knowledge.

Barth describes Paul's situation in existential terms shared by all today. The question "Is there a God?" is entirely relevant and indeed inevitable! But the answer to this question, that is to say, our desire to comprehend the world in relation to G*d, must proceed either from the criminal arrogance of religion or from the final apprehension of truth which lies beyond birth and death—this is what is meant by a perspective that proceeds from G*d outwards.[5]

Given this theocentrism, prayer remains an intangible human experience. For Barth, prayer is impossible for humans to initiate on their own and words of prayer are gifts unconditionally given from G*d. For a human even to stand still in the presence of G*d is impossible without G*d being there first.[6] As Barth understands, when mystics or seculars

---

4. Barth writes the famous introduction to Feuerbach's *The Essence of Christianity*, where he considers Stirner's "individual" as a step closer to real thinking. Stirner writes that Feuerbach's weakness as an inauthentic consideration of "evil and death" with respect to G*d. Barth writes what he believes Feuerbach does not: "Are we willing to admit that even in our relation to God, we are and remain liars, and that we can lay claim to His truth, His certainty, His salvation as *grace* and *only* as grace?" Barth, "Introduction," xxvii.

5. Barth, *The Epistle to the Romans*, 37.

6. Ibid., 59.

believe they "know how to pray," it is a prayer that falls short of communion with G*d.[7] In prayer, "we do not possess him—he us."[8]

Therefore, if prayer is presented as a discourse it is one different than other economies of language because the knowledge and possession of the object of language escapes human grasp; in prayer, at least in this precise prayer, there is no manipulation of the object.[9] In contrast, typical human speech strives to manipulate an object by a repetition of understanding; by saying "rock" repeatedly while referring to the same object(s), usual meaning is understood. A corresponding relation between the object and the sign takes root within a public consciousness or memory over time, which then transcends particular usages. So one is able to verify whether *it* is a rock or not. But prayer is a qualitatively different relation in speech to G*d and about G*d because it is made in the wake of G*d's self-revelation. Thus prayer is like a window from which to be seen, it is disclosure. Prayer then is being discovered in G*d's plan of salvation rather than to discover salvation oneself. As Barth writes, "In human fashion no man and no thing can make intercession for us. We stand alone, and are lost."[10] So then he writes that only in G*d's naming are there saints. Or, in other words, the holiness and freedom of G*d is our simultaneous destruction and salvation.

Paul is able to write a letter to the Romans as one continual prayer because the letter points beyond any human ability, it is a sign of a new and eternal age.[11] Here, the end of time is understood immanently when there is a denial of a human capacity to know G*d or any constructions to attain understandings of G*d's ways. For Barth, G*d's utter mercy is apparent in every word of Paul's letter. The most true response is a quiet waiting, as though something is beyond the present brokenness.

7. Ibid., 316.

8. Ibid., 315.

9. Ibid., 441.

10. Ibid., 317.

11. Barth uses the trope of an apocalypse to speak of a "new creation" which is a mysterious work of G*d. "There is no question here of contrasting a particular epoch in the life of a single individual, or of a group, or indeed of all mankind, with some other epoch, past or future." Ibid., 249. "The Spirit thinks and acts and works. Thou doest not know what this means. Neither do I. He has already spoken, already acted. But He has acted in direct contradiction of everything that I can say or thou canst hear—He contradicts even our questioning. He is completely Other. Confronting Him we are confronted with perfected speech and with perfected action." Ibid., 275.

There is no doubt that Barth is speaking of a common experience found in everyday life. There is a profound opportunity within the mundane. "To wait is the most profound truth of our normal, everyday life and work. Every agricultural laborer, every mother, every truly active or truly suffering man knows the necessity of waiting. And we must wait, as though there were something lying beyond good and evil, joy and sorrow, life and death; as though in happiness and disappointment, in growth and decay, in the 'Yes' and the 'No' of our life in the world, we were expecting something."[12] Similarly, everyday prayer is fundamentally waiting for something, described here as a profundity apart from religion.

No one, including Paul, knows how to pray. In fact prayer itself is singled out by Barth as particularly important while commenting on Rom 8:26. If prayer be thought of as a tangible experience and glorified as such, the objection is justified which Feuerbach brought against all religion: "we do not know." Beyond this "we-not" lies the reality of communion with G*d.[13] For Barth, prayer is more than "species-being" and human projection; his radical theocentricity allows for an incorporation of the brokenness of history as an element of prayer. It is the possibility that brokenness and that which is beyond brokenness coincide. Then how might this coincidence of opposites in Barth's understanding of prayer be inscribed as knowledge or even as a norm from which a cooperative community can truly act to alleviate suffering in its full soteriological sense? By describing an alienation that is not overcome by any knowledge, is the only alternative then an acceptance in quietude?

Some interpreters of Barth take issue with an abstraction of history but there is a spectrum of assessments here. Johann Baptist Metz finds an inadequate politics in Barth while Eberhard Jüngel appreciates his political foundation and dialectic precisely because it is not anthropocentric and not a predicate for theological reflection. Catherine Keller finds Barth to be "suspended somewhere between anti- and neo-apocalyptic theology" but nevertheless patriarchal and parochial.[14] Neither rejecting nor embracing his political foundations, she suggests a "post-Barthian theology of Barthian hope" which manifests itself in three characteristics; 1) hope is not to be bound to optimism, 2) it is always found in action,

---

12. Ibid., 314.
13. Ibid., 316.
14. Keller, *Apocalypse Now and Then*, 126.

3) and always performed in and with the community and the world. These characteristics seem to be a fair starting place for assessment and will be brought back into the analysis toward the end of this work to assess whether an apocalyptical prayer as described here meets these criteria.

While all these readers of Barth will admit that for him it is in prayer that hope is made real, it is not always understood how prayer is considered not in terms of its worshipful meaning but in its concrete occurrence. The concrete or everyday calling upon G*d remains problematic insofar as prayer's apocalyptical aporias remain questionable themselves, but this differs from the issuance of a paradox, which issues from the incommensurability of divinity and humanity. Barth describes a double aporia concerning prayer: one cannot avoid prayer and yet prayer is the most questionable act of all. "Placed as we are and grievously oppressed, how can we avoid calling upon God? . . . Uncomfortably this energy of prayer presses into the world of men. It is almost as though the normally parabolic action of men were in prayer disturbed by the intrusion of the absolute human act. And yet what a paradox it is! For is there any human activity so utterly questionable as the busy praying of men?"[15]

This double aporia refuses any validation of prayer itself except that which questions whether there is any action so questionable as prayer, which opens prayer as an everyday questioning of ethics. Prayer and ethics are intertwined insofar as the questions, "Why?" and "What now?" continually disturb any human understanding of its own grievous oppression and suffering. Therefore prayer questions all conceptions of community and any conception of neighbor, insofar as they address human suffering. In prayer all ethics are unfinished parable, a narrative where the status of "community" and "neighbor" are precisely the point for the grievously oppressed. Parabolic action offers a completed interpretation of itself, but prayer's questioning lends itself to an ongoing discourse about any narrative. Such prayer is apocalyptical and discursive because it asks these questions while also being open to any questioning itself.

For now there is one main question that I find most appropriate about this questioning questionable prayer. This question comes from reading Barth from the perspective of Metz who rejects an "argumentative" discourse because it ultimately fails to fully recognize human suffer-

15. Barth, *The Epistle to the Romans*, 458.

ing in the process of redemption, and who differentiates an apocalyptical discourse from a systematic one. Metz writes in an apology for narrative theology:

> The non-identity of the history of suffering cannot be canceled out in a dialectical process of the Trinitarian history of salvation in such a way that it preserves its historical character. This is because this non-identity is not the same as the negativity of the dialectical process . . . A purely conceptual reconciliation between the history of salvation, as an expression of the history of redemption accomplished in Jesus Christ, and the history of man's suffering is, in my opinion, not possible because it can lead either to a dualistic gnostic perpetuation of suffering in God or to a reduction of suffering in the level of a concept.[16]

There are two wrong turns difficult to avoid. One is dualism that eternalizes suffering and the other wrong turn is a false filtering of it. In either case, prayer then would cease to be discursive and more a matter of ideological rigor and an application of didactics. So for Metz an indispensable issue for prayer is its involvement in the political landscape. Prayer must be critical of its own involvement in suffering and injustice. Metz is not far from Barth's description of prayer as we will see, but the distinctions may be most important. Both agree that prayer cannot conceptualize redemption without ceasing to be a prayer of hope, even by the criteria Keller sets down. So with Metz and Keller, one must inquire whether Barth's description of prayer sufficiently exposes its own purposes and self-interests, even while speaking of a theocentric origin of prayerful language. One must then ask what constitutes a *sufficient exposure* of purpose and self-interest where a prayerful discourse is concerned in a global society?

Barth's G*d speaks always in "eternal silence" and any direct communication with G*d is for Barth "altogether destroyed."[17] The eternal and vast chasm between G*d and humanity is marked only by a consuming silence. This is a typical dualism that marks apocalyptic texts, and which contrasts the way of G*d with the way of humanity or in this case the message of G*d with the words of humanity. Barth's dilemma of human speech and G*d is stated succinctly in a 1922 lecture, "As theo-

---

16. Metz, "A Short Apology for Narrative," 258.
17. Barth, *The Epistle to the Romans*, 98.

logians we ought to speak of God, we are human however, we can never speak of God."[18]

Some observers see here confirmation of an eschatological perspective of Barth insofar as he is focused upon an impossibility of human speech. I suggest that an apocalyptical trope is more suited. Since eschatology relates to a history that exists as an order of human communications born and brought into view by reason, Barth's point about human words is apocalyptical in that all such ordering of history is already understood as destroyed by G*d's freedom. Here Barth recognizes another process of enlightenment, one not viewable as history and not reducible or criticizable from any known viewpoint.[19] An order of new creation is initiated by the speech of those like Paul who pray for a new order of creation different from an enlightenment or process of human reason. Such prayer creates anew by a light of utter and complete questionability, even the questionability of all questions. If one calls this an eschatological perspective, it is important to understand that Barth is not speaking of a future of human making or participation. He is speaking of an always possible complete collapse of every time and every possible history.

Walter Lowe calls this aspect of Barth's theology a *wound* of reason. By this word *wound*, Lowe makes the point, "Barth could hardly be more explicit that what he has meant by contradiction up to this point has *not* been opposition; and that is only now, now that one considers the absence of faith that it becomes *a sorrowful opposition.*"[20] Along this same line Barth writes: "This, however, is not secured by means of some Entelechy or perfecting of the whole natural organism, but by his being confronted by that which is common to all humans, namely, by the eternal distinction of God."[21] Barth is in agreement with Immanuel Kant in the sense that there is *no mediation* between G*d and humanity. For Barth religious mediation is problematic to morality and freedom, much as it is for Kant, because it confuses eternity with time, G*d with humanity. Barth even makes plain his agreement with Kant in the Romans com-

---

18. Barth, *The Word of God and the Task of Theology*. Jüngel comments that this "recognition" as Barth calls it, is above all "aporetic" in the systematic sense, which is fundamentally different from making G*d the escape from traps of logic. Jüngel, *Karl Barth: A Theological Legacy*, 69.

19. Barth, *The Epistle to the Romans*, 435.

20. Lowe, *Theology and Difference: The Wound of Reason*, 39–40.

21. Barth, *The Epistle to the Romans*, 442.

mentary: "Pure ethics require—and here we are in complete agreement with Kant—that there should be no mixing of heaven and earth in the sphere of morals. Pure ethical behavior depends upon its primal origin, an origin that needs to be protected by a determination on our part to call God and man, man, however much we may be tempted to stray into romanticism."[22]

As it is important to see how Kant's practical concerns are not rejected by Barth, it is also helpful to see where the departure from Kant is underlined. Barth holds Kant's feet to the fire by holding him to his word and remembering the problem of *all* human speech, even his own and even if it is well intentioned. "It is not for us to add to God's right against every person the right of one person against another! . . . Nothing what we call peace—here we are unable to follow Kant—is even a preparation for eternal peace, for the kingdom of practical reason."[23] Unlike Kant, Barth brings the eternal distinction of G*d to bear upon himself first, and thus also any practical reason or judgment. Barth accepts no cunning of reason as admitted by Kant and then applied by Hegel to history. Thus, human naming of any eternal peace or any good action remains impossible even after the recognition of an eternal distinction.[24]

There is no naming of peace in light of the eternal distinction and no human economy of interaction that can be given over to idealism; G*d remains hidden from human conception. So any community of human discourse need be continually disturbed when it names or makes unify-

22. I see here an allusion to one of Kant's essays, "The mechanisms of nature, in which self-seeking inclinations naturally counteract one another in their external relations, can be used by reason as a means to prepare the way for its own end, the rule of right, as well as to promote and secure the nation's internal and external peace." Kant, "To Perpetual Peace: a Philosophical Sketch," 367. Whether or not a federation of nations may exist today for the cause of keeping peace (Kant calls for a United Nations), for Barth the realization of peace is always by G*d's action. Neither human nor natural reason can even name peace. Barth's optimism always rests entirely on G*d's Otherness. Barth, *The Epistle to the Romans*, 432.

23. Ibid., 470.

24. Thucydides' "The War of the Peloponnesians and the Athenians" is the first and best statement on this matter, for me. It describes well how the rational but prideful Athenians become mad with aspirations of justice, their own justice. The Athenian Generals to the Melians who are besieged, "If you have met to reason about presentiments of the future, or for anything else than to consult for the safety of your state upon the facts that you see before you, we will cease talking; otherwise we will go on." Thucydides, *The Landmark Thucydides: A Comprehensive Guide to the Peloponnesian War*, 351.

ing assumptions of communication, or from within its own life-world. Barth's moral-ethical discourse is different from Kant's not because it requires that G*d be G*d, but because it casts out in an apocalyptical manner the no-G*d that pretends to liberate by questioning but in reality closes existence into a ghetto of rationalism.

Paul's words are read as a participation in solidarity with others through Christ, one based in practical and fundamental discourse. A universal discourse proceeds from Paul's recognition of G*d as G*d that always disturbs any human ability to speak of G*d, and therefore any human discourse, but this is a sign of communal solidarity, not contrary to it. "The reality of the righteousness of God is attested by its universality. It is not irrelevant that it is precisely Paul, who daring in Jesus, to put his trust boldly in grace alone, is able, in Jesus, also to perceive the divine breaking down of all human distinctions . . . The Pharisee who prays can indeed become a missionary, but not a missionary of the Kingdom of God."[25] This is why the criticism of religion is the beginning of all criticism.

The political import of such a sphere of discourse centers around an apocalyptical awareness of every word and the breaking down of all human distinctions. Barth can agree with Metz that suffering is not explainable or justifiable, but then what happens to suffering in prayer, or from the perspective of prayer? If human identity remains aporetic insofar as the separation of G*d from humanity is always maintained, so human reason is always wounded insofar as prayerful discourse remains disturbed by its own inability to know how to pray, then what?[26] It seems the individual is now the irreducible category of redemption. For this reason, Barth warns against a fall into romanticism when the individual is thought of as something autonomous from eternity or finally able to pray on one's own. But unlike romanticism, which builds upon and pro-

---

25. Barth, *The Epistle to the Romans*, 100.

26. Eberhard Jüngel comments on this lecture, "This recognition is a matter of aporia (perplexity or doubt). The theology he had learned recognized no systematic theological apori; it only knew how to escape before getting trapped in a situation from which there was no escape. Barth thought these means of escape were too commonplace, an all to smoothly paved boulevard which he was not prepared to travel. He sought paths that stood up to aporia. For this reason his thought became above all aporetic. And with this aporetic knowledge his theological beginnings came to an end." If Jüngel means that aporia was left behind in Barth's later stages, I would disagree. The aporia of prayer remains underneath everything Barth did later. Jüngel, *Karl Barth: A Theological Legacy*, 69.

tects the freedom of the person, Barth calls for an individuality that is "nothing but sacrifice and demonstration: and which does not also, in claiming this 'nothing but,' impinge upon the freedom of God."[27] This "nothing but" can also become a historicism if it enables some other naming of the good that is not questionable, or in any way usurps the place of G*d. For Barth, "nothing but sacrifice" remains an indispensable position of humanity eternally distinct from G*d.[28]

Our solidarity with other men is alone adequately grounded, when with others—or apart from them, since we may not wait for them!—we stretch out beyond everything that we are and have, and behold the wholly problematical character of our present position. The need of forgiveness of sin might in fact be regarded as a Dionysiac enthusiasm, were it not that it can be placed in no such human category. True negation is directed as much against the denial of this life as it is in acceptance of it.[29]

Barth proposes an end of all human justification that will not always already accept its problematic nature. In other words, Barth describes an apocalyptical discourse that is always aware of the brokenness and suffering in life, and also does not turn this awareness into a feeling or fact that may then be systematically elucidated. He attempts to describe a discourse that is neither grounded in relations that are constructed by rational or metaphysical argument nor any romantic or mystical understanding of life and death.[30] Rather a discourse of prayer is first of all already seen and heard by G*d; one speaks and acts only by G*d's loving providence for creation. So prayer is an utter questioning of existence within G*d's freedom and by G*d's will.

All our action and relation is secondary to this original relation rediscovered as *being discovered in prayer*. This is crucial for moral development because it is in prayer that we are discovered with a purpose in and for *relation*, while yet in a mode of utter questioning. It is this secondary ethical action of self-recollection bent backwards to its origin, to

27. Barth, *The Epistle to the Romans*, 433.

28. McCormack cites Ingrid Spiekermann at this point, who argues that this ties with an "analogy of the cross." However, as I will argue later, an analogy like this is tied to a narrative and is insufficient itself as a representation of something which itself excludes human language. McCormack, *Karl Barth's Critically Realistic Dialectical Theology*, 261.

29. Barth, *The Epistle to the Romans*, 101.

30. "What we can see in the other is here totally irrelevant . . . The Body in the parable is therefore neither the sum of its particular members, nor the consequence of their interaction." Ibid., 442–43.

the primary ethical action, where it participates in the power and dignity of its origin. The secondary action of demonstrating its own transcendental purpose is itself fulfilled when the individual stands before G*d.[31]

This may be Barth's most remarkable description of prayer. He means something different from an Aristotelian prudence or moderation by which the human pays homage to the gods. Rather, to act soberly is to act in the presence of G*d, already conscious of one's origin in G*d's freedom and thus also in the light of G*d's judgment. Prayer is like a meditative envisioning by the light of G*d's original purposes. There is no direct governance of individual human ethics, but an indirect governance discernible only when prayer is both an act of rethinking and also a veritable worship or acknowledgement of G*d as beyond. "Repentance, as the primary ethical action, is the act of rethinking . . . There is an act of thinking which, because it dissolves itself and every act, is identical with the *veritable worship of God*, with utter, bowed adoration of Him."[32] G*d is revealed as the possibility of a human autonomy that is inclusive of others as an apocalyptical perspective upon of every human action. The historical impossibility of human solidarity is a possibility when the freedom of G*d is not diminished by human purposes and justifications, or when a new epoch has begun. Thus he writes the strange words, "Human exhortation is justified only when it is seen to be void of human justification: that is to say when it is grounded upon the *mercies of God*."[33]

One continues to ask whether human suffering is taken seriously when discourse and thereby any community rejects its own justification in an apocalyptical manner. In other words, without trying to reduce it into the non-identity of an over-determined dialectic. Barth's prayerful and apocalyptical perspective is an attempt to be more true and more relevant to each instance of suffering; to address each instance without falling into a systematizing form of eschatology. G*d's coming is a merciful apocalypse. It destroys all human constructions of history and thus is the comfort of a coming day of justice to people who suffer without witness or understanding. The marginalized of history find consolation in apocalyptic texts which speak of G*d's ending to things. These who are lost in any explanation of history especially find mercy and hope in an in-

31. Ibid., 444.
32. Ibid.
33. Ibid., 429.

terruption of the flow of time that is more of the same.[34] Barth brings this future ending into the present by describing an apocalyptic perspective upon human discourse which is interrupted by the revelatory event of an everyday prayer that makes space for a re-thinking, even repentance. He describes human discourse and community as a consequence of such revelation, which breaks into our midst and which need be understood as "destructive of fellowship."[35] This is in contrast to a community of communication that is a consequence of a history of knowledge, as we will discuss later in Jürgen Habermas. For this reason Barth speaks of the virtue of *in*tolerance rather than tolerance. "Tolerance is, no doubt, a virtue without which none of us can live; but we must, nevertheless, at least understand that it is, strictly speaking, destructive of fellowship, for it is a gesture by which the divine disturbance is rejected. The one in whom we are veritably united is himself the great intolerance."[36]

Barth's description of an apocalyptical prayerful discourse is one of a pervasive questioning of all non-theocentric meaning.[37] This description of prayer remained a constant starting point throughout his career. While some interpreters may see the development of the anhypostatic-enhypostatic Election/Christology as a material departure from an earlier period, a focus on Barth's work as prayer leads readers to see a *continuity* that supersedes the usual segmentation of his earlier and later periods of thought. He is best understood as *first of all* a person of prayer. The apocalyptical discourse of prayer is more than a "red thread" which ties together his whole development as Bruce McCormack suggests of his neo-Kantian background. But I suggest that Barth's remnant of Kant is no longer what can be called Kantian idealist epistemology because

---

34. This reminds one of Walter Benjamin's use of a *weak messianism*. "Thinking involves not only the flow of thoughts, but their arrest as well. Where thinking suddenly stops in a configuration pregnant with tensions, it gives that configuration a shock, by which it crystallizes into a monad. A historical materialist approaches a historical subject only where he encounters it as a monad. In this structure he recognizes the sign of a Messianic cessation of happening, or put differently, a revolutionary chance in the fight for the oppressed past." In the next paragraph, Benjamin states that the experience of this "Messianic time . . . coincides exactly with the stature which the history of mankind has in the universe." I am suggesting that in Barth a similar parallel or analogy between prayer and the history of humanity, which is more adequately understood as an expectation of the One yet to come. Benjamin, *Illuminations*, 262–63.

35. Ibid., 445.

36. Ibid.

37. Ibid., 502.

the Kantian rejection of heteronomous reason is itself rejected while the Kantian affirmation of moral autonomy or good will is also rejected. What is left is prayer given as an interruption of all human will *and/or* reason.

Prayer is like an ongoing and everyday historiography, but one that questions all interests of will *and* reason. So that later in *The Holy Spirit and the Christian Life*, Barth can write of prayer as a peculiarly non-justified but warranted description of a dynamic reality that is an opening of human discourse, which is, in turn, creative.

> The wonder of prayer—and this is something quite different from the "infused grace" of ability to pray aright—is the incoming of the Holy Spirit to the help of the person who is praying. It is the Spirit's sighing, which, to be sure is in our mouth; yet as his groaning, who creates out of the man who is sober or drunken or finical, or even the *homo religiosus* who has utterly collapsed (I mean by that, the man who prays in himself and to himself): out of a man of that kind, the Holy Spirit makes a person who *actually, really* prays.[38]

Like Paul who prays without knowing how to pray, a person actually really prays from G*d; one thus lives life in disturbance, and also as a new creation. Prayer as an apocalyptical encounter by G*d is a new creation, a new ordering of the person. Elsewhere, he goes further to describe how this encounter works itself into an ecclesial discourse in his *Church Dogmatics*.

A Community of Discourse in Prayer

Karl Barth's criticism of Kant's epistemology, his apocalyptical wounding of reason that nevertheless recognizes each history as transitory, begins our exploration of prayer as a discourse. While he reaffirms a Kantian commitment that reason cannot understand the ways of G*d, he rejects that which limits the freedom of G*d in any way, even *piety*. So it is the disclosure of this divine freedom that, in turn, becomes the basis for human action. He reasons only as a result of a disclosure of G*d; a revelation from beyond the knowable. Thus, prayer unites humanity as no other ideology, because prayer is an appreciation of the questionability of all human perspectives, it is a great leveling. For Barth even the non-sincere

---

38. Barth, *The Holy Spirit and the Christian Life: The Theological Basis of Ethics*, 68.

can pray, but only true believers receive the disclosure of G*d that is the foundation of Christian community, which is fundamentally a discursive union. So if the rich Christian does not suffer with, in solidarity with the poor, then their prayers are heard more as escapism and amnesia rather than as the truth of a unity heard only in silence. "The Pharisee who prays can indeed become a missionary, but not a missionary of the Kingdom of God. The strange UNION—of men one with another—must assert and expose the strange, yet saving, SEPARATION—between God and man . . . Nothing must be allowed to disturb this paradox . . . All flesh must be silent before the inconspicuousness of God, in order that all flesh may see his salvation."[39] But then is Barth's own prayer sufficient? Must not prayer that questions the rational foundations of human society also demand the silence of all flesh? This seems to ostracize conceptions of human freedom, as Barth writes: "The freedom of the man under grace is founded on the good pleasure of God; and has no other foundation . . . Free in God, ye are imprisoned in Him. This is the categorical imperative of grace and of the existential belonging-to-God. Knowledge here emerges as the distinction between the old and new man; a distinction which is, however, immediately dissolved in the oneness of the new man."[40]

Step one in answering how Barth's own prayers have a sufficiency, is to keep in mind this is a rewriting of the categorical imperative into soteriological terms. In the next paragraph he states that all language is insufficient to the extent it is non-paradoxical. This is why in Christianity there is no longer any direct communication.

Now, if one summarizes Barth's description of prayer as an apocalyptical event that disturbs all discourse—which calls into question all legitimacy by recognition of an always deeper gap between G*d and humanity—then prayer is G*d's coming, a messianic moment.[41] And if the "no-G*d" of all human constructions is cast out, then all truly prayerful economies of meaning are counter-religious. They are not reliant upon orders of nature, society, or personhood, which always tend to confuse time and eternity.

---

39. Barth, *The Epistle to the Romans*, 100.

40. Ibid., 220.

41. Sallie McFague writes, "Barth saw creation as totally enclosed within election and totally defined by it." McFague, *The Body of God*, 221.

However helpful as a starting place, Barth's description of prayer opens a bevy of issues for us. For example, how then does one mediate between conflicting revelatory events? Certainly different prayers do not lead different people to one conclusion—often prayers conflict. In a global society that calls for a global discourse, can prayer provide a universal starting point? Later Barth refocuses material aspects of his theology to answer this type of question from within Christianity, but never does he diminish the importance of prayer as a universal foundation for discourse.

Barth's interpreters see a discontinuity between an earlier and later Barth that has lost an understanding of how prayer as apocalyptical. He describes a discourse important to the sustenance of community as it is described in *Church Dogmatics*. This is, all in all, a critique of prayers by Barth's own prayer. The *Church Dogmatics* distinguishes between true and false prayers by presuming words of the church to be signs of grace and thereby aporetic and therefore contingent upon an apocalyptical Word of G*d. While at the same time the *Dogmatics* do not presume all words of the church to be equal or most efficient representations of this impossible conversion. "The Church's prayers and hymns and confessions of faith obviously are what they purport to be only to the extent that so far as possible they cease to attempt *the impossible task of proclaiming something to God or the unworthy one of incidentally proclaiming one to humanity*"[42] (italics mine). These opposing aporetic criteria of prayer continue to set the right and left banks of a community of discourse. The right bank is the impossibility of prayer, which is the apocalyptical theme in Romans. The left bank an exhortation to a prayerful discourse like that described by Anselm. Barth envisions an entire community as a river of prayer between these two banks, an accumulation of authentic and effective prayers by individuals that represent a conversation about conversion. Community thus conceived is fundamentally a soteriological project; individuals and groups participate in a common pursuit of a new unity.

Important to understanding the relation of the earlier to the later understanding of prayer, I would like to comment on the 1930 book, *Anselm: Fides Quaerens Intellectum*. Many interpreters of Barth pay attention to this particular volume as a shift. One sees however, as in *Romans*, that the entire commentary on Anselm is based on a presup-

42. Barth, *Church Dogmatics*, 49.

position of prayer, which frames Barth's understanding of Anselm. Barth explains, "Anselm speaks about God while speaking to him. The knowledge which the proof seeks to expound and impart is the knowledge that is peculiar to faith, knowledge of what is believed from what is believed. It is—and this is why it has to be sought in prayer—a knowledge that must be bestowed on humans."[43] Barth recognizes Anselm's evangelical prayer as one lacking a certain certainty of G*d; his faith is unfinished. Thus, a vision of G*d that is partially eclipsed by others disbelief calls for conversation with those others. Anselm's faith in G*d is never doubted itself, but it submits to a questioning by others who doubt that it submits to reason. "It is the presupposition of all theological inquiry that faith as such remains undisturbed by the theological yes and no."[44] Theology remains a description undisturbed.

So what Barth finds most interesting about the *intellectus fidei* of Anselm's prayer is not only G*d's confrontation of Anselm, but also G*d's indwelling of Anselm's reasons to converse at all, his intellectual commitments. "It [*intellectus*] cannot establish this object of faith as such but rather has to understand it in its very incomprehensibility. Yet nevertheless, it has to progress at the level of reflection, expressing in symbols what in itself cannot be expressed . . . In the end the fact that it reaches its goal is grace, both with regard to the perception of the goal and the human effort to reach it; and therefore in the last analysis it is a question of prayer and the answer to prayer."[45] The end is not achieved yet, nor can one claim it in any form other than it's questioning. But Anselm claims his questioning is an *investigare,* directed by G*d's absence as a dog tracks by scent and not sight.[46] Prayer continues to be anti-metaphysical and strangely eschatological in the apocalyptic sense. This is reminiscent

43. Barth, *Anselm*, 100.

44. Ibid., 18.

45. Ibid., 40.

46. Anselm uses the Latin word *investigare* to describe his own research; the Latin has the double meaning that can refer to a dog following a trail on a scent. So always coming afterward, as the thing pursued is gone, only leaving a trace. All this could sound like a philosophical or metaphysical closure of deduction, as one relentlessly drives toward a foreordained conclusion. But here it is the *"ratione necessariae"* which is not an *apriori*, but always comes after a given text and always is pursued on the same field as the questions are raised, within "the *Credo* itself". "And so, not mastering the object but being mastered by it, he achieves true noetic ration—a real comprehension of the ontic ratio of the object of faith; he attains to the *intellectus fidei.*" Barth, *Anselm*, 55.

of Romans, in the sense that the questionability of all existence remains at hand as prayer's own eschaton. But how can utter questioning also be an investigation drawn forward, progressing on a path of knowledge? Is not the path itself questioned, or the idea of forward and backwards? How can a questioning of "what is" from the perspective of "what cannot fail to be" refrain from ideologizing the real and the good, while at the same time not falling into a solipsism of faith?

Barth distinguishes between the inner and outer text of Scripture and creed. Stated succinctly, the tradition of interpretation exceeds itself and is thus related to a *veritas rationes*, or Truth itself. Because unbelievers today may be believers tomorrow (and the reverse), so also theology cannot dissolve the relation of faith and knowledge "by virtue of which faith is obedience to authority which must be prior to knowledge."[47] Anselm's discourse claims no qualitative difference from the doubter. Barth underlines that Anselm chooses to speak to the *insipiens or fool* contrary to biblical injunction, "in which case all discussion with him is pointless and meaningless."[48] Anselm throws pearls to the swine with the confidence that the fool and himself are on different parts of the same path. Anselm and the fool walk the path from *credere* to *inteligere*, as the fool cannot deny this as the nature of all truth. But the conversation is foremost an act of faith for Anselm, it is a prayer. Anselm's interpretation of the quest of the unbeliever enables him then to engage in a discussion with him without either accepting the unbeliever's criterion—such a universal human reason—or stipulating that in order for the unbeliever to be competent to discuss he must first be converted into a believer.[49] So Anselm's crusade is for the inclusion of the other. One could say that there are finally no infidels within Anselm's prayer.

This prayerful perspective enables Barth to reflect upon Anselm's ontic and noetic economies. Simply put ontic rationality—or the necessary relation between the "object of faith" and knowledge of it—precedes any noetic rationality or even noetic necessity. As he states, "ontic rationality is not ultimate but is only true rationality measured along side the *summa veritas*, the same is true for the ontic necessity that is consistent with it."[50] Perhaps Anselm's use of necessity is intended to give him in-

47. Ibid., 64.
48. Ibid., 65.
49. Ibid., 67.
50. Then in a footnote Barth states of Anselm, "Ontic necessity is ascribed in *Cur Deus Homo* to the incarnation and to the atoning death of Christ. It should never have

sight into the being of G*d and Barth asks if this is *apriori* theology. He will not venture to guess but notes that "The road taken by Anselm's later writings (and it is in *Cur Deus homo* that this is most clearly seen), leads in the opposite direction."[51] Is Barth alluding that Anselm may have changed his mind on the nature of necessity? Perhaps, but it is clear that Barth believes that even in the *Monologian* "we are confronted by a very pronounced rejection of speculation that does not respect the incomprehensibility of the reality of the object of faith, by a recognition of the indirectness of all knowledge of God, and also, though more clearly in the *Proslogian*, by the reference to the pattern of faith which is the basis of everything."[52]

Neither Barth nor Anselm want to confuse knowledge of faith for faith itself, while at the same time they always are remembering that knowledge is inseparable from faith. Anselm describes his procedure, moving from the relative to the final and real "as a *conciere* such that the question *sive sit in re aliquid huius modi* might remain an open question."[53] For this to remain an open question, the existence of G*d is a question that is necessary in itself. However, this necessity is not to be combined, or is inexplicable if combined with the unity and aseity of G*d, and or creation.[54] Rather, this formula remains only as a prayer, existent only by the mercy of G*d. Because it remains only as a prayer it opens all rationality, ecclesial and secular, to a faithful Truth beyond human reason.

This conversation between believer and unbeliever sounds a note of resonance that informs any human discourse. Anselm's knowledge in faith, rather than faith in knowledge, comes always after G*d as prayer investigates all unknowns. Anselm offers a performative proof that knowledge contextualized within ontic necessity walks a common path shared by all humans. At the same time, Anselm's practice is a participation within a conversation capable of opening a path to salvation for all,

---

been overlooked that ontic necessity in Anselm can as little be a final word as any other word that is not the inexpressible Word of the One and Only God, glorious in himself." Ibid., 51.

51. Ibid., 56.

52. Ibid., 57.

53. Ibid.

54. Thus Anselm shows us a "reality of Revelation which cannot be analyzed by any causal or teleological construction but which is rational and necessary in itself." Ibid., 58.

or so he believes. Prayer is thus a discourse accessible to all interested in opening the question of G*d as "that than which nothing greater can be conceived." This means that prayer's conversation can never settle upon a particular ontic necessity without closing conversion off to someone and thus off to oneself. Anselm's conversation with the fool (*insipiens*) is the advent of one's own conversion as well.

Church Dogmatics

From 1932 to 1968 Barth continually published fourteen volumes of *Church Dogmatics*. It is widely regarded the most important theological work of the twentieth century. After one sees that Romans is a letter written as an apocalyptical prayer and that Anselm's proof-investigation is also understood as a performance of prayer, one can begin to address the *Church Dogmatics* as an inscription *of* prayer *by* prayer. The fourteen massive volumes are simply the discourse of a community that is closed off to no questioning. This performance of prayer claims no knowledge of how to pray. Barth participates in a conversation with/about G*d that necessitates no particular metaphysics within prayer. Instead he describes a course of inter-subjectivity discovered pursuing conversion or an awakening to reality. In other words, he takes an organic approach to history/reality or historiography. Barth's view of inter-subjectivity is when all human pretensions to presence are given back to G*d. Barth frames this inter-subjectivity within an eschatological reality, which Paul's prayer attempts to convey by an inadequate participation. The relation of knowledge and faith is then understood within this same reality where sinners become saints and saints become sinners, as modeled by Anselm's prayerful theology. In *Church Dogmatics* it is in prayer that the elements of an inter-subjectivity are read as the church's humble and audacious economy of meaning, always revealed within ambiguities.

As far as a prayerful discourse is concerned, the *Church Dogmatics* need not be segregated from the prayerful method of the Romans commentary.

Bruce McCormack describes the *Dogmatics* as an impossible and thus dialectical performance of discourse, similar to my description of an apocalyptical prayer as found in the *Romans* commentary. McCormack describes the *Dogmatics* in terms that are familiar to us from *Romans*. The object of the *Dogmatics* is G*d; *Deus dixit*—G*d speaking in person. "And that means that the object of this science is not given over to human hands. Human beings have no power of disposal over it. It is this that makes dogmatics an impossible task (humanly speaking!)."[55] McCormack sees that Barth's focus on G*d, as the object of science, entail's delimitation on four sides so as not to be given over to human hands. The first is a denial of any abstraction of revelation. Second, there is no mixture of revelation with its medium. Third, there is no quantification of revelation that is wholly given. Fourth, there is no continuity between humans and revelation, thus no economy of an analogy between G*d's action and human actions, but there are fragments and degrees of analogy.[56] When taken as a picture-framing of theological perspective, the parameters of a "needles eye" come into better focus.[57] These are now a framing of prayer as discourse and one can see the similarities with what I have described as an apocalyptical prayer.

When these four parameters are seen as a window frame, the communicative-action taking place within it is a prayer itself. Thoughts, words, and actions are perceived as prayers and so Barth is able to write; "Prayer can be the recognition that we accomplish nothing by our intentions, even though they be intentions to pray. Prayer can be the expression of our human willing of the will of God. Prayer can be the expression that for good or evil man justifies God and not himself. Prayer can be the human answer to the divine hearing already granted, the epitome of the true faith which we cannot assume of ourselves. We do not speak of true prayer if we say 'must' instead of 'can.'"[58] The reader is here duly reminded that prayer is not a guarantee of successful theological work but Barth is unable to see any other possible way to think and act theologically except as a prayerful discourse.

---

55. McCormack, *Karl Barth's Critically Realistic Dialectical Theology*, 345.

56. Ibid., 352–54.

57. Jüngel describes Barth's theological beginnings, which are nonetheless recognizable later. "The assertion that such thoughts are impossible is posted like a guard at the shrine. The category of "impossible possibility" in this phase of Barth's thought does not mean to stifle theological thinking itself. Rather, the process of thought should be set right: the divine possibility in question can only be conceived (and therefore should be conceived) through the *needle's eye* of recognizing its human and earthly impossibility . . . For this reason his thought, his knowledge, became above all *aporetic*."(italics mine) Jüngel, *Karl Barth: A Theological Legacy*, 69.

58. Barth, *Church Dogmatics I.1*, 23.

Like Augustine and Anselm, discourse after prayer is gift, the thought that is thought which is a *donum Spiritus sancti*, and thusly can be "understood only from the standpoint of the divine Subject."[59] Augustine prays when he realizes how hazardous his speech and his thinking are in the presence of G*d.[60] This realization is similar to Anselm's recognition of the unrest of faith.[61] Augustine's exposition of the triunity of G*d is from the perspective of prayer that risks a "fullness of vision." It is in prayer that the fullness of vision connects identity with conversion. As when Augustine prays, "Where did I learn of you? How could I know what I didn't know, save in yourself and above myself."[62] The fullness of vision is the prayer that supplants all metaphysics with soteriology. Reality is a prayer made by G*d for the sake of humanity. This amounts to a continually new giving, "the *donum Spiritus sancti*, which refuses to be abstracted from its Giver. But the Giver is God."[63] Any notion of our own understanding of good and bad personhood is left behind in light of this Gift. Any publicanism or self-justification is here outlawed, but this may never outlaw or diminish any personality or subjectivity, instead an authentic diversity is the object of the Gift of renewing prayer. Thus, church narrative is not a process of identity by which G*d is named God, but rather it is a prayer begun in G*d's hearing.[64] The Christian life is the continuing birth of discussion between G*d and humanity that is the Word of G*d for us.

The *Dogmatics* are a prayerful questioning of prayers as an ongoing apocalyptical event of giving by G*d. The so-called church is criticized insofar as it interjects within the apocalyptical meta-narrative and thus

---

59. Ibid., 489.

60. Ibid.

61. "If we take seriously the fact that Anselm prayed in this unrest and that he suffered this unrest in prayer, one will evaluate the chapter as in its own way a distinctive illustration of the truth that authentic, utterly certain and hidden faith is always in transition from expectation to fresh expectation. All faith's unrest is in fact set aside in prayer, but its prayer is its profound unrest." Ibid., 231.

62. Ibid., 489.

63. Ibid.

64. Augustine prays, "You do not change as the circumstances change but are the self-same, of the self-same of the self-same: Holy, Holy, Holy." But he is also tormented by this vision; he is unable to speak because he asks "Who am I?" He loses his voice. But then he reads Psalm 4 and gives himself and his voice over to G*d. Psalm 4 put him "at large," a feeling of being set free. It gives him a new speech situation that allows himself to speak with himself again. He writes, "I cried out aloud as I realized this within."

usurps G*d's freedom.[65] For example, Barth critiques seventeenth-century Protestantism for, "splitting up the unity of this act and regarding it
synergistically, with an objective divine giving on one hand, and on the
other a subjective human taking and assimilation."[66] Another important
example is how an "awakening to conversion" plays out as *said* and *saying*
in volume IV of the *Dogmatics*, and how Scripture operates as a prayer
itself. "An awakening to conversion" is perceived within prayers. Here
we see the fruit of Barth's so called doctrine of eternal election found in
the prayerful eschatology of Romans. The apocalyptical thread is that
G*d's election through Christ is an opening of ambiguity to a purpose of
salvation; it is G*d's own prayer.

For Barth, this is what humans discover in prayer. That prayer is
possible as G*d's word for us, our truest humanity is continually asleep
and only awakened by G*d. "We can not, therefore, define Christians
simply as those who are awake while the rest sleep, but more cautiously
as those who waken up in the sense that they are awakened a first time
and then again to their shame and good fortune. They are, in fact, those
who constantly stand in need of reawakening and who depend on the
fact that they are continually reawakened."[67] Our awakening from our
slumber is made possible by G*d's speaking to us through Scripture, despite our will not to hear.

Barth is most of all mindful of the Christian's blind and deaf approach to "the Bible which is a witness to a reality which impinges upon
it as a problem posed for itself."[68] The focus or purpose of the scriptural
discourse is the great need for conversion, for awakening, for alteration.
This problem is made more serious in the church, which ignores its own
need for conversion and instead merely talks about progress, reform, or
the ennobled life. Conversion can never be mere talk, it takes place only
in the "whole life" of the believer; thus there can be no repetition of it,
no implementation, nor any understanding. So when prayer is a matter of conversion it must engage the whole life, but how this takes place
remains a mystery to believers: a mystery that needs to be distinguished

65. This would constitute an essential mark of proclamation, as it endeavors always
to limit this illegitimacy of itself. Ibid., 764.

66. Ibid., 768.

67. Ibid., Vol. IV.2, 559.

68. Ibid.

from a magical or mechanical process, and understood, rather, as a living aporia.[69]

This involves the movement from the past to a new future, described by Barth as an ongoing argument or "falling out with ourselves" because we are undergoing conversion, which is itself the gift of recognition of ambiguity from the prayerful perspective that we are *simul (totus) justus, simul (totus) peccator.*[70] Barth makes the point that the antinomies of John (light and darkness, etc.) and those of Paul (the old and new man, etc.) are all references to the community of faith in the present, between past and future.

> We are never given to understand that the one determination of the person engaged in conversion, the Christian, is seen or regarded only as his heathen past or Jewish past, and the other only as her future. On the contrary, it is the life of the believers, the Christian present, which is here pitilessly but resolutely set in light of this twofold determination, as illustrated by the concrete admonitions and promises of the epistles. Again, however, we are nowhere given to understand that there will arise even momentarily a state of rest or equipoise as between coordinated factors. Christians are forcefully ejected from any fanciful equipoise or coordination by the fact that in this *simul* there are addressed to them very concrete warnings and promises concerning their present.[71]

This understanding of our present is too often ignored in our slumber. This conversion is what Barth calls "the teleology of falling out with oneself," which entails a participation in Christ that can never be reduced to any speculative metaphysics or dogma. In other words the present is discovered as being discovered—in its participation with G*d in prayer.[72]

The prayerful perspective of *Romans* and *Anselm* continues here, resurfaced as an absolute interruption. So, if it is agreed that election and Christology are material themes in the *Dogmatics*, it is because of an eschatology of prayer that is not diminished but rather is more than ever a meeting place for G*d and humanity. Communion with G*d here opens a new future of honest awareness of our own ambiguity and utter

69. Ibid., Vol. IV.2, 578.
70. Ibid., Vol. IV.2, 572.
71. Ibid., Vol. IV.2, 574.
72. Ibid., Vol. IV.2, 581.

dependence on the mercy of G*d even to pray. Although it can also be agreed that it is the person of Jesus who teaches us to pray.

In Karl Barth's 1946–47 lectures, the perspective of prayer is made more clear. Barth describes prayer as, first of all, an eschatological confrontation that unites all humanity in an aporetic condition of moral ethics. "On the one hand, there is our inward life, that of weak wily persons. On the other hand, there is our outward life, in this world, with all of its enigmas and difficulties. There is also the judgment of God, who encounters us and says to us at every moment, 'This is not enough.' . . . Deep is the abyss. The core of our being is put into question at the very moment we believe and obey as well as we can."[73] Prayer then is first of all a matter of *solidarity*. It is the recognition of our situation face to face with G*d as one of torment and utter inadequacy in the face of life's exigencies. Only then can prayer be a moving forward through life's exigencies by God's help, that tells us "the first thing is to pray."[74]

For example, Barth writes that the Reformers did not even ask what prayer is because it was their certitude that G*d always answers prayer. It was not an important question. Barth says that "from a logical standpoint" it is a quandary that the Reformers prayers were effective. But prayer is a matter of gift and weak prayers are often more effective because what matters is not the argumentative force of the prayer but that G*d listens and answers prayer.

How does G*d answer our inadequate prayer? Calvin's Christology is here purposefully advanced by Barth. "We can not better understand God's answer than by keeping in mind this thought: Jesus Christ is our brother, we belong to him; he is the head of the body of which we are members; and at the same time, he is the Son of God, of God himself . . . We are not separated from God, and, more important still, God is not separated from us. We may be without God, but God is not without humanity."[75] Here it is interesting that Barth uses his Christology to explain how prayer works. Prayer is not an explanation of how Christ works salvation, but the reverse. Again, the hint is taken that prayer is Barth's dynamic of reality and truth. It is because G*d is already revealed in Christ that G*d is able to be understood within our prayer; that makes prayer more than a mechanical operation on our part. Prayers are an

73. Karl Barth, *Prayer*, 18.
74. Ibid., 20.
75. Ibid., 22.

actual participation in G*d. "Thus it is not possible to say, 'I shall pray'
or, 'I shall not pray,' as if it were an act according to our own good pleasure . . . It is a need, a kind of breathing necessary to life."[76] One can say
that prayer is life that is both morally autonomous and ethically active,
and thus a mixture of past and future that is known by G*d. The path
one walks in life, as a citizen of the City of G*d, is one given to us and
thus is prayer. It is described by Barth as the first act of *reconnaissance*,
or remembering our debt to G*d by giving to others.[77] This means that
prayer is a trembling as one rethinks and remembers in solidarity with
all others, that takes the same path retread with all humans—a common
path given by G*d. This is what Anselm called an investigation, the Latin
investigare referred to dogs on the hunt. This prayer *on the hunt*, is always
between a double aporia and amounts to a humble audacity. "Luther is
right: the position of the person at prayer is utter humility as well as
an attitude of boldness and virility. There is a good kind of humility; it
consists in accepting, through liberty, this place that we have in Jesus
vis-à-vis God."[78] The prayerful person boldly speaks as if the life-world
at one's back that can never be known pertains directly to that which is
known. So when we pray the human condition is unveiled as much as
our hope. Prayer then is the possibility of an opening of the future that
may thus be different than the past. Prayer is thus conversion. Prayer is
the revolution of reality to the extent the present is discovered by a presence beyond our knowledge and experience that opens the future. So
prayer is at once humble and audacious, "prayer is not an act that comes
naturally to us" but nonetheless it is the power to participate with G*d.[79]

Here, prayer is not a human performance, nor a religio-magical incantation intended to manipulate or exert some control over our reality.
Rather, control or manipulation need be the last intention of the person
of prayer. Prayer, instead, begins with the supposition that reality is a gift
received, and a person's present is a path that must be tread with audacious humility.

Later, Barth writes how thoughtful theologians must begin and end
always with the misery of humanity but a real difference is conceived

76. Ibid., 23.

77. *Reconnaissance* is the French word used by Barth here. Barth speaks in French
throughout this lecture on prayer. Ibid., 24.

78. Ibid., 26.

79. Ibid., 28–29.

only in prayer. "But a radical turnabout begins with the invocation 'Our Father . . .' This is why it is imperative to recognize the essence of theology as lying in the liturgical action of adoration, thanksgiving, and petition."[80] Thus, Barth explicitly states that prayer is the prior and posterior of theology and states further, "The first and basic act of theological work is prayer . . . But theological work does not merely begin with prayer and is not merely accompanied by it; in its totality it is peculiar and characteristic of theology that it can be performed only in the act of prayer."[81] So one begins to sense a confusion of prayer if one considers these later statements with the apocalyptical meaning of prayer as that which questions all social meanings. Is prayer beyond human ability or not? Here it is theological work, and a source of a new meaning. How can this be reconciled? Before addressing these issues, let us surmise generally the importance of prayer for Barth and state some of the issues to be addressed later in this work.

Critical Issues

I have shown that prayer is the perspective from which to read Barth's *ouvre*—it is how he would read his own work. There is no break of method between and earlier and later works insofar as this point is concerned. Whether theology be process or a critical realism, eschatology or Christology, dialectic or analogical, all of Barth's work is approached from the same angle of prayer. It is prayer, rather than human interpretations, that unifies his work. So does prayer exclude modern hermeneutics or historiography? If modernity is understood as a courageous use of reason in pursuit of fairness and decency for society then can prayer be a deepening of modernity? Perhaps modern historiography amounts to a stepping back from prayer, or a fullness of vision. But is history's reality taken seriously enough by prayer?

Let me be clear, I have followed a continuity of prayer throughout Barth's whole theology that is distinguishable from Bruce McCormack's description of a Kantian "red thread which runs through the whole of the development, making it to be a unified whole in spite of the differing models of explication employed from one phase to the next."[82] Like

80. Barth, *The Humanity of God*, 90.
81. Barth, *Evangelical Theology*, 160.
82. McCormack, *Karl Barth's Critically Realistic Dialectical Theology*, 464.

McCormack's dialectical critical idealism, prayer can hear the content of direct experience as known only from within limited perspectives. Like Kantian epistemology, prayer may inscribe public reality as much as personal intuition. So, while I can agree with most of McCormack's proposed observations about the complexity and sum total of Barth's thought as critically realistic, there is another issue relating to prayer at the foundation of all of it. This would seem to me to address the points about Barth as a consistently dialectical thinker. To this point, I will show that it is Barth's foundational act of prayer, less than his methods of thought, that move him beyond Feuerbach's critique of religion as a human projection of "species-being." As Barth himself writes to us: "Only when God is thought of abstractly, when his predicates are thought of as philosophic abstraction, there arises the distinction between subject and predicate, existence and nature . . . But this is only a fiction. A God who has abstract predicates has also abstract existence."[83] If McCormack's Barth does not retreat behind Kant, the question remains whether he retreats behind Feuerbach. In other words, is this an abstraction of history which amounts to a modern gnosticism? This may be the case, at least with some prayers, but there is also the possibility that marks other prayers. I have suggested that the meaning that stems from an apocalyptical questioning in prayer is the mark of a more authentic prayer. In this way the present suffering of existence is addressed in prayer.

In partial summation, let us reiterate three main points gleaned from Barth's use of prayer as discourse.

- First, prayer is *an apocalyptic event* where all is questioned, whereby human reason and will are destroyed as foundations for discourse.

- Second, prayer is *a conversation about conversion* or a new existence and as such is open to all and in solidarity with all.

- Third, community is a matter of being discovered in relation, by the grace of G*d. This *community of prayer is an address of suffering.*

All this makes prayer's apocalyptical character indispensable to Barth because it sounds the end of all human dualism, gnosticism, or abstraction. It is the note that disallows any escapism of religion from itself while it denies all human ability to predicate G*d. A *reconnaissance* of prayer speaks as a political theology and theological politics to the extent

83. Feuerbach, *The Essence of Christianity*, 20.

it represents a new thinking and action, both as confession and supplication. Barth reminds us that prayer uncovers our inability to know how to pray while at the same time announcing the gift of prayer and prayerful conversation. If Paul's prayer is a questioning of all human relations by G*d, then prayer is a disturbing apocalyptical note that calls all to salvation, calls all to a qualitatively different existence. In this way, our individual prayers may also be the sigh of G*d. Prayer is then a "breath of life" as Barth calls it in his lecture on prayer.

If one is permitted to step back from Karl Barth's commitments to the proclamation of an already occurred salvation, a question can pose itself about a critical science of limits discovered in an apocalyptical prayer. Where does McCormack's ability to describe Barth's understanding of limits as a critically realistic dialectic connect with prayer? Dialectically, revelation is given always between left and right orthodoxy, internal and external rationality, past and future. All these may be helpful in delimiting a zone where G*d may act within a dialectic.[84] But, I suspect that Karl Barth's threefold form of the Word of G*d and his commitment to proclamation of this Word is more fully enabled by an embrace and questioning of all liminality in prayer.

The basic structure of Barth's doctrine of the Word is a linguistic version of the *analogia fidei*, which argues by modeling communication as always located within a dialectic of hidden/revealed meaning. In other words, the church is a community of truth by sacrificing its own words as prayer, *reconnaissance*. In this sense the church community is called to live according to the mercies of G*d. It is itself a text to be read as a sign of an apocalyptical questioning and meaning. It is a word written for the purpose of a new future.

Of course, the Christian church is also always human and thus comprised of acentric structures, not only in a state of constant flux but often comprised of elements seeking their own political advantages. Thus its performance as a sign is never completely settled within G*d's Word until the event of conversion is complete. In other words, the goals of the church are never fully in accord with G*d's locutionary act and therefore it must confess this in every way possible. When it confronts all pretension and questions ceaselessly then prayer can be an opening to a different future. It is this history of prayer that interrupts human striving and economy. In other words, illocutionary action is illumined as from

84. McCormack, *Karl Barth's Critically Realistic Dialectical Theology*, 464–66.

behind the text, even if one brings supplications into public view, when the church confesses all.

Barth prayerfully reads human economies of meaning within the Christian community as they are illumined from behind. In this way, G*d's perlocutionary goal of conversion, to which we remain blind, is nonetheless a light that shines through a history of prayer. Barth shows that prayer can also be a conversation, which is a falling out with ourselves, when it is a discourse between and within ontic and noetic texts. Prayer is a trembling resonance, an exchange between Word and words, but in prayer there is no getting behind the text, only conversation with(in) the text. In prayer there is no economy of exchange or rules of translation except those that permit a participation in conversation with others. These aspects of prayer inform an organic historiography, neither determined by the past nor proposed for future purposes, but rather apocalyptical in that the present is the place where suffering is destroyed.

But does prayer really perform this way for most? Is this so much wishful thinking? Or does prayer truly solidify the communal mores and values that are often for self-interested purposes? We are returned to the specter of Martin Jaffee's *parole* of elective monotheism. When does prayer bestow a presence in the present for the other? Do prayers speak for the alien?—or even the subaltern?

Let us return to our questioning borrowed from J. B. Metz who wonders if Barth proposes a "conceptual reconciliation" that leads "either to a dualistic gnostic perpetuation of suffering in God or to a reduction of suffering in the level of the concept."[85] Another issue that reappears is the relation of rhetoric about G*d to an emancipatory discourse begun within prayer. Can prayer expose its own participation in language and history and thus become so conscious of sin and finitude as to begin a discourse that operates both as an accountable criticism and as moral transformation? If not, then a Barthian rhetoric is like the old imperial strategy that is announced as a new order but gives more of the same. It is a prayer that attempts to control its own sense of apocalypse. Jaffee's elective monotheism reappears as prayer falls back into the application of a banal efficiency and a bourgeois community, which seeks no difference in the future.

Two general problems come into view when considering prayer's apocalyptical perspective on reason and society. One general problem,

85. Metz, "A Short Apology for Narrative," 258.

which is actually a group of problems, centers on the relation of ethical action and religious sensibility. Barth's description of prayer illustrates for us an ethical problematic that arises when an utter questionability of reason is asserted. How then to communicate and thereby avert open conflict? Even if the "no-God" of human conception is cast out by a universal embrace of paradox, in order to let the wholly other disclose or reveal a truth beyond knowledge, practical interests that are not dependent upon metaphysical interpretation will lead to differing views about what constitutes fairness. This set of problems occupies Barth for his whole career and continues to occupy living thinkers involved with the communicative-action theory of Jürgen Habermas.

A second general problem arises in Barth's description of prayer when one considers reconciliation and the spiritual need to pray. Once the origin of prayer is described, even as theocentric or aporetic, then isn't this at odds with the spiritual sense of one's need to pray? This is related to the question why pray at all, especially if G*d is always already all knowing? This second set of issues are helpfully addressed, I will recommend, primarily in dialogue with the deconstruction of Jacques Derrida.

Certainly today many are motivated by their prayers to bomb and kill. Prayer need take some responsibility for itself and not always remain above criticism or contain within itself a "black box" impervious to outsiders. This entails that faiths learn from each other's prayers, and not be satisfied with a solipsism of prayer by which either a stoic or utopian view of the world is encouraged. Only such a faith, which prays to learn from others prayer, can hope to begin the work of community and the discourse necessary to it.

Toward this end, I will return to Metz' description of prayer which questions pervasively as Barth describes, but which is also involved in an inter-faith and polycentric discourse. As a supplement to the counter-religious, Metz describes prayer that works from within all religious narratives. But before revisiting these questions of Metz, I will lay out recent philosophical criticisms of religious uses of language.

Recent philosophy of discourse and language questions religion from two opposing sides. From one side the criticism is that religious language is prone to an uncriticizable rhetoric and another side criticizes that it is always corrupted by systems of knowledge. The former criticism describes a universal moral discourse accountable as an emancipatory communication that enables mutual cooperation. The power of reason is unforced by virtue of criticizable knowledge as the only or best way to make ethics more universally fair and just. This side will suspect Barth for serving the interests of a particular group rather than being accountable to a universal criterion of ethical responsibility. The later side finds religion and matters of faith susceptible to corruption when surrendered to knowledge or criticizable interests because the rhetorical ambiguities necessary for an enlightened and worldly discourse are reduced.

The next two chapters lay out these perspectives on religious language, so as to inform a reconsideration of a relation between prayer and discourse so that a framework for the comparative study of prayer will be elaborated.

4

Public Reason and Religious Discourse

THE PREVIOUS CHAPTER DISCUSSES HOW KARL BARTH WAS A FORERUN-
ner of much of the twentieth-century reassessment of enlightenment
rationality. In some ways the impulse toward postmodernism began
with his commentary on Romans. It is most interesting that his understanding of prayer can be understood as an apocalyptical discourse (as
described in chapter 2). Throughout his career Barth performs his criticisms as prayer, a pursuit of understanding the meaning of others also
in prayer as well. This performative approach to prayer is what replaces
anthropocentric foundations of reasoning. His prayerful approach is
like a paradoxical restatement of the categorical imperative in relation
to the non-knowability of G*d. Later he makes this point again in his
description of Christology, the point of contact and exchange between
the creator and the creation.

The issues raised in Barth's *Römerbrief* continue unanswered
throughout the bloody twentieth century. Whether knowledge enlight-
ens society, as Kant envisioned, continues to be the major debate in
social ethics to this day. Caught between reason and the reality of contin-
ued social conflict, responses often go in one of two different directions.
Either in the direction of an increase in the leveling, secularization of
reason, or towards a mystical deepening of existential meaning, as in
Romanticism and other counter-movements.

Today, current reassessments of Kant and religious language can be
summarized by a description of the critical theories of Jürgen Habermas
and Jacques Derrida. Some will think it strange that these two theorists
are chosen but like Barth both have an appreciation for human suffering
in its fundamental role in understanding the relation between reason
and meaning. However, they have distinct perspectives on how prayer
and faith may take part in community discourse. Our framework for the

comparative study of prayer is called to focus on the unique criticisms of religious language presented today. For this the two most distinct projects of thought informing this framework are represented in the reconstructed project of rationality of Jürgen Habermas and the unending acts of deconstruction of Jacques Derrida. Both will be discussed in this project, always with an eye toward apocalyptical suffering and divine freedom as discussed in the previous chapter. These descriptions will help lay out issues and options for a framework for the comparative study of prayer and especially its role in collective memory.

A Two-Edged Rejection of Paradox

Jürgen Habermas rejects both a *leveling* secularization and an *appropriating* language of mysticism. He explains how these opposing uses of language fail to include "the other *in his otherness.*"[1] His work is massive and a complete appraisal is outside the bounds of this book. However, his rejection of the paradox of rationalization provides important observations for a reconsideration of prayer. First, he underlines issues and criticisms of both a secular leveling of language and its opposite mystification. For the purposes of this book it is most interesting to note how Habermas *protects* prayer as a discourse. He neither allows for its marginalization by secularization nor its mystical enthronement over discourse. Second, his fundamental insights of language as communication are useful to prayerful interaction within society. Habermas has indirectly valued a type of prayer that rejects dehumanizing divisions between reason and meaning while at the same time being a prayer that performs as a separation between humanity and G*d. Regardless, the relation of reason and faith within discourse will be reconsidered as a reinvigoration of the project of enlightenment as a peaceful betterment of a global society. More specifically, I am asking if Habermas may accept a Barthian critique of Kant, or will refuse to limit a universal principle of reason by an aporetic rephrasing of the categorical imperative.

The issue of rational foundations for discourse is taken up by Jürgen Habermas. His central problem is that both romantic and heteronomous reason are non-criticizable foundations of social arrangement and thereby contribute to systemic misunderstandings. To use

1. Habermas, *The Inclusion of the Other: Studies in Political Theory*, 40.

the metaphor described at the beginning of the book, they each contain a "black box."

Jürgen Habermas exemplifies supreme confidence in reason to arbitrate conflicting views, most notably in his reworking of the categorical imperative of Kant. Also he deepens critical theory by always setting about the task of reconsidering historical and social situations of reason, a habit inherited from Hegel. So many thinkers in the last 200 years have found themselves choosing between these two perspectives. But rather than trying to separate or filter background assumptions found in every assertion, Habermas follows a path laid out elsewhere.

This path is a reflection on how the labor of language entails within each person a cognitive learning of two different roles—speaker and hearer. Each of us inevitably perform and incorporate interests and background assumptions in any process of legitimation. As creatures of language and culture, there is no individuation without socialization and no system of knowledge without an assumed life-world; no knowledge without memory.

What is notably rejected is any use of paradox as a hermeneutical ambulance for reasoning. Paradox often leads to systemic misinterpretations of unavoidable ambiguities at play between life-world assumptions and any systemization of knowledge. Paradox is sometimes used as a wounding of reason. This is used by many theorists of religious ethics, notably Reinhold Niebuhr and Albrecht Wellmer, who understand paradox as an expression of Christian truth. Habermas summarizes this and critiques it in one sentence, "The paradox of rationalization would be that a rationalization of the life-world is the precondition and the starting point for a process of systemic rationalization and differentiation, which then has become more and more autonomous vis-à-vis the normative constraints embodied in the life-world, until in the end the systematic imperatives begin to instrumentalize the life-world and threaten to destroy it."[2] Paradox threatens the broader cultural exchange by developing a formula of when and where to expect itself. Instead, on a fundamental level, Habermas wants to develop a rational perspective on how personal and social action can work as an organic unfolding of rational exchange. Reason is neither something imposed nor external.

Rationality is internal to the exchange, a transcendence from within. There is a progression represented to the extent a full criticizability

2. Habermas, "A Reply to My Critics," 324.

is advanced, or in fact our eyes are opened to the world in front of us.[3] Paradoxical reason or any mechanization of reasoning becomes inadequate foundations for a sustainable community of discourse as history has shown. In history one finds romantic notions embraced by some particular group or exhibited in a type of behavior that makes claims of being able to imagine a more perfect of even utopian society. An imagined society where all differentiations will be overcome leads instead to disillusion that either falls into defeatism or a reactionary ideological zealotry. More recently this has taken the form of dystopia that imagines society as utterly problematic.

For Habermas, in order that humanity might be truly free and live in community, the rules of a society must be reasoned from within yet also transparent and universally accessible to criticism.

> Traditionally established obligations rooted in communicative action do not of themselves reach beyond the limits of the family, the tribe, the city, or the nation. However, the reflexive form of communicative action behaves differently: argumentation of its very nature points beyond all particular forms of life . . . [T]he practice of deliberation is extended to an inclusive community that does not in principle exclude any subject capable of speech and action who can make contributions. This idea points to a way out of the modern dilemma, since the participants have lost their metaphysical guarantees and must so to speak derive their normative orientations from themselves alone.[4]

A reasoned approach to community has its origin in a common sense reflection on the dynamics of communication. The discourse remains inclusive of the other by giving no metaphysical guarantees. This brings new possibilities into view. Some conflicts between faith and reason are defused. It remains to be seen whether religious conceptions of community based in traditional faith, can sufficiently speak without recourse to metaphysical or specific orders of salvation. Recently Habermas ac-

---

3. Early in his career, Habermas is involved in describing the processes of rationalization of society, where he begins to relate labor and interaction, moral and ethical reasoning, without letting these relations harden "into quasi-natural forms, according to the model of technically progressive systems of rational and goal-directed action, we have reason enough to keep these two dimensions more rigorously separated . . . *Liberation from hunger and misery* does not necessarily converge with *liberation from servitude and degradation*, for there is no automatic developmental relation between labor and interaction." Habermas, *Theory and Practice*, 142–69.

4. Habermas, *The Inclusion of the Other: Studies in Political Theory*, 41.

knowledged that this places a greater burden on the religious person. Albeit a burden that still benefits the secular society and I think one might consider as a sacrifice.

In an interview Habermas states that traditional religion is a source of continuing sustenance to conceptions of community and the good life that communicative reason cannot do without, at least for now. He tells the interviewer, "For me, the basic concepts of philosophical ethics, as they have developed up to this point, also fail to capture all the intuitions which have already found a more nuanced expression in the language of the Bible, and which we have only come to know by means of a halfway religious socialization. In light of this shortcoming, discourse ethics attempts a translation of the categorical imperative into a language that also lets us do justice to another intuition—I mean the feeling of 'solidarity,' the bond of a member of a community to her fellow members."[5] Thus, Habermas attempts to describe a public discourse that is able to be lasting and sustain mutual community. He uses the word *post-metaphysical* to describe the nature of discourse that I believe finds some affinity with Barth's apocalyptical rejection of teleological or religious constructions of history.

Also in some affinity with Barth, Habermas wants to make questionable the political consequences of all hermeneutical perspectives, recognizing that each justification hides or filters aspects of reality and thereby debilitates reason. However, post-metaphysical thought relies on communication in a way that Barth's conception of language might make impossible. His strategy of bringing the same criteria to both sides of every paradox, reconstructs reason by an affirmation of the elements present in successful instances of communication. He wants to understand how successful acts of communication, found in everyday life, teach humanity to live in community and not in relations based in coercion.

Habermas describes within the practice of communication itself "a stubbornly transcending power, because it is renewed with each act of unconstrained understanding, with each moment of living together in solidarity, of successful individuation, and of saving emancipation."[6] In his response to a group of theologians in Chicago in 1988, he calls attention to "transcendence from within, transcendence in the world."[7] This rejects positivist rationality either in favor of relativistic terms or

5. Medieta, "A Conversation about God and the World," 162–63.

6. Habermas, "A Reply to My Critics," 227.

7. Browning and Fiorenza, *Habermas, Modernity, and Public Theology,* 226.

in religious terms, both of which exclude other perspectives of reason. Habermas thus states explicitly in this text that his perspective is to be understood in contrast to Barth. Rather he proposes a universal or *formal pragmatics* that continues an enlightenment rationalization of society, which enables mutual decisions regardless of background or religious perspective. This proposal is furthered by recognition that validity and truth claims can only be redeemed by the unforced force of a universal reason Thus, his main task is to describe the conditions of "mutual understanding" [*Verständigung*] and this entails an inclusion and participation of others who are traditionally left out of discourse.

Prayer from a Habermasian approach is as much about temporal redemption as an eternal one. From the perspective of mutual understanding, the question arises concerning the relation between what is promised in each prayer and its performance. To the extent that prayer takes part in the situation of language, and seeks to create an understanding of others and myself as well as G*d's self-revelation, then it is observable as a process of communication. If prayer is communication with G*d—or language out of brokenness to beyond brokenness as I have defined it—then it is participating in its meaning by an involvement in a process of redemption of this world, and it thus cannot avoid the question of neighbor or community. Habermas opens the door to a consideration of the validity of prayer that may or may not involve a performative contradiction of itself.

In order to begin a consideration of this understanding of prayer I will first outline two essays that illustrate the Habermasian relation between religion and discourse. In both essays, Habermas refuses to allow the category of prayer and its participation in redemption to be pre-decided. When taken together, these essays point to an interpretation of prayer that asks how a performance of prayer may contribute to valid understandings of normative rightness. The first essay critiques Karl Jaspers's *philosophical faith*, and the second essay critiques Michael Theunissen's *negative theology*. When taken together, they demonstrate how reason that is based in events of communication will reject *both* secularization *and* mystification of religious language. However, in both essays Habermas's appreciation of existential suffering as an original element in the process humanization and solidarity is nonetheless affirmed. Thus, one may find similarities between Habermas's description and the origin of religion in prayer that speaks from brokenness.

Cutting against Philosophical Leveling

Habermas underlines that Karl Jaspers's "philosophical faith" is a *substantive* hope for a common ground between various religious traditions. Instead of settling religious differences by armed brutality, Jaspers believes that the enlightened alternative does not have to be the abandonment of faith, even faith that is based in revelation. Habermas quotes Jaspers from 1962, which is just as timely fifty years later:

> Today we are in search of the basis on which human beings from all various religious traditions could encounter each other in a meaningful way across the entire world, ready to reappropriate, purify, and transform their own historical traditions, but not to abandon them. Such common ground for the (plurality of) faiths could only be clarity of thought, truthfulness, and a shared basic knowledge. Only these (three elements) would permit that boundless communication in which the well-springs of faith could draw each other closer, by virtue of their essential commitment.[8]

Jaspers was coming out of the experience of the Holocaust and struggle to come to grips with German guilt but his words are just as meaningful in the twenty-first century, tormented as it is by the twin problems of global terrorism and poverty. Habermas agrees with these stated goals and states his concern about the intercultural understanding between Islam and the Judeo-Christian West. He also shares Jaspers's idea of a discursive mediation, a form of communication capable of lessening the tension between antagonistic beliefs. This is manifest by a courageous and discordant type of tolerance that delegitimates armed conflict and which fosters a sense of community where "legitimate oppositions" are not erased.[9]

However, in the essay *The Conflict of Beliefs*, Habermas rejects Jaspers's dialogical model insofar as it places too much emphasis upon an existential leveling of faith that abandons too easily normative resources for communication.[10] Religious persons are convinced that

8. Jaspers, *Der Philosophische Glaube Angesichts der Offenbarung*, 7. Quoted by Habermas, "The Conflict of Beliefs: Karl Jaspers and the Clash of Cultures," 30.

9. Habermas, "The Conflict of Beliefs," 31.

10. "Of course, Jaspers was alert to the fact that hermeneutical insights have political consequences. He perceives that reason, which tames fundamentalism, is built into the communicative constitution of our socio-cultural forms of life . . . Yet, as a philosopher

philosophers "who describe faith as an *ethical* conception miss the *redemptive* significance and binding character of prophetically disclosed truths, and deprive their lives of an essential dimension."[11] But in a global society in which disparate religions all claim an essential truth and also live and work together then different norms for social interaction are sure to arise.

How then does religious faith and ethical construction of society interact? Modernity deepens this problem of disparity by defining enlightenment, which interprets each religion as "communities of interpretation, each of which is united in its own conception of the good life."[12] Jaspers's solution of faith is that if each becomes a participant in an existential discourse, then they will be convinced of the authenticity of other religions as another form of life—whose self-understanding they do not need to share but can nonetheless respect.

Habermas contrasts this dialogical model with an apologetic model. He notes that those like Alastair MacIntyre enter into discourse because they hold open the possibility that one religion will prove itself superior to others, even if it is strictly by virtue of the fact that in times of *epistemological crisis* other religions eventually will abandon their own standards of rationality. A third manner of inter-religious discourse is an evangelistic model, which Habermas calls the *nonchalant ethnocentrism* of Richard Rorty who openly attempts to assimilate the other into *our* worldview. The dialogical model of Jaspers's philosophical hermeneutics, like Gadamer's, intends to respond to cultural relativism without dismissing its insights. Rather than avoid competing paradoxical notions of the good life rightly found in different conceptions of revelation, Jaspers contends that only a full blown substantive discourse can enable the pacifying power of reason to work without falling into apologetics or ethnocentric evangelism. Habermas affirms aspects of this dialogical model of understanding insofar as Jaspers characterizes it by a relational symmetry. Habermas writes: "Understanding is only possible between parties who expect to learn from each other. Through the exchange of first- and second-person perspectives, which are reciprocally related to each other, they are able to effect a *rapprochement* between divergent

of existence, Jaspers was so obsessed with ethical self-understanding, with communication in the domain of unconditional truths, that he failed to exploit the normative resources of communicative reason in the domains of morality, law, and politics." Ibid., 44.

11. Ibid., 42.
12. Ibid.

horizons of their linguistic understanding. Thus, hermeneutics wrests the universalistic potential of a linguistically embodied reason from the conditions of successful communication as such, and encourages us in the quest for intercultural understanding."[13] So, the question he asks of Jaspers's hermeneutical model is, "Toward what end?" Given the paradigm of a hermeneutically sensitive exchange that might inform an intercultural listening, it is still unclear whether there should eventually be a substantive agreement or some other goal of the discourse, which both the apologetic and evangelistic models have. One asks, why are we talking and listening? Toward what outcome? Will this be endless, or is there some point to the discourse? I am reminded of the police negotiator who tries to keep the hostage-taker talking, as long as there is some negotiation happening then there is hope of averting tragedy.

Habermas finds the line between faith and knowledge in a triple relation. He outlines relations that again need to be continually discussed. The triple relation that distinguishes faith and knowledge is between philosophy and its own history, to the interconnection between Scriptures within the Western tradition, and to other world religions in general. These guiding questions for continual study can be briefly summarized:

1. Does the history of philosophy seek to *level out* the transition from tradition to modernity (like Heidegger) or does it *intensify* the break (like Kant) and dismiss classical knowledge claims from the standpoint of a critique of metaphysics?

2. Which of three possible relations between philosophy and religion, with regard to Scripture? Either philosophy is put in the service of religion (either by negative or positive method of theology, or a division between natural reason and revelation), religion asserts its independence (either polemically or by indifference), or it claims a cognitive superiority by trying to salvage religious truth in its own terms?

3. The third relation involves the sympathetic or generous attitude toward world religions. Does one expect to *learn from others*?

Habermas's assessment of Jaspers is that he is able to listen to other world religions most sympathetically (question 3) because he emphasizes the intense break between modernity and religious tradition (question 1) by placing Greek metaphysics alongside other traditions in the

13. Ibid., 34.

process of overcoming myth. Thus for Jaspers modern philosophy is primarily a matter of faith, rather than knowledge. Habermas observes that Jaspers "draws an unusual line between faith and knowledge. He recognizes in the self-critical confrontation of modern thought with its own metaphysical beginnings one instance of a more general problem. How can there be rational communication with those faiths which are articulated in strong traditions and in comprehensive doctrines, and which appear to the unbeliever only in the form of ciphers?"[14] Jaspers describes modernity as caught between two challenges. On the one hand, it is given the task of continuing the rationalization and disenchantment of metaphysics and religion, even as metaphysics and religion were once directed against myth. On the other hand, the risk then is that as the lifeworld is reduced to the domain of the knowable, then this results in the translated ciphers no longer being taken seriously as "the living embodiment of transcendence" and thus no longer able to "illuminate the space of existence."[15] The danger of the modern disenchantment of reality is ultimately meaninglessness, or the problem of a Heideggerian project of de-mythology. As Habermas states it, "One's own existence cannot be illuminated without an enlightened account of *transcendence*."[16]

Jaspers's proposal to solve this dilemma of modernity is an authentic existence that acknowledges that "[b]eing a self and being in communication are inseparable."[17] Habermas is quick to notice that the character of this intersubjectivity is not conceived and described as therapeutic, which is notable since Jaspers was a psychiatrist. Rather, Habermas underlines that the intersubjective communication here is described as friendly and polemical, between competing life projects. Even antagonistic forms of belief "encounter each other in an ambivalence of attraction and repulsion."[18] The truth of such a commitment to dialogue is that partners can choose to not let disagreements and hostility break off their communication with one another.

Habermas's criticism of Jaspers, even as their agreement is profound, is that philosophy is co-opted by his substantive faith commitment to competition of existential dialogue, for which he also lays down

14. Ibid., 36.
15. Ibid., 37.
16. Ibid., 38.
17. Ibid.
18. Ibid., 39.

the rules. Jaspers describes his faith: "this philosophical faith, which appears in many forms . . . cannot [become] an authority or a dogma, [it] remains dependent on communication between human beings, who are obliged to talk to each other, but not necessarily to pray with each other."[19] The universal nature of philosophical reason is surrendered to an existential faith in dialogue, which is more salvatory than prayer. Habermas objects because then there is no impartial criterion by which to legitimate various contributions to the social discourse. Jaspers has surrendered all philosophical arbitration of social discourse in order to become a player in an inter-religious discourse. "For if fundamental philosophical knowledge is distinguished from comprehensive doctrines of tradition only by virtue of its undogmatic posture, then it lacks the impartiality which is needed if it is to establish the rational basis on which contrary faiths can enter into a fruitful communication with each other."[20] Jaspers's philosophical faith enters into the religious fray, and insofar as philosophy can enable an ethical society based in authentic and truthful existence, then it outlines a level playing field on which all religions and worldviews may compete within the social discourse. "But in so far as it analyzes the condition of successful communication between essentially competing faiths, then its arguments must be directed towards an agreement concerning the rules of the game; in other words, they must point beyond substantive ethical questions, concerning which there can always be reasonable dissent.[21]

So philosophy may not be a competitor with religion and a referee at the same time.[22] Whether one agrees or not with the Habermas assessment of Jaspers in particular, it is important to notice that the place of religion as a participant in public discourse is protected from a philosophical incursion that would privilege dialogue over prayer. From Habermas's perspective, an inter-subjective discourse need be protected from the confusion of truth and reality caused by a strictly existential authenticity that then abandons reason's role as arbitrator. However, this also leaves open a possibility for prayer if it refrains from the confusion of truth and reality and admits its fallibility. Yet this is only one side of Habermas's relation to religion.

19. Ibid., 40.

20. Ibid.

21. Ibid.

22. Habermas notes that this is the same criticism that he has with John Rawls, which we won't detail here.

And against the Mystical

The other edge that swipes against paradoxical reasoning is directed toward mystical deepening of the dialogic exchange. Habermas performs this for us by explaining how Michael Theunissen, like Jaspers but from a different direction, describes the inter-subjective center of a dialogical reality. For Theunissen the essential relation is defined as that "which is opened by the dialogical encounter and in turn enables the dialogical self-becoming of the self and the other, as the Kingdom of God which underlies the sphere of subjectivity."[23] Habermas reads Theunissen as the attempt to capture philosophically the meaning of the words of the Gospel of Luke where Jesus says, "the kingdom of G*d is in the midst of you." So Habermas discusses Theunissen's argument that a theological description of this type of community is based on a will to communicate. As Theunissen writes, "it is *the* [only] side of the kingdom of God that philosophy can grasp at all: this is not the side of 'grace' but that of the 'will.'" It is the will to dialogue that is a "striving after the kingdom of God in such a way that the future is promised in the present love of human beings for one another." [24]

Theunissen describes an unimpaired or undamaged [*unversehrte*] intersubjective space characterized by the coincidence of freedom and love in "a relation of symmetrical and reciprocal recognition."[25] In order that communicative relations be more than competitive games, a mutual recognition of the freedom of the other must be consistently manifested in words and actions. Habermas describes Theunissen's concept of communicative freedom, which grounds his dialogical model, and writes, "In this interrelation the one is not a barrier to the other's freedom but rather a condition for the other's self-realization. And the communicative freedom of the one cannot be complete without the realized freedom of all others . . . Theunissen is indeed convinced that every interpersonal relation is embedded in the relation to a wholly other that precedes the relation to the concrete other. The wholly other embodies an absolute freedom which we must presuppose in order to explain how our communicative freedom is possible at all."[26] Additionally Habermas notices

23. Habermas, "Communicative Freedom and Negative Theology," 182.
24. Ibid., 183.
25. Ibid., 185.
26. Ibid., 186–87.

that this way of thinking goes back to Jewish and Protestant mysticism, where G*d is confirmed as G*d by releasing humanity into freedom to enable their self-becoming.

Thus, G*d is always already present in the enabling and orienting structure of reconciliation. As Habermas states it, "God is present as the promise as well as the existing presence of a fulfilled future."[27] I might add that this is comparable to a prevenient presence, not a justifying presence, as Theunissen also credits Walter Benjamin for observing the incredible sadness evoked by "the sight of history fossilized into nature."[28] Habermas notices that this explains an additional theme of the forgetfulness of time in metaphysics, and Theunissen's desire to find an appropriate conception of *prolepsis*, an eschaton or the future presence of eternity and thus achieved reconciliation. But this always remains unfinished and therefore it is undecided how to fully understand the possibility admitted in the structure of undistorted intersubjectivity.

Habermas questions how this point can be understood philosophically. "In which sense can we understand such an expectation? Should we understand it as an idealized surplus that demands from the participants in communicative action that they engage in acts of transcending all by themselves, or as the breakthrough of an occurring event [*vorgangiges Geschehen*] of communicative liberation that requires self-abandon from those who have been emancipated into freedom?"[29] In the first option the myth of the self-limiting G*d will ultimately melt into the process of profanation, and in the second option if G*d remains the only guarantor in history who liberates the past into a new future, "then the concept of the absolute-already presupposed in every act of successful mutual understanding, stands in need of an adequate philosophical explanation."[30] In a manner reminiscent of his three points in reply to Jaspers, Habermas can agree that this is not accomplished by a destruction of the history of metaphysics. How this history is understood remains open for discussion.

In reply Habermas asks how Theunissen pursues a "postmetaphysical" description of communicative freedom in connection with Kierkegaard's *Sickness unto Death*. How can discourse contribute to justice and freedom, given the method of negation?

27. Ibid., 187.
28. Ibid., 184.
29. Ibid.
30. Ibid., 187–89.

First, the negative mode of reason replaces an objective teleology. Normative contents are reconstructed "from the necessary subjective conditions of the objective validity of our experiences and judgments."[31] Generally this is affirmed in Habermas's own critical theory, whereby normative ground is discovered in a formal validating procedure of communicative action oriented toward mutual understanding. However, Theunissen rejects what he calls "normativism," not because he suspects traces of essential determinations still held over from an objective teleology but because of his understanding of the life-world and life history. Because humans experience being in its negativity, he does not describe negation in terms of an objective teleology like Heidegger but from the point of view of an inverted history of suffering—from the perspective of the everyday life of the powerless and the marginalized.

Second, because Theunissen's method of negation is organic in the sense that he describes everyday life as it is experienced, despair says something about successful self-hood in everyday life. Thus he tries to avoid transcendental issues or over-conceptualizations of existence, where nobody actually lives. As in Kierkegaard, despair offers an initial subject matter from which to consider the sickness of the self, "even before he determines a normative concept of self."[32] Nonetheless, Habermas still recognizes the well known dialectic of despair: (a) the despair of not willing to be oneself, life condemned to freedom; (b) the despair of willing to be oneself, life posited as a self; (c) despair aware of the finitude of our freedom, life of reflexivity and therefore cognizant of one's dependence upon an infinite power. Thus Theunissen writes, "That in positing oneself one must presuppose the other, who posited one in this very self-positing, thus defines ones selfhood."[33] Existence is defined in terms of a prayer—a situation of brokenness and despair that is accepted and thereby also perceived as a providence.

In another book, *Postmetaphysical Thinking*, Habermas continues this discussion by assessing Kierkegaard's authentic selfhood precisely as a prayer, an internal dialogue with G*d. He writes, "Kierkegaard's Either-Or poses itself ineluctably in the conversation of the lone soul with God. The ethical stage of life is only a gateway to the religious stage, where the dialogue with oneself proves to be a mask behind which has

31. Ibid., 91.
32. Ibid., 189.
33. Ibid., 190.

been concealed the prayer, the dialogue with God."[34] Regardless of the organic nature of Theunissen's everyday despair and faith, Habermas can recognize that Theunissen, like Kierkegaard, incorporates a faith in a future reconciliation with or by G*d, which enables despair to be moved beyond despair to dialogue. Thus, the stages of despair are finally only gateways through which there is movement toward reconciliation with G*d. Habermas does not question the theological validity of this assertion, but he does question how prayer may then function in an ethical life.

Is it sufficient to ground mutual communication in a selfhood that always will despair in its finitude, and that must then necessarily be cognizant of a power beyond finitude? Habermas does not think so but he tries to explain carefully how this is the case for Kierkegaard. "The Christian consciousness of sin and the Protestant hunger for grace therefore form the real spur for the return to a life that takes on form and coherence only in relation to the justification, due at the last Judgment, of an irreplaceable and unique existence."[35] Consciousness of sin may spur a return, a hunger for coherence and form that will finally reconcile one's irreplaceable existence in an eternal scheme. But until that final judgment and reconciliation, what now? One might answer live as a knight of faith, but what of the reconciliation with other faiths? Is not prayer then rhetorical, and a matter temporal and strategic concerns?

This is complicated further by what Habermas points out as another form of prayerful existence. He contrasts Kierkegaard's internal life of prayer with Jean-Jacques Rousseau's prayer as described in his letters to M. de Malesherbes. Habermas notes that the form of letter writing indicates the private nature of the contents, but also the claim to a radical sincerity. So Rousseau claims to require an unrestricted audience, a universal public.[36]

The juxtaposition of these two forms of prayer raises an issue for Habermas. Must the liberating power of despair wait to actualize itself at a final judgment or eschaton, or is an emancipation available in the act of *any given time* of address? So here again one comes back to the meaning of Benjamin's eternal remembering of history and the weak form of messianicity. Theunissen describes "self-hood in faith," that one can be

34. Habermas, *Postmetaphysical Thinking*, 165.

35. Ibid., 165–66.

36. Ibid., 166–67.

oneself in one's finite freedom only to the extent one recognizes G*d's absolute freedom and thereby liberated by communication grounded in the wholly other. But even if one concedes as much, Habermas argues that this still needs a supplementation "with regard to the communicative constitution of the potentiality for one's selfhood."[37] Because in some manner the final judgment on one's existence is "not yet" or suspended, then this opens a problem of ambiguity for prayer. What claims here can be mutual and precise with regard to a foundation for communication? Isn't the line between a private validation of truth and a public validation of truth become fluid and indeterminable? Confidence in social institutions discovered in prayer might vanish in prayer tomorrow. Especially given the possible equivocation of prayer that might be looking for a final reconciliation with G*d, or might also be looking for a validation from a public audience.

In contrast, Karl Barth completely delegitimates a publicly verified prayer because it fails to recognize the universality of G*d's righteousness and thereby the sin of all. A prayer that is based in knowledge then erects barriers between humans is like that of a "Pharisee" who prays according to lingual distinctions of intellect, morality, and religion. "The Pharisee who prays can indeed become a missionary, but not a missionary of the Kingdom of God. The strange UNION-of men with one another—must assert and expose the strange, and yet saving, SEPARATION—between God and man. In this separation is displayed the righteousness of God. The paradox must be maintained absolutely."[38] The issue for Barth is that prayer is only capable of grasping the paradox of the Kingdom of G*d and not any rationalization of the saving righteousness of G*d. In the same paragraph Barth affirms and radicalizes Kierkegaard's description of existence as prayer, and sees paradox at the center of a universal imperative for human reconciliation. "All must proceed along the road of faith, and must proceed only along this road; yet it is a road along which no man can go. All flesh must be silent before the inconspicuousness of God, in order that all flesh may see His salvation."[39]

It is very important to recognize here that Barth's silence of all flesh, is a *quietism* of prayer that Habermas does not deny, but which he must qualify in relation to a more *pietist* understanding. He will not separate

37. Habermas, "Communicative Freedom and Negative Theology," 190.
38. Barth, *Romans*, 100.
39. Ibid.

an understanding of silence from verbalized and actionable speech. The issue for him is whether prayer is always already paradoxical as an exchange with G*d's eternal righteousness, or is prayer more a matter of reconciliation taking place within selfhood?

The point of contention for Habermas is that selfhood is always already a matter of individuation through socialization, and Barth can agree that any prayerful quietism of the vertical must also be combined with a horizontal life in community. In fact it is a universal perspective that both men are attempting to describe so that a human individuation in community might be possible. However, the crux of the matter is that community must be based in a universal recognition of a reciprocity where all can take up the perspective of all, an eternally unresolved paradox only creates a "consciousness of crisis" which is the underside of endemic utopian currents within modernity.[40] The next section of the paper will return to this issue of prayer's social perspective and Habermas's criticism of utopia.

Theunissen also criticizes Kierkegaard for his "worldless" character of selfhood, and for this reason he recommends a Hegelian reading where selfhood is always already in-another. Theunissen concludes that when freedom of selfhood in reflexivity is thus understood in relation with others, then an original dimension of communication is revealed by love and is represented in faith. He believes that the freedom of G*d is also the ground of all communicative freedom. Thus, prayer will act in constant respect for others freedom as well. Habermas notes that Kant also saw the logic of this type of questioning, but only posits G*d as a practical postulate of reason. Habermas's question is clear and direct: "Under the conditions of postmetaphysical thinking, can we reply to the classical question of the good life (in its modern rendition as a question of successful selfhood) not merely formally but in a fashion that, for example, we draw a philosophical silhouette of the evangelical message?"[41]

His answer is that Theunissen's description of dialogue overemphasizes or relies too heavily on a particular description of intersubjectivity. Like Jaspers, Theunissen makes metaphysical beliefs operative by conceptualizing self-relation in terms of self-observation, but then the practical relation to another is described in terms of an I-Thou relation, which takes the place of the previous reflexive model. "The philosophy of

40. Habermas, *Postmetaphysical Thinking*, 188.
41. Habermas, "Communicative Freedom and Negative Theology," 193.

dialogue de-emphasizes the structure of mutual understanding itself and shifts attention onto the existential self-experience of the participants in dialogue which occurs as a consequence of successful communication . . . thereby neglecting the relation to the objective world or to that *about which* we communicate. In this fashion the dimension of truth claims is closed off in favor of authenticity."[42] One can not overemphasize the importance of this observation.

So his critique of a mystical negative theology is not entirely unlike his criticism of Karl Jaspers's philosophy of dialogue. Both neglect a third person attitude necessary for mutual decision and action. Dialogue becomes a way to describe metaphysical assertions about the importance on an experience of selfhood and existence, whether it be a faithful commitment to a discordant plurality or to a community of faithful dialogue. In Theunissen's case the criticism goes further insofar as authenticity is held open and hopes for a universal public validation. Nonetheless this is established "behind our backs but which ought to first make communication as such possible."[43]

In short, Habermas finds that Theunissen strays from his negative method and evokes a particular concept of G*d to support the practice of communicative freedom. Instead everyday experiences of successful communication are enough to establish a sense of universality which allows for participants to criticize and enter into the sense of stability and reciprocity. A use of a theological construction of G*d is unnecessary.[44] Habermas observes that if we *integrate* a third-person attitude about the world then even a fallible and shifting set of facts has a unifying force. In such an attitude, rather than a faithful performative attitude that Theunissen describes, the complimentarity that is claimed as the exclusive domain of freedom falls apart. I might add that a tragic brand of communitarianism results.

For Habermas all that is necessary for freedom to be ascribed within discourse is for the participants to have a competence of responsibility, and this does not rely upon a substantive faith commitment or mystical appreciations. "This freedom consists in the following: That the participants are able to orient their actions toward validity claims and, in doing

42. Ibid., 194.

43. Ibid.

44. See also his critique of Max Horkheimer on this point. Habermas, *Justification and Application: Remarks on Discourse Ethics*, 133.

so, they raise validity claims, adopt a yes or no position toward other validity claims, and enter into illocutionary obligations."[45] This would seem to suggest that communicative freedom is an easy achievement.

Is communicative freedom more pervasive among humans than Theunissen's theory may recognize? Habermas does not deny that each person is dominated by the past, which acts as a stigma on the future. However, the recognition that no one person or group has possession of all the facts or a special access to a hidden reality clears the space for a communication that is liberative. This is always accessible, regardless of the status of our despair (whether it be cynical, submissive, or melancholic) we all gain insight and information from all experiences of suffering, or the damaged life, which reminds one of one's finitude and can propel one into a mutual participation in discourse. While both philosophy and theology have access to an experience of suffering, they are different according to how they make claims about these experiences. As Habermas states, "We recognize philosophical discourses by the fact that they remain on this side of the rhetoric of fate and promise."[46] Therefore unnecessary metaphysical claims about dialogue or intersubjectivity are an insufficient grounding of discourse because they are often dependent upon an eternal or secret reality that cannot be verified by temporal and public rationality.

Just as Habermas does not allow public dialogue to circumvent prayer in Jaspers, here he does not allow Theunissen's sense of prayer to circumvent discourse. In either theoretical context the inclusion of prayer is an issue but he distinguishes problems with both a secularization of discourse and a mystification of prayer. One may surmise that prayer's inclusion in discourse is not to be discounted nor overplayed.

So one revisits prayer's questioning that Barth takes as foundational. Does prayer take part in human morality claims and, if so, how? Isn't prayer, as language, inevitably a process of distinction? Yet, as a discourse of redemption, or speech with G*d, isn't prayer also a language of salvation and eternal righteousness? Where the imperative of paradox identifies apocalyptical prayer finally as a silence before G*d, this enables both extreme secularizations and mystification of prayer. Habermas sees prayer's sincerity in its willingness to engage itself in a public discourse, as well as access substantive theological expressions. A clarification of

45. Habermas, "Communicative Freedom and Negative Theology," 195.
46. Ibid.

this public engagement of prayer is important, as it remains to be understood how this discursive engagement may be more than a contextualized practice while also not universally enthroning religious identity by
way of metaphysical or soteriological absolutes.

Universal Community, Communicative-Action, and Prayer

Habermas critiques two problematic perspectives on prayer and brings
some clarity to the ambiguities of religious language in a modern age. A
key insight is that Habermas goes in two different directions simultaneously and refuses any non-criticizable polarity between a philosophical
faith and mystical discourse, which may result from Kantian and Barthian
perspectives. His deep dissatisfaction with paradox as a hermeneutical
crutch is because it intensifies romantic illusions and disillusions with
enlightenment and an individual's ability to transcend their society.

The critique of the two above relations within reason, between faith
and despair, is in line with what Habermas writes about a history of reason in *The Philosophical Discourse of Modernity*. "The parties that have
contended about the correct self-understanding of modernity since the
days of the Young Hegelians all agree on one point: that a far reaching
process of self-illusion was connected with the learning process concep-
tualized in the eighteenth century as 'enlightenment.'"[47] While Habermas
names Marx, Kierkegaard, Feuerbach, and Nietzsche as examples in this
context, I might add Barth, Jaspers, and Theunissen who all "protest
against false mediations" between subjective and objective realities. In
the judgment of Habermas: "They insist on a desublimation of a spirit
that merely draws the real oppositions emerging at a given time into
the suction of an absolute relation to self, so as to deactualize them, to
transpose them into the mode of the shadowy self-transparency of a remembered past, and to strip them of all seriousness."[48] Thus, an authentic subjectivity becomes a false absolute when all rational relations to the
world become a means to an end, a functionalism or instrumentalization
of selfhood, by which to complete in history what is already decided.

The defatalizing of history is short-circuited by a "shadowy" memory caught up in itself rather than the "seriousness" of real oppositions.

47. Habermas, *Philosophical Discourse of Modernity*, 55.
48. Ibid., 54.

One sees how this critique of memory might also apply to some prayers to the extent they either instrumentalize selfhood or fatalize history by way of a religious identity where prayer as an act of language is hardwired into the situation of dialogue. So when prayer takes part in what is described by Max Weber as "this worldly asceticism" then the paradox of rationalization is unavoidable.

Whether it is Jaspers's Sisyphus-like faith, which continues to present itself in an always discordant plurality, or Theunissen's negative understanding of G*d, each tends to present modern short-cuts to an authentic dialogue by way of a systemization of despair. But each contradicts their stated goal of fair and emancipatory dialogue by performing as an absolute understanding, what Habermas calls a performative contradiction. Each is interesting and truthful as an expression of the author's perspective, but they fail to provide a ground that is acceptable to all. But in both cases, these performances confuse the relation between identity and knowledge, which in turn privilege certain social understandings that attempt to evangelize or act as an apologetic.

Although Habermas is in profound agreement about the importance of dialogue, he frames it in the formal pragmatic terms of universally successful communication that may validate social action by a "postmetaphysical" version of the categorical imperative—his U principle. This section will briefly describe his version of the categorical imperative, in order to compare and contrast it with Barth's own version especially with prayer in mind.

As an alternative, Habermas suggests a "transcendence from within" which is discovered in successful instances of communication, and thus would not try to reduce religious understandings to the aesthetic. He and Karl-Otto Apel refer to the transcendence inherent to validity claims, a claim about some set of facts that opens the question of the relation between the present and future. In his reply to the theologians in Chicago, he quotes Charles S. Pierce: "Thus, thought is rational only so far as it recommends itself to a possible future thought. Or in other words the rationality of thought lies in its reference to a possible future."[49] Thus a temporal transcendence is made available in language because it makes claims that are possible. Habermas states in this article that he has always steered between a transcendence-less empiricism and an idealism that glorifies transcendence. This moderate transcendence in relation to

49. Habermas, "Transcendence from Within, Transcendence in This World," 241.

faith and religion is perceptible as one relates his readings of Jaspers and Theunissen.

Inherent here is a non-Lockean conception of memory, which is inadequately described as a decaying sense of experience. Rather, C. S. Peirce in America and Edmund Husserl and Gottlob Frege in Germany begin another conception of memory which refuses to allow empirical psychology to become the foundation for all truth claims. He quotes Frege as the summary of his alternative view, "We are not owners of our thoughts as we are owners of our representations."[50] Habermas sees this as the first step in the linguistic turn, which is able to differentiate expressed perceptions from stated facts about the world. Whether in everyday speech acts or in expert cultures, participants claim validity for their utterances and thereby through a process of listening and speaking. All can attempt to reach a shared understanding about a set of facts in the world.[51] "The idea of the redeemability of criticizable validity claims requires idealizations that, as adopted by the communicating actors themselves, are thereby brought down from transcendental heaven to the earth of the life-world. The theory of communicative action *detranscendentalizes* the noumenal realm only to have the idealizing force of context-transcending anticipations settle in the unavoidable pragmatic presuppositions of speech acts, and hence in the heart of everyday communicative practice."[52] His point is that all language that calls for some response, whether yes or no, relies at least on potential reasons that the speaker may, at any time, be called upon to make clear. The act of speech is inherently a show of confidence in the other and that there are reasons available if needed, which may provide the basis for mutual understanding and thereby coordinated reconciliation.

Where did this originary speech come from? Habermas rejects the Heideggerian *ursprung* as a mythic narrative of origin, and instead credits the originary conception of God. "Unlike the range of early mythic narratives, the idea of God—that is, the idea of the unified, invisible God the Creator and Redeemer—signified a breakthrough to an entirely new perspective. With this idea, finite spirit acquired a standpoint that utterly transcends the this-worldly."[53] This directly relates to modernity when

---

50. Habermas, *Between Facts and Norms: Contributions to a Theory of Law and Democracy*, 10. The translator uses "representations" from the German *Vorstellungen*.

51. Ibid., 17.

52. Ibid., 19.

53. Medieta, "A Conversation About God and the World," 148.

the knowing and morally judging subject assumes the divine standpoint of transcendence, albeit diminished to a "transcendence from within." Individuality means an ability to objectify nature as a totality connected in a law-like manner, and simultaneously express an expanded familiar moral responsibility to an unbounded communication community.

> The idealizing supposition of a universalistic form of life, in which everyone can take the perspective of everyone else and can count on reciprocal recognition by everybody, makes it possible for individuated beings to exist within a community—individualism as the flip-side of universalism . . . The self-critical appropriation and reflexive continuation of my life history would have to remain a non-binding or even indeterminate idea so long as I could not encounter myself before the eyes of all . . . Thus, the relationship between the "I" and the "me" *remains* the key for an analysis of the socially imputed postconventional ego-identity. But at this stage the relationship between the two is reversed.[54]

This means a pervasive questionability of any so called fact because each "ego-identity" is always already indebted to provide an explanation in response to any criticism. Thus, this manner of reason enables the person to *interpenetrate* both the "cognitive rationalization of an objectified nature" with the "rationalization of the totality of morally regulated interpersonal relationships."[55] A level of integrity is possible once a person recognizes how both a set of mutually accepted facts and subjective relations mutually constitute an authentic personhood.

Where Heidegger argued for a radical interiority where self-knowledge and decision interpenetrate, Habermas finds a relational interpenetration available through communication. Instead of authenticity of the individual, one seeks a life of integrity to the extent ones actions and expressed purposes are not contradictory to others they involve, or those who question. In this way Habermas advances beyond earlier critical theorists who find only a reification in the paradox of modern rationalizations of society. In addition he describes a resolution of the paradox of rationalization within the temporal dimension by virtue of the community that is implied in each communicative-act.[56] This implied or inherent universal communication community enables society

54. Habermas, *Postmetaphysical Thinking*, 186–87.
55. Medieta, "A Conversation about God and the World," 148.
56. Habermas, *Postmetaphysical Thinking*, 187.

to advance toward its own emancipation, which modernity has set in motion but has inadequately described or institutionalized for now.

So Habermas describes the sacred as "a world behind us" and as uncriticizable but he also describes "sacramental practice (and prayers) of the congregation" as a point along a path of disenchanting religious practice, and as "less and less carried on in the consciousness that a divine power can be forced to do something."[57] Thus prayer may function as an act of communication when there is an evident "transcendence from within" that is present as the distinguishing of an intersubjective validation of norms and values.[58] It is more than plausible, given that he credits the conceptualization of G*d as the originary form of transcendence from within, and that he also describes a communicative reason as an always already universal questionability that enables a life of integrity and meaning, that this might also describe a prayerful life.

It is not necessary to decide upon G*d as a given fact or not, nor to make a commitment to a particular religious community, all that is necessary to prayer is for it to be speech out of brokenness directed toward something beyond brokenness. In this way, if prayer participates within the universal communication community as an apocalyptical prayer, a process of myth or de-myth is unnecessary. This refrains from any irreversible polarizations of the ego-identity of an "I" and the "me" that is encountered before the eyes of all. "Here *myself* means: my existence as a whole—in full concretion and breadth of the life contexts and formative processes that shape identity."[59]

Perhaps then the validity of prayer can be asked in terms of its performance as an action of successful communication which is neither completely a matter of an expressed selfhood nor an assertion of a community system. Habermas may help along this line by describing com-

57. Habermas, *Theory of Communicative Action*, 190.

58. Here, I will have to disagree with a statement made by Habermas in his *Theory of Communicative Action*, which is unnecessary to his main argument and is also incorrect. He writes, "The distinction between communicative and purposive activity is not relevant to the sacred realm. In my view there is no point to contrasting religious cults and magical practices from this perspective." Habermas, *Theory of Communicative Action*, 192. My point is that some prayers may function as a furtherance of purposive or strategic goals, rather than a participation in a validation of norms, but this is not always the case. Prayers are also reflexive and sometimes involve a reciprocating reconsideration of worldviews, and prayer may also be normatively unbound and valued as communicative-action from the perspective of a sacred seer.

59. Ibid., 186.

munication as criticizable interaction between all possible individuals involved. A prayer may be said to be valid insofar as it is also universally criticizable as a questioning of social norms and shared agendas of social action. The performance of prayer in this way can contribute a universal consensus community.

Before describing how this interaction may involve prayer, we can verify the possibility of this interpretation of Habermas thus far by his own words in response to a recent interview when he was asked about two contradictory perspectives in his philosophy of religion. He answers: "in one tendency religion is liquefied and sublated in discourse ethics and the theory of rationality; in the other, religion is given the function of preserving and even nurturing a particular type of semantic content that remains indispensable for ethics and morality, but also for philosophy in general."[60] His reply is revealing of his rejection of paradoxical conceptions at the center of religion and yet also open to some religious content. His reply is direct, "I see no contradiction there." He states that, on one hand, he desires "to show that unconditioned meaning or truth" is not dependent on "strong theological premises," as we have noticed already in his criticism of Theunissen. On the other hand, he "expresses the conviction that indispensable potentials for meaning are preserved in religious language."[61] This is apparent in his essay on Karl Jaspers. Importantly, notice here that he says "to show" and "to express." Habermas is clear about what he knows and who he is, and the arch enemy is when "who we are" determines "what we know" and the reverse; thereby we cease to hear the other and we cease to collect data to correct propositions about the world. The rationalization of social action must be discursive and thereby postmetaphysical and oriented to a mutually accepted description of the facts. When identity is solidified within a certain description of reality, then society becomes organized by a brutish rhetoric or coercion and is reduced to conflict between ideologies and finally never really emancipatory.

Habermas describes this problem of the rationalization of society in terms of a religious fundamentalism that reacts to materialistic modernization, both of which can become rhetorical continuations of the false dilemmas and offered solution of paradox arising between secularization and mystification. He describes fundamentalism as one reaction,

60. Medieta, "A Conversation about God and the World," 162.
61. Ibid.

to the "very real experiences of loss, suffered by populations torn out of their cultural traditions during processes of accelerated modernization."[62] These losses cannot be repaid "within the horizon of future generations." The fundamentalist reaction gains plausibility when it is perceived that Western consumerism trivializes these losses in a materialist non-normative culture, except insofar as it is concerned with opening new markets. While some might call for either increased secularization of reason or a liberalization of religion, instead Habermas calls for religious contributions to a discursive re-structuring of a global society. But in order to contribute responsibly, religion need be "self-reflexive" and also able to accept rather than repress the "cognitive dissonance" caused in a plural society. In other words, religious identity must not solidify itself nor work within a fallibility of all social norms and validity questions. This must be complete. The exemption of one value claim within one community can lead to prejudiced action against other communities.

This is a tacit explanation or theory of how prayer functions as an apocalyptical discourse of brokenness in both fundamentalist and secular material-oriented societies. The problem becomes the systemic approaches to apocalyptic issues that then orient each society to itself rather than the other. This "Habermasian" attitude of prayer is pertinent to an apocalyptical origin of prayer, but also an opening of eschatological understanding to discursive validations rather than to inter-faith conflict.

As an illustration, I am reminded of the character of Thomas More in the 1960 play *A Man for All Seasons*. His life is presented in the play as a man of faith grounded in prayer and the questioning of all social agendas and thus also in reason. Toward this end he refuses to submit to a polarization of his identity, neither the "I" of his faith in G*d nor his "me" in loyalty to the King will be separated. This is climactically stated by More, in jail for years and threatened with beheading, when his daughter visits and tries to argue that he should submit to an oath to the King as the Supreme Head of the Church.

> Margaret: "God more regards the thoughts of the heart than the words of the mouth" or so you've always told me.
>
> More: Yes.

62. Borradori, *Philosophy in a Time of Terror: Dialogues with Jürgen Habermas and Jacques Derrida*, 31.

Margaret: Then say the words of the oath and in your heart think otherwise.

More: What is an oath then but words we say to God?

Margaret: That's very neat.

More: Do you mean it isn't true?

Margaret: No, it's true.

More: Then it's a poor argument to call it "neat," Meg. When a man takes an oath, Meg, he's holding his own self in his own hands. Like water. (He cups his hands) And if he opens his fingers then he needn't hope to find himself again. Some men aren't capable of this, but I'd be loathe to think your father one of them.[63]

More states that his "self" is a matter of an integrity between his values and the facts as he knows them. Certainly he is willing to enter into argument, and willing to be convinced by the unforced force of a better argument, but finally his personhood would be lost if he surrendered this integrity. But also the character describes his prior "I" seriously, when earlier he expresses his faith to his friend Norfolk about the Church, "What matters is not the I *believe* it, but that *I* believe it." And yet he also explains to Cardinal Cranmer during an interrogation that he can accept the King's sovereignty only insofar as the King does not claim to command truth itself. More states, "If the world is flat, will the King's command make it round? And if it is round, will the King's command flatten it?"[64] If read from a Habermasian perspective, an appreciation both for a 1st person subjectivity and also a 3rd person view of facts makes room for More's "words we say to God" where meaning and action can not be separated. He then states to his Son-in-Law that he is able to give the devil benefit of law for his own safety's sake.

For our purposes one may already note how a final judgment on prayer is disallowed, especially if such a judgment is connected to the description of transcendental reason, which either amounts to a secularization or mystification of dialogue. It was stated above how the relation of faith and knowledge should not be solidified in a way that closes possibilities of reconciliation because this amounts to a non-criticizable performance of reason based in metaphysical absolutes. Habermas will not make prayer itself an all or nothing proposition to be "wired" into a

63. Bolt, *A Man for All Seasons*, 140.
64. Ibid., 133.

description of the transcendental. Instead, the question of the authenticity of prayer is a matter of its particular performance. He asks indirectly if prayer can allow for questions of reconciliation to be answered both with faith and knowledge without confusing or privileging these perspectives. This is the same structural problematic described earlier by Martin S. Jaffee. Although Jaffee describes the problem of monotheism, which is structured in eschatological claims, Habermas notices a parallel problem for any description of dialogue that pre-decides its claim to authenticity and sets itself up for conflict with other substantive descriptions. Perhaps as responsible creatures of history we must pray for reconciliation in rational terms if we hope to avoid coercion or exclusion of others.

Returning then to Habermas's main criticism that Kant has set within modern rationality a foundationalism of epistemological reason, which allows metaphysical assumptions and hidden interests to go unchallenged. "In championing the idea of cognition before cognition, Kantian philosophy sets up a domain between itself and the natural sciences, arrogating authority to itself."[65] Habermas's perception of Kant may be analogous what he would say about Karl Barth's ideal of prayer, which sets up divine freedom as an uncriticizable foundation. But regardless, he contributes to the consideration of an apocalyptical prayer because in either case the permissibility of a noncriticizable criterion becomes problematic to issues of justice in a polycentric world.

Like Barth who narrates the differences of the old and new man, Kant contrasts the present age with the past when reason was not courageously implemented nor society rationalized. Kant's present reason is liberated by a moral autonomy, legitimate because it has the capacity of a universal implementation for all. "Ordinances and formulles, the mechanical instruments of a rational use, or rather misuse, of his gifts of nature, are the fetters of an everlasting minority."[66] Present injustice and conflict, for both Kant and Barth, is explained ultimately in terms of the ongoing struggle between forces of light and darkness. So the problem for Habermas and a global society is that a conceptual system is thus still rhetorically imposed across various cultures, religions, and spheres of reason. Religious language becomes easily mired in this dilemma to the extent the decision to pray or not pray becomes an ideological one, pre-decided from both secular and mystical perspectives.

65. Habermas, *Moral Consciousness and Communicative Action*, 2.
66. Kant, "What is Enlightening?" 34.

So at this stage, we can place three versions of a categorical imperative: the autonomous, the paradoxical, and the communicative. The
Habermasian version is a return to Kant insofar as the value of prayer is
not pre-decided; however, it also takes the Barthian problem of paradox
seriously by addressing morality and reason in terms of an autonomous
subject insofar as one is able to communicate. The communicative version of the imperative states, "For a norm to be valid, the consequences
and side effects of its general observance for the satisfaction of each person's particular interests must be acceptable to all."[67] I read Habermas's
version as a type of prayer, but one that participates within a transcendence from within, taking both seriously the brokenness of history and
the freedom attainable by a reason which is the consequence of successful communication. Thus, a pragmatic defusion of the dilemma between
a materialized ordering of society and an absolute conceptualization of
it is furthered by a prayer that in each circumstance nonetheless participates in a universal communication community. In Habermasian terms,
one speaks in a belief or reasoning that one will be understood. Just as
the speech act itself participates in a universal reasoning, prayer is also
a speech action in the belief of being understood. One prays with some
conviction that there is reason to pray, it is a personhood in touch with
some being, some meaning of action. It is this reasoning which moves
Habermas beyond Barth's paradoxical description of G*d and man.

However, a further question need be posed about the nature of
such a universal community claimed in every event of communication.
It has to do with a problem of memory, which always seems to perme-
ate itself. As our example of apocalypse, Sethe from Beloved, "having
never had the map to discover what she was like."[68] How do those like
Sethe experience themselves within a theory of communicative-action?
In one sense she is proof of the importance of communication, as Sethe
portrays a person's inability to address others truthfully and also unable
come to any resolution of an unspeakable past. And in another sense,
Sethe reminds us that each of us have some memories, and memories
forgotten, that are constantly hindering a conscious participation in
communicative action. These permeations of memory are not avoided
by Habermas's rejection of paradox.

When the idealization of a universal standard is used to categorize
remembrances—necessary for any use of language, written or spoken—

67. Habermas, *Moral Consciousness and Communicative Action*, 197.
68. Morrison, *Beloved*, 140.

then doesn't the qualification of "successful" communication serve as a manipulation? A standard is imposed nonetheless upon the act of communication by memory and its idealization of itself, in whatever form. The next section will describe this as a problem of knowledge in prayer, which may amount to a return of paradox or not. Even once a third person perspective is enthroned and a set of facts is agreed upon, and even in the mode of a stabilized reciprocation, prayer may not be successful in the sense that Habermas describes a mutual success.

Habermas's proposition of a Principle of Universalization within communicative action theory is important to a consideration of prayer because of his observations of how culturally laden and normatively oriented truth claims affect social practice. His hope is to be able to legitimate claims, which would not exclude claims made in prayer, according to their objects and consequences. Perlocutionary acts need be distinguished from the illocutionary, or, in other words, communicative action that allows itself to be criticized in a pervasive manner contributes to a reciprocal and structured communication that has the potential for mutual understanding. However, communicative action that keeps aspects secret or away from criticism, creates opportunity for strategic or manipulative rhetoric that is contrary to a mutual procedure of decision.[69] Thus, when communicative freedom's transcendence can be understood as "post-metaphysical" (in the sense that it is criticizable as a universal foundation of discourse) such freedom may be seen by its fruit, or by its happening within the process. Communicative freedom's fruits are individuals reinforced as individuals in community by their respective arguments made and questions asked according to standards of universal discourse, rather than necessity.[70] A pragmatic discourse is then to be decided by the "unforced force of the better argument" rather than the metaphysically pre-decided rules.

When standards of a metaphysically operative necessity orient the discourse, such as often are found in prayers, then the polarity of popular sovereignty and human rights is irresolvable, and democracy and mutual understanding are short-circuited by an uncritizable ought. As Habermas would say, one would admit as metaphysical necessity the impossibility of a balance between "freedom of the ancients" and "free-

69. Habermas, *Theory of Communicative Action*, 288–90.
70. Habermas, *Between Facts and Norms*, 33–38.

dom of the moderns."[71] But rather than imposing freedom externally or instrumentalizing it as human rights, Habermas suggests that communicative freedom is intrinsically good in the "thin" sense that it remains a discourse. It is the possibility of communicative action that is respectful of the others freedom to respond, that is, a balance of the ancients and the moderns—discursively established.

This mutuality of freedom is a universal moral value in the sense that validity claims are admissible to the discourse, legitimated, when these claims do not detract from the universal discourse operative within a moral consciousness.[72] Habermas is attempting to keep a sphere of intersubjectivity, a social and public field of reason, from being colonized. Neither by cultural or subjective values borrowed from any particular life-world, nor by systems of commodity or objectification. He identifies a sphere of discourse that keeps open criticisms of both the value laden life-world and the factually oriented economy of systems. Usually this sphere is that of speculative metaphysics or some description of reality that relates these two normatively. Thus social virtues like "trust" or "family" can be understood as having a productive foundational role in situating social reality or as having priority in society.

Habermas's theory of communicative action is meant as a corrective of the often-criticized problem of Hegelian enthronement of the present, from a perspective of a Kantian formal universality of morality. In this case the universal is essentially intersubjective discourse, and that is to say that universalizability is understood as that which does not diminish or subvert the engagement of others by myself or myself by others. It seems to me that Habermas describes what an inter-religious dialogue has often attempted, which is to dialogue carefully, taking the discourse and the other religion most seriously by mutually respecting each other's freedom. Isn't this how Barth approaches prayer, in the freedom of G*d? Whether in discourse or in prayer, one speaks knowing that each word may be the last, especially if the other can break off conversation.

Then prayer has an ability to negotiate the pitfalls of plurality when it is an act of prayer that is capable of the criticizable "transcendence from within" that Habermas describes. This happens when prayer develops or contributes to mutual understanding. The prayerful person need realize how "transcendence from within" or communicative freedom is easily

71. Habermas, *The Inclusion of the Other*, 258.
72. Habermas, *Moral Consciousness and Communicative Action*, 197.

co-opted by a transcendental positing of an "outside." The establishment of a metaphysical frame that then prejudices the field of discourse as well as the discursive relations themselves in a way that excludes possible participants and pre-decides valid actions.

Can it be claimed that prayer does this always? There are many like Karl Rahner who argue that a transcendental consciousness is part of what it means to exist. But if prayer is transcendentally undecidable as a discourse then prayer gives one no new knowledge of the transcendental outside, as if one now knows best how to dial up G*d. If it did then prayer would be more like a magical manipulation of transcendental being. Rather, prayer is more like a questioning discourse that arrives at always-new questions. When questions are outlawed metaphysically or doctrinally—for instance, when it is said that a grieving parent need realize G*d knows what are the best interests of their dead child and therefore anger at G*d is inappropriate—then this guts prayer that questions seriously. Rather no lamentation, no words of anger, no doubt or question is inappropriate in a prayer, at least by virtue of prayer.

Prayer rather than trying to set up an economy of exchange with G*d or an Other, is more fruitfully pursued as a communicative act made with the freedom of the Other's response most prevalent. In other words, one never knows what response if any one will receive in return. Prayer cannot be magical, cannot be coercive, nor systemically generated. However, like Habermas's description of an intersubjective discourse that contains within it "an ideal speech community," prayer also offers one's values up for consideration and criticism. Prayer is then post-metaphysical in its form.

For an example, one that comes to mind is Gerhard Ebeling's description of prayer as a praxis. Ebeling writes: "Those who know how to pray ought also to know that at best they are in the process of learning how to pray. This presupposes that God is taken seriously. But all praying takes God seriously."[73] There are at least two points alluded to by Ebeling that dovetail with a Habermasian theory of communicative-action. The first is that speech acts, including prayer, are an ongoing process of learning how to interact. There is no one way to communicate and no ultimate form of language nor any magical formula of prayer, only a temporally marked praxis. The second point is that this "learning how" presupposes that G*d is taken seriously. An ongoing practice of prayer need be more

73. Ebeling, *The Lord's Prayer*, 6.

concerned with history *as it is lived* than history as it should be. The great historical theologian underlines here that it is not necessary to define G*d normatively, *via positiva, via negativa* or *via analogia*, in order to talk with G*d. In fact, the necessity of such an understanding of G*d is problematic to a serious prayer, one that is learning and serious, questioning and questionable.[74]

There is enough evidence here to hypothesize that prayer is a *via media* of the apocalyptical, a way of mediation in the sense that prayer engages G*d and others undecidedly, without introducing necessary presuppositions about either brokenness or G*d. That is to say, prayer is simultaneously a discursive questioning of all reality claims and a discourse engaged ethically with the other. To surrender either aspect of prayer is to surrender prayer itself, to fall into magical thinking or ideology.

Could it be that prayer itself is an intersubjective discourse that is marked by the communicative freedom essential to universal community? Can a religious discourse engage itself by a universal fallible procedure of rationality, not a reason of metaphysical necessity, by which an enlightened transcendence of sociality is operative rather than other worldly dreams? This is not to say prayer need be syncretistic nor do I suggest what Habermas calls "methodical atheism" but rather prayer is an opening of all identity to a communicative action, an interaction which is always questionable, and therefore contributing to a reciprocity of viewpoints, and thereby a mutual understanding and "transcended from within." By taking others seriously, then one also takes G*d seriously as well.

A brief comparison of Habermas to Barth is helpful. Remembering Barth's prayer is identified by a categorical paradox that always adjusts knowledge to the unknowableness of G*d, an ongoing experience of apocalypse. Habermas, however, identifies valid communication by its categorical contribution to community, which cannot be structured by paradoxical terms, nor as a secular dismissal, nor as a mystical knowledge in G*d. Keeping both positions in mind for now, a conception of prayer may want to consider both perspectives, united by a sense that the filtering of experience and systemizing knowledge is a problem for those who desire to address brokenness. Whether a prayerful preparation for

74. Gerhard Ebeling's lecture on Dietrich Bonhoeffer is for further discussion of what he calls "revelational positivism." Ebeling, *Word and Faith*, 98–161.

an ultimate salvation or the implementation of an emancipatory interaction, a common thread between the two comes into relief by considering how both open language to wider realities, unknown for now. So whether it is the destruction of metaphysical understandings by understanding their ends, or it is a paradoxical suspension of existence under G*d, or an evaluation of the performance of understandings within communicative-action, in each case the venue of an apocalyptical perspective acts as an originary location for prayer. The brokenness of existence and the conception of something beyond brokenness is utterly necessary for any spoken truth, from both perspectives. Although Barth as a theologian offers only an unspeakable concept of G*d, absolutely free and beyond brokenness, Habermas's transcendence from within communication already implies a universal community only when it is spoken or made explicit. While Barth's practice of a paradoxical imperative exemplifies a quietistic or non-public approach to prayer, a Habermasian practice of a universal speech imperative may be described as a form of pietism where public action becomes the fundamental avenue of any possibility of prayer. While the former advocates continually listening in prayer, the other would interpret prayer in light of its action.

Various spheres of discourse should not be allowed to dominate or colonize one another. As discussed already, premature preference for either secularization or mystical understandings of reality are the result of false mediations that do not sufficiently take into account the 3rd person perspective upon acceptable facts. A norming process by which a community criticizes itself needs to keep in mind that both individuation and socialization are mediated in light of a transcendence from within; a reasoning that moves beyond paradoxical conceptions or religiously implemented structure (*parole*) that will limit criticism. We have described how communication contains within itself a stubborn transcendence, an unlimited capacity to enlighten rules of accountability from the perspective of a performative non-contradiction, or, in other words, a life lived in integrity with the community. One might also begin to see how an individual can live a life interpreted simply as a type of service or sacrifice.

This performative approach to prayer is cognizant not only of its effects upon social structures, but in turn hopes to enact social structures necessary for mutual decisions and actions. Such prayer would not secularize dialogue, nor does it permit theology to necessarily validate a proper manner of intersubjective communication. However, it has also been recognized how this performative prayer has a pietistic sense that is concerned with the accountability to its performance within society. Toward this end, a prayer's inherent identity and knowledge need be sufficiently interactive and reflexive to inform shared norms of mutual accountability. Society may then be, and has been, transformed by the prayers of individuals willing to be vulnerable to all criticism and actually accountable to accepted knowledge, especially within prayer. Such prayer can inform and inspire the rationality that combines a realistic fallibility with an emancipatory hope for a universal community, already present but not yet achieved.

However, Habermas's (U)niversalization principle may take us only so far as a description of prayer, especially if one wants to pray as a communication, where both listening and acting are imperative to prayer. While a pragmatic movement beyond paradox is helpfully made accountable to an always already community present in a reciprocating communicative action, it is an insufficient description insofar as some reciprocations or mutual understandings are not a matter of procedure or structured communication. One does not even have to go so far as to conceptualize G*d, or a transcendental, or the sacred, to understand this problem, which arises even in an accounting of history and is therefore also problematic for a transcendence from within.

For instance, if one recalls the exchange of letters between Max Horkheimer and Walter Benjamin, where the former states that the past is decidedly closed, while the latter refuses to finalize or reify the past, especially as it admits undisclosed and outstanding injustices. Habermas's criticism of the theologians still echoes the perspective of Horkheimer's advice to Benjamin: "Past injustice has occurred and is closed. Those who were slain in it were truly slain."[75] A fundamental question is raised in the context of brokenness and suffering, whether human reflection begins in continuity with the past in order to understand?

Is there a praxis of prayerful action in solidarity with the past or does prayer break with the past? This is a crucial question when prayer becomes serious about its implementations of faith, because Habermas shows us how all systemization of human brokenness amounts to false mediation that filters out many perspectives. Where a practice of faith is concerned, if a prayerful interaction helps guard against an apocalypticism that reduces prayer to a socializing of one ideology, which reduces

---

75. Peukert, *Science, Action, and Fundamental Theology: Toward a Theology of Communicative Action*, 206.

the diversity of voices in reason, shouldn't this include an opening of the past and a willingness to include the voices of the dead in present conversations? Helmut Peukert makes this criticism of communicative action theory, even though he agrees with communicative action theory as a progress beyond "science" insofar as it an emancipation of humanity is theorized. However, Peukert restates the problem between Benjamin and Horkheimer.

> If the other is viewed as a reciprocally recognized and recognizing partner in action, his death can no longer be ascertained as a matter of fact. The memory of the other as the one who has acted for the benefit of the one who is now remembering is only possible in such a way that one returns to the possibilities of action opened up by the one who has gone to his death; hence, he is present, remembered and affirmed as an actor in the other's presence and affirmation is the well established fact that the other has ultimately been annihilated in his innocence and that one benefits from his annihilation. To simply direct one's solidarity to others and finally to future generations does not resolve this inner contradiction.[76]

The death of the other is a problem to prayer that is exacerbated by a strictly pietistic approach. The memory of any other, in order to be approached in a truly universalistic way, need be liberated from restrictions imposed when the past is remembered as my benefit. Sacrifice must be recognized and in a way that also recognizes I continue to benefit from the slaughter. This brings one to the re-consideration of prayer's intersubjective exchange that is not only an act of communicative freedom but also a continuing stigma of memory and thus a stigma on all present reasoning.

76. Ibid., 232–33.

5

Reconsidering Knowledge as Memory in Prayer

I HAVE SHOWN THAT IT IS POSSIBLE TO THINK ABOUT PRAYER AS A discourse that cuts against leveling secularizations and mysterious exchange, by developing transcendence from within that is displayed in social action. Such a prayerful participant works along the road from unjust social structures to emancipation by the recognition of a moral or universal consciousness that arises from reciprocal acts of communication. This is criticizable as a communicative freedom rooted in the recognition of our shared humanity with all.

It is not only ethical decision making that orients a life of prayer. The performance of prayer also claims to order the relation between an ongoing experience-of-brokenness and prayer's object-which-is-beyond-brokenness, the source of salvation. In this way prayer is capable of turning its pietistic sense inside out and upside down. Rather than a given performance, it is the quiet of prayer that is the moment of re-orientation. The quietism of a continuing memory of apocalypse, a remembering of the forgotten, not only limits accountability but potentially transforms it into a wider responsibility.

This is an address of the apocalyptic(al) question that we have asked from the beginning of this project, what is prayer an experience *of*? Or in other words, how is prayer applied to any future, especially recognizing a religious past that even Habermas describes as a stigma on the present? This relates directly to the status of suffering in any plan of salvation, and explains how prayer may make a difference. This is an especially difficult and important question for a prayer that affirms a transcendent divinity. It is especially difficult for Abrahamic prayers that faithfully address one G*d, holy and loving. One example of this is Karl Barth who takes many years to wind through the complex discursive nature of prayer in his *Dogmatics*. He patiently describes an experience of G*d within Christian tradition, an experience that amounts to a disturbance of all words by the Word that is complete(d) gift. Barth repeats that all reduction or symbolization of G*d's gift is for him an apocalyptic utterance, an act of sacrifice, the recognition of the judgment of G*d.[1]

Parallel, may not all prayer be described as the discourse of ultimate ends, an address out of utter brokenness to something beyond any utterance of our own? This would be an approach to prayer that suspends an assortment of positions within the phenomenology of religion. For example, on one hand, transcendental experience is sometimes taken as a reflection if not a proof of something beyond, as by Karl Rahner. On the other hand, it might be asked if the subject is then more radical than G*d, experientially understood as by Paul Ricoeur? Somewhat mediating the two, Maurice Merleau-Ponty describes reflection always already within a reality. A mediating reflection on experience must work as if it is horizontal even if it can't finally comprehend and decide upon a vertical transcendence. So again, *if epistemically* the self is more original than G*d so as to respect the boundless nature of a wholly Other, then what might this mean for a discourse directed to the Other? Or more to the point, what kind of prayer is appropriate to this situation? A re-consideration of all these positions permits one to question whether prayer, or speaking with G*d, is possible without hubris or arrogance.

For prayer, an inadequacy of *episteme* has often amounted to the theme "manifestation is not Revelation." This two tiered mediation plays out in various manners by the work of Emmanuel Levinas, Jacques Derrida, David Tracy, and Jean-Luc Marion, among others. These recent approaches constantly question enlightenment reason as a metaphysics of presence that privileges verifiable and visible knowledge, and neglects undecidable aspects of a spiritual humanity. Remembering Catherine Keller's appreciation and frustration with this apocalyptic element within Barth, I will describe prayer as the discourse of religious ends, an address out of brokenness to something beyond.

In this vein, the deconstructive approach by Jacques Derrida can be described as an appreciation of *aporia*, a form of quietism that always suspends judgment upon relations of identity and knowledge, especially within performances of language.

Like Habermas, Derrida is interested in a pragmatic deepening of enlightenment, but for him this is in contrast to accountability to per-

1. Barth, *Church Dogmatics* I.1, 49, 75–76, 230–31.

formance. Instead he performs a pragmatic approach to language with a sense of responsibility that is akin to a prayerful sense of the unknowable. He describes a pragmatic sensibility of that which is beyond any final economy of meaning or accountability. I would add that one needs to be able to pray and say things to G*d without fear that it may be counted against one.

Reduction and Messianicity

Jacques Derrida describes economies of exchange that take place as language, where Habermas describes a reciprocating structure of discursive communication. His view of inter-personal exchanges is always marked by *familial* understandings that provide both identity and non-identity, knowledge and non-knowledge; an inter-subjectivity marked indelibly by ambiguity. So Derrida describes acts of language that have a capacity to distinguish identity and knowledge, but also to confuse, even insofar as they come to further understandings. He disagrees or resists a practice of proper communication according to so-called *necessities* of a reciprocal procedure. This refusal of any permanent ordering or economy of responsible decisions is important for a reconsideration of how prayer works today if there can be no holding back of religion from within language, no forgetting of forgetting. Rather language is *messianicity*, as will be explained. This also recognizes that all prayer is inevitably a reduction but one construed as a disquietude of being. What I call an apocalyptical resistance.

If an implicit universal community within communication arises from a pious spirit of history (the good interaction which builds reasoned community everywhere) then a natural question is whether discourse characterized by "transcendence from within" also communicates and therefore makes criticizable the community's eventual *end.* More succinctly stated, is the "post" of *post*-metaphysical thinking presumptuous by replacing descriptions of being with a third person perspective upon the agreed facts? If so, this may be another form of coercion insofar as a different privileging of perspective arises or if it means that traditional interactions must be eventually subsumed under an unending modernity. In either case, the past is forgotten insofar as it does not contribute to the present. The forgotten are truly forgotten.

In contrast to a post-metaphysical thinking, Derrida hopes to perform an *opening* of metaphysics (*cloture*) that takes place in the relations
between past and future, within acts of memory. It is by making the
ultimate purposes or ends of cultural movements criticizable through
literature, religion, and other institutions of memory that preserve and
alter trajectories toward an end. His task is to understand understanding, or find some perspective given upon inter-subjective exchange
without making any one perspective sovereign, therefore each is to be
deconstructed or criticized from within. Although a complete render-
ing of Derrida is beyond the scope of this work, I will incorporate this
Derridean *opening* as it may relate to prayer. This is important to the
responsibility of the person in prayer who strives to be accountable to
a universal communication community. Derrida describes this opening
from which prayer may be given, rather than made, where any alignment
of identity and knowledge is a matter of decision not necessity and thus
also a matter of sacrifice; but where the non-purity of this sacrifice may
not be held against the giver.

From the beginning of the career of Jacques Derrida, the topic of
an opening of metaphysics is always implied. To explain what is meant
by this one can return as early as 1962. His *Introduction to the "Origin of
Geometry"* comments upon Husserl's description of geometry. It is helpful for us to consider geometry because it operates like a metaphysics,
for it originates from a system of axioms that *govern* a multiplicity. In
this commentary Derrida points out that Husserl mentions a perspective
upon this *governing* which includes what Gödel describes as the possibility of "undecidable" propositions within any system, and thus supple-
ments any governance by metaphysics or sovereign ontology. So Derrida
reads Husserl as questioning whether knowledge is always a result of the
decidable or rather includes a category of the undecidable. He answers
that it depends upon whether one is "within the horizon" of a tradition.

Geometry is an example of a tradition of knowledge "whose unity is
still *to come* on the basis of what is announced in its origin."[2] The history
of geometry has involved different theories of reality that today include
euclidian rules and corollaries, to fractal geometry, that everything is reducible to equations, to string theory, that everything is interconnected.
The proof of one's hypothesis, the attainment of knowledge, entails a
bracketing of existence. Thus singular examples may be known in their

2. Derrida, *Edmund Husserl's Origin of Geometry: An Introduction*, 53.

essential meaning and thus governed from within by a set of rules that are in turn verifiable by experimentation. This second bracketing is important because it is not possible to know the end of tradition *in general*, or what is "to come" of that which is announced in tradition's origin. Within two concentric brackets [( )], Husserl suggests a procession of a "zig-zag" pattern both forward and backward, which he calls a "return inquiry" (German, *Rückfrage*; French, *question en retour*) which Derrida describes in detail. Husserl theorizes and conducts a suspension of suspension from within phenomenology that relates particulars to a sense of their origin. Thus the present is presumed contextualized by an origin yet to be discovered.

> Thus only under the cover of static phenomenology's reductions can we make other infinitely more subtle and hazardous reductions, which yield both the singular essences of institutive acts and, in their exemplary web, the whole sense of an open history in *general*. Without the *Wechselspiel* [interplay, alternating performance, or play, *my trans.*] of this double reduction, the phenomenology of historicity would be an exercise in vanity, as would all phenomenology. If we take for granted the philosophical non-sense of a purely empirical history and the impotence of an ahistorical rationalism, then we realize the seriousness of what is at stake.[3] (Italics mine)

Derrida is entertaining the idea that for there to be an "open history in *general*" the decidable and the undecidable are not mutually exclusive, but each contaminates each decision of knowledge. While reduction makes knowledge possible, it is nonetheless a reduction of reality. Decision cannot be understood without the perspective of the undecidable at the same time. So a phenomenology need to suspend judgment and allow the interplay or playful exchange between reductions for the sake of a coming essential meaning. This means that phenomenology is limited where human ends are concerned or at play; history is incomplete for now.

Presumed presences always have at least two sources of undecidable supplement. An interior and exterior as the "double" bind of intersubjectivity, between the unknowability of singular essences and the unknown outcome of their play through history. Therefore, while reductions are necessary for the sake of knowing for now, yet they are most

3. Ibid., 51.

dangerous if one does not have a sense of their limited horizon. We see in this earliest work how Derrida speaks, will speak, of the "to come" [avenant] of the future in the ambiguous terms of presence and meaning, so as to also speak of an advent, the future that is yet to come. "Horizon is the always-already-there of a future which keeps the indetermination of its infinite openness intact (even though this future was *announced* to consciousness). As the structural determination of every material indeterminacy, a horizon is always virtually present in every experience, for it is at once the unity and incompletion for that experience—the anticipated unity in every incompletion."[4] The person of prayer does not know if this is a happy circumstance or not; the future, like a stranger, may bring happiness or misery to the person of faith. The present burns with an indeterminacy between its own unity and incompletion. Where Husserl posits intentionality as the highest source of value and thus he "locates the space where consciousness notifies itself of the Idea's prescription . . . It is on the basis of this horizon-certainty that the historicity of sense and the development of Reason are set free."[5] Instead, Derrida suspends final judgments about any such positing or location, although communication between individuals who have different experiences use references to their respective horizons. Here there is some agreement with Habermas who is quick to describe the procedure of reciprocation that distinguishes perlocutionary and illocutionary statements until individuals may meld their horizons. Derrida's focus is upon a depth of equivocity that may not be sacrificed for the sake of what seems a placid premature univocity of the already present.

As long as there is inescapable ambiguity between cultural manners of distinguishing and so-called eternal distinctions, then the constant temptation within this ambiguity is to sacrifice either finitude or infinitude in order to have clarity. An example of an undecidable position is one that is caught between either universal categories of being or specific irreducible events of revelation. This is the general structure of messianicity, where religious discourse finds itself. To decide on religious knowledge, its messianicity, then one of two options has to happen. "You would have to go back from these religions to the fundamental ontological conditions of possibilities of religions, to describe the structure of messianicity on the groundless ground on which religions have been

4. Ibid., 117.
5. Ibid., 140.

made possible . . . The other hypothesis is that the events of revelation, the biblical traditions, the Jewish, Christian, and Islamic traditions, have been absolute events, irreducible events which have unveiled this messianicity."[6]

The choice between the two, between a fundamental ontology and a religious conversion, is a temptation to know once and for all; to blatantly delegitimize and therefore remove the brackets. The temptation of this sacrifice not only haunts Derrida but is the temptation of anyone everyday. Religion does not avert this aporetic temptation, as soon as one speaks then one attests to one form of economy or another, one language or one religion, without knowing the final answer as to whether one speaks the truth or ultimately lies. The answer can ultimately come only as an absolute event, the unity announced in its origin, and whatever combination of the above two schemes is impossible to know. Everyday speech is the experience of this teleological aporetic, a pure anticipation for an impossible answer. So Derrida can say that this is the "least bad" definition of deconstruction, "experience of the impossible."[7]

The issue of an origin that is inaccessible in its unity is forgotten but must not be entirely forgotten and this makes all knowledge a matter of general knowledge, or somehow always in need to be contextualized. If one forgets origins, or forgets that there is an origin, then one buries the past forever. This is the temptation of Discourse where the end is reduced to today's purposes and the stigma of memory is forgotten.

> We need to conclude this propaedeutic de jure or anticipate its factual end, so that we may pass from the question *how* to the question *why*—to know of what we speak. It is in this respect that all philosophical discourse must derive its authority from phenomenology . . . The *why* can emerge only from the *possible* (in the metaphysical or ontological sense, and not in the phenomenological) nonbeing of historical factuality; and nonbeing *as* nonhistory only discloses its *eventuality* on the basis of a consciousness of *possibility* in the phenomenological sense. As we have sufficiently seen, this consciousness (which phenomenology alone can bring to light) can only be a teleological consciousness . . . Teleology is the threatened unity of sense and being, of phenomenology and ontology. However, this teleology, which never ceased to ground and animate Husserl's thought, cannot

---

6. Caputo, *Deconstruction in a Nutshell*, 168–69.

7. Derrida, *Deconstruction and the Possibility of Justice*, 15.

> be determined in a philosophical language without provisionally
> breaking this unity for the benefit of phenomenology.[8]

The teleological reduction of the future, is both the "threatened unity of sense and being" and is also "provisionally" broken for the benefit of a description. Reduction is a danger but also an opportunity to meaning. The unity of sense and being is threatened because its absence is noticed as soon as one looks for it—which those questioning origins-ends tend to do. But the provision is that so-called reduction may then lead to a new end, or change direction. The zigzagging questioning of reduction makes the possibility of a previously impossible justice part of the consideration.

With regard to human knowledge of the past, memory can have multiple directions, it makes possible both the inclusion or exclusion of the other.[9] With regard to the relation of "We" and "You," then, memory is not a zero-sum game or a competition between different identities. Rather a questioning such as this, within a double suspension, can be reconceived over and over again, sometimes more inclusive or sometimes exclusive forms of history. Michael Rothberg sees this view of memory predicated on the rejection of two often-made assumptions about our relation to the past. He rejects the notion of "a straight line that runs between memory and identity" and he equally rejects the idea that the only kinds of memory that are possible are ones that exclude elements of alterity and forms of commonality with others."[10] Simply, the claim here is that "why" can be asked only once it is realized that it is not answered; unless the *unity* of sense and being is *broken* then "why" is not questioned and the past is too easily sacrificed, such is the way to an easy conscience.

Along this line of broken unity, which is also possibility, twenty-five years later Derrida also shows what he means by a closure of metaphysics in the Heideggerian frame of being (*Dasein*) committed to its own radical questionability as the procession toward its end.[11] He states his hypothesis about Heidegger in his book *On Spirit*: "Such at least is my hypothesis—to recognize in it [Heidegger's interpretation of the word

---

8. Ibid., 150–51.
9. Rothberg, *Multidirectional Memory*, 44–46.
10. Ibid., 4–5.
11. Derrida, *Of Grammatology*, 4.

Spirit, *Geist*], in its very equivocation or indecision, the edging or dividing path [*le chernin de bordure ou the partage*] which ought, according to Heidegger, to pass between Greek or Christian—even onto-theological—determination of *pneuma* or *spiritus*, and a thinking of *Geist* that would be other and more originary."[12]

The indecision or equivocation is perceived in the way Heidegger approaches a question of the meaning of being (*die Frage nach Sinn von Sein*), the question that acquaints one with a possible nothingness of being which is necessary for one to *be* in the fullest sense (*Dasein*). Heidegger calls questioning the "piety" of thinking, and such is his piety that he also questions questioning in 1957, and explains that a certain listening always precedes the question of being. Heidegger explains that the question "was already in the ambiance of the realization that the true stance of thinking cannot be to put questions, but must be listening to the grant or the pledge (*das Horen der Zusage*)."[13] There is no questioning possible without listening first. The alternative is some pre-determined reason why to question, and if this is pre-determinable then it is unquestionable and therefore surrenders being to self-ignorance.

Derrida wants to understand the relation of this questioning and listening.[14] He questions this *indecision* of listening/questioning as an example of one caught between quietism and a piety of thought. If there is an analogy between "hearing the promise as being" and a prayer which "listens in the absolute freedom of God," then there is also an analogy between the questioning of being and the performative approach to communicative-action.[15] A full treatment of this comparison takes this work off course, for now it is important to see Derrida's question about Heidegger as it relates to an inter-subjective communication cognizant of its purpose.

The response to the other and responsibility to the promise are, for Derrida, inseparable from any placement of exchange. Language entails listening to the temporalization of being, which always already appears

12. Derrida, *Of Spirit*, 81–82.

13. Heidegger, *On the Way to Language*, 72.

14. Is this indecision simply a humbling of selfhood in the older philosopher? I am reminded of the quietism of Karl Barth, and the silence that is only appropriate to listening for G*d. Although much has been written about the similarities of Heidegger and Barth, this may be more true of the later Heidegger and the early Barth.

15. A famous volume of essays that makes this comparison. Robinson and Cobb, *The Later Heidegger and Theology*.

as the promise or pledge that is implied in all language, but is also the uncompleted task of language. So universal categories of thought or "transcendence from within" is too much. This must be balanced with reflection about an "auto-immunity" or "the principle of sacrificial self-destruction ruining the principle of self-protection."[16] Derrida sets up an opposing force to Heideggerian being, which reappears at the edge of language or on the border between knowledge and identity. Instead Derrida describes an *eGodicy*, analogous to theodicy, as the cynical wound of all the unkept promises and the unkept promise of words, varieties of death. Universal principles cannot be a form of self-protection, according to Derrida, rather a zigzagging of selfhood or immunity by phenomenological questioning, may stitch together and tear apart again, in an ongoing reassessment of selfhood. This is an ongoing emancipation of being, framed as messianicity; it is the possibility that one may (not) presume to know too much. One speaks as if it were a prayer when one understands a giftedness of the present exchange, and place of exchange. Derrida call this, "A Dasein liberated to find itself."[17] This means a presenting of the present presence, thus opening the present communities to a future yet to come, a radically new future.

This messianicity represents Derrida's most important disagreement with Habermas upon the issues of time and being. Where Habermas does not permit "false mediations" of being—those that do not accept universality as the criterion of reason—so as also not to admit the Zeitgeist that continually arises in rhetorical battles, Derrida remains undecided upon the relation between these same spirits or regional ontologies. He will not presume judgment upon them as true or false. Each is its own realm of prayer. This is to retain a sense of infinite responsibility at stake here between time and being. So Derrida calls for "messianicity without messianism," if there will be renewal of being or new being. For Habermas nothing is more dangerous because it opens the door to ambiguities of rhetoric, and thus new prophets of myth and coercion,

---

16. "The immunitary reaction protects the 'indemn-ity' of the body proper in producing antibodies against foreign antigens. As for the process of auto-immunization, which interests us particularly here, it consists for a living organism, as is well known and in short, of protecting itself against its self-protection by destroying its own immune system . . . It seems indispensible to us today for thinking the relations between faith and knowledge, religion and science, as well as the duplicity of sources in general." Derrida, "Faith and Knowledge," 73 n. 27.

17. Derrida, *Of Spirit*, 15.

while Habermas desires instead to draw preconditions, like lines on a soccer field, that will permit playful response and thus a freedom within continual, unending discourse. Derrida finds this potentially tiresome; not so much that he desires a knight of rhetoric to announce the origin of virtue, as Benjamin may, but that dialogue secured by ongoing response eventually loses hope for anything more than the same. Perhaps it can be stated thus: no different pasts then no new future; drawing *new* lines on the field are not only a possible saving grace, but also unavoidable.

The messianicity of each discursive event is marked by its own deconstruction, exposing the event as being both knowledge and non-knowledge and the unpredictable shifts between what these two categories represent. What we know with certainty may not be known tomorrow or as I change even within the same conversation. So Derrida appreciates Socrates' dialogue for its maieutic sense of something *to come,* rather than the performance of reciprocity as described by Habermas. Derrida writes something that must be understood with inflection: "To give back, to leave, or to give the floor to the other amounts to saying; you have (a) place, have (a) place, come. The duplicity of this self-exclusion, the simulacrum of this withdrawal, plays on the belonging to the proper place, as a political place and as a habitation. Only this belonging to place authorizes the truth of the logos, that is also its political effectivity, its pragmatic and praxical (*praxique*) efficiency, which Socrates regularly associates with the logos in this context."[18] While it is crucial to have a place, occupy the place for a time, because there is no language or dialogue without such occupation, which marks a possibility of an authorization of truth. However, this is not the truth of social norms or laws, already sovereign truth, but rather the truth of that which is yet to be known. Derrida will not allow meaning to be completely surrendered to performance; rather place and context provide a capacity for meaning and performance. Thus, he consciously straddles between the pledge of being and being's performance, in a way he calls messianic, or messianicity without messianism. Only thus can one avoid a finalized reduction of historical purpose, which is a closure of death as evil rather than death as irreducible possibility.

This all speaks to the everyday experience of language, as an act of memory, which is always rhetorical, a magic trick with words insofar as it presumes that the promise is performed. If the promise behind lan-

18. Derrida, *On the Name*, 108.

guage could be exposed by a performance, no words would be necessary, maybe no witness to the promise but only being fulfilled. In contrast, Derrida describes language as not only disseminating but *dissemination itself.*

> An immanent structure of promise or desire, an expectation without horizon of expectation, informs all speech. As soon as I speak, before even formulating a promise, an expectation, or a desire *as such*, and when I still do not know what will happen to me or what awaits me at the end of the sentence, neither *who* or *what* awaits whom or what, I am within this promise or this threat, which from then one gathers the language together, the promised or threatened language, promising all the way to the point of threatening and *vice versa*, thus gathered together in its very dissemination.[19]

The use of language is both identity and non-identity, humanizing and de-humanizing, it is attestation to either a promise or a threat to be decided, thus it is a horizon without horizon; a description of a future which is always yet to come. Language itself remains incomplete; any presence of language is gathered together by positing a future as either differing or deferred. The danger of language is that it is always forgetting that it is a preference based in decision (which is to say, in faith without determination). "Whether we like it or not, and whether we know it or not, when we ask others to take our word for it, we are already in the order of what is merely believable. It is always a matter of what is offered to faith and of appealing to faith, a matter of what is only believable and hence as unbelievable as miracle. Unbelievable because merely "credible." . . . Even in false testimony, this truth presupposes veracity—and not the reverse."[20] The origin of language is promise; otherwise there would be no speech necessary. Language, or any economy of meaning, is a placement of an exchange where faith is offered and appealed to, which in turn makes veracity possible. So language is always *of the other*; it is never mine and I am possessed by it; the reverse of being concerned with credibility before believability.

Response is an infinite responsibility to faith; an indeterminable faith because religion as such is a matter of reduction, of making credible that which is incredible, that which is beyond any economy of question-

19. Derrida, *Monolingualism of the Other or the Prosthesis of Origin*, 21–22.
20. Ibid., 20.

ing or listening. The question then is whether my aims are sufficiently, or proximately, open to the aims of the other? As Derrida asks, am I hospitable to the stranger regardless of what the stranger brings? It is this that distinguishes a mechanical response from one with an infinite sense of responsibility.

When modernity or society denies time's temporality, often by presencing the present and privileging the now, this sovereignty of time and space is forgetful of an infinite responsibility for the sake of a piety as the appearance of rightness, found within proper interaction. Modernity thus builds a machine of knowledge by which responsibilities may be maintained, an accountability mechanism. In so doing it forgets that responsibility is an event that is never assured in any time, nor in any response. Derrida writes, "In debates concerning responsibility one must always take into account this original and irreducible complexity of consciousness that links theoretical consciousness to 'practical' consciousness (ethical, legal, political) if only to avoid the arrogance of so many 'clean consciences.' We must continually remind ourselves that some part of irresponsibility insinuates itself wherever one demands responsibility without sufficiently conceptualizing and thematizing what 'responsibility' means; that is to say everywhere."[21] When mechanizations of knowledge set the conditions of the possibility of responsibility, then they also provide ready-made alibis, blinders to responsibility for those who can say, "It is the system." This is why Derrida writes that Socrates is what a responsible knowledge looks like, because he knows that knowledge always is marked by a not knowing. One is caught between responsibility and irresponsibility, and this is especially true for religion, which defines the conditions for responsibility according to revelation. "In its most abstract form, then, the aporia in which we are struggling would perhaps be the following: is revealability (*Offenbarkeit*) more originary than revelation (*Offenbarung*), and hence independent of all religion?"[22] This is the question of a post-religious prayer.

This question reminds one of Karl Barth's description of the *disturbance* of all human words by the eternal Word. Both men speak of a promise of meaning anterior to every word or communication; there is a "to come" in every act of language. For Derrida, the apocalyptic disturbance of each word is combined with an emancipatory appreciation for

21. Derrida, *The Gift of Death*, 26.
22. Derrida, "Faith and Knowledge," 16.

public reason's performance. So where Barth describes a *krisis* of reason that makes way for revelation, Derrida would still be suspicious to the extent it may alibi a privileged quietude. All language is a performance of the promise and, as such, it transcends the *krisis* of reason. It is the experience of an ongoing apocalypse. Not only can one speak out of brokenness, but it is brokenness which language represents as an originary brokenness.

> There is no language without the performative dimension of the promise, the moment I open my mouth I am in the dimension of the promise. Even if I say that "I don't believe in truth" or whatever, the minute I open my mouth there is a "believe me" at work. Even when I lie, and perhaps especially when I lie, there is a "believe me" at play. And this "I promise you that I am speaking the truth" is a messianic *apriori*, a promise which, even if it is not kept, even if one knows that it cannot be kept, takes place and qua promise is messianic.[23]

Not unlike Habermas, an emancipation is at hand by a performance of language; yet not an already present freedom but a freedom *yet to be*, witnessed as absent. Derrida often reminds his interpreters that deconstruction is not a renunciation of the critical idea and its emancipatory powers. But unlike Habermas, it is not conditioned by a successful interaction that institutes economies whereby there can be appropriate reciprocation. Nor is it finally a shared 3rd person set of facts that offers an emancipation from within the circumstances provided by well-intentioned interlocutors. In response, Derrida points to an infinite irreducibility of the promise that is always reduced in language. Interaction is the happy exchange of unequal partners, their intentions saved by the possibility to come. Thus Derrida can reply to Rorty that he is a pragmatist "all the way down" and also that he believes in "happiness."[24]

The promise allows attestation to community, but not community itself. When I say x, do I mean x? For Habermas the answer is a matter of differentiating perlocutionary and illocutionary goals. When there is doubt, then questions must be asked and conversation may ensue until all parties have arrived at a common understanding of x. This procedure of questioning can clarify what x is at the moment, and it may even institute some confidence in the person attesting to x if s/he has some history

23. Derrida, "Remarks on Deconstruction and Pragmatism," 82.
24. Ibid., 77–79.

of trustworthy attestation. Derrida reads every event of attestation to be different, a new danger and a new opportunity, and any institution of attestation is both a matter of knowledge and faith. The circumstances of the event are constantly changing, also each person may change even as they are engaged in the same conversation; this is so if they are listening. This is why Derrida will not permit deconstruction to be discussed as one method and prefers to speak of it in the plural. Deconstructions occur in all manners of understanding, and history itself is deconstruction. Any attestation or manifestation of that which language represents is never the same or reliable. Even when the same words are repeated, that which the words manifest or point toward has moved.

So Derrida, reads, listens, writes, and speaks about the movement of words, as specters, what words do when they move and are moved by an end of time. He describes an apocalyptic tone in philosophy of those who speak of the end as their ends, who desire to make their ends always apparent in order to achieve a new community, even with a certain piety of knowledge that claims to be different. The classics of the end, "the cannon of the modern apocalypse" includes Hegel, Marx, Nietzsche, Heidegger, Kojeve.[25] He explains that he grew up with "this bread of apocalypse in his mouth," a "daily bread," and yet everyday the realization of Stalinism and totalitarian terror. This is the period of historical entanglement in which he developed deconstruction, and also a sense of modern fatigue, a tiresomeness that is always "late to the end of history."

Nonetheless, what still calls him today from within modernity is the thinking of an event after the end of history. One is obliged to question whether what one calls history is really only a concept of history. "Here is perhaps one of the questions that should be asked of those who are not content just to arrive late to the apocalypse and to the last train to the end, if I can put it like that, without being out of breath, but who have the means to puff out their chests with the good conscience of capitalism, liberalism, and the virtues of parliamentary democracy—a term with which we designate not parliamentarism and political representation in general, but the present, which is to say, in fact, past forms of the electoral and parliamentary apparatus.[26] By questioning the ends of certain histories, intent not to arrive late to the apocalypse, there is a renewal of a sense of tradition within modernity. Could this be the

25. Derrida, *Spectres of Marx*, 15.
26. Ibid.

sustaining breath of traditions and languages, even when a traditional-ism forgets past forms of itself, remembering selectively; a representative democracy even when parliamentarism forgets past forms of itself? He describes "the presenting of the presence of the present." I am reminded here of something written by Karl Rahner, "Metaphysics, which is already a philosophy of religion, must acknowledge God as the one who is free and unknown; it must understand persons as beings who, in our innermost spirit, live in history; it must refer us to our history and bid us listen in it to an eventual revelation of this free unknown God."[27] Such is the phenomenological-metaphysical *quietism* of Derrida that will always refrain from privileging any form of listening, as well as forms of communication.

The important contribution made to prayer is that he describes the horizons of claims made in order to apply them for the sake of a future revelation of community not taken for granted. While Habermas argues that a universal community transcends from within an ongoing interaction between distinct horizons (a discourse that wants to differentiate identity and knowledge), Derrida reminds that such differentiation is never clear, nor completed, nor can it be presumed that discourse will always be appropriate.

When new ideas are called for, the inappropriate is also appropriate. "The question here is whether it is through the decision that one becomes a subject who decides something. At the risk of appearing provocative, I would say that once one poses the question in that form and one imagines that the who and the what of the subject can be determined in advance, then there is no decision. In other words, the decision, if there is such a thing, must neutralize if not render impossible in advance the who and the what."[28] This is how deconstruction becomes indispensible to a pragmatic approach to community. There is a continual interruption of every identity, every decision. "Every time I decide, if a decision is possible, I invent the who, and I decide who decides what; at that moment the question is not the who or the what but rather of the decision, if there is such a thing. I agree that identification is indispensable, but this is also a process of disidentification, because if the decision is identification then the decision also destroys itself."[29] Rather, for Derrida, this separation of

27. Rahner, *Hearer of the Word*, 8.
28. Derrida, "Remarks on Deconstruction and Pragmatism," 84.
29. Ibid.

the "who" and the "what" is for now untenable. Knowledge and identity cannot be indissociable from each other, from each end today.

All societies are marked by their particular intermingling of knowledge and identity, and so the question for Derrida becomes whether one recognizes how identity and knowledge are bound together in each determinate context. He therefore embarks upon a project of deconstructions of onto-theology, which is always a matter of reading between the shifting lines, so to speak. So he writes, "There is no maintaining and no depth to, this bottomless chess board on which Being is put into play."[30] This takes us to a place of prayer that is called disquietude, in that it interrupts any piety or confidence that prayer is adequate in itself. In other words, an approach to suffering must be apocalyptical suspension, speech from out of brokenness to something beyond.

Prayers of Disquietude

The concluding paragraph of one of Derrida's earliest publications alludes to a sense of the future. This is the "to come" which advances on the Origin, "a procession of a *Rückfrage*." He describes this procession as "a disquietude."

> The pure and interminable disquietude of thought striving to "reduce" Difference by going beyond factual infinity toward the infinity of its sense and value, i.e., while maintaining Difference— that disquietude would be transcendental. And Thought's pure certainty would be transcendental, since it can look forward to the already announced *Telos* only by advancing on (or being in advance of [*en avancant sur*]) the Origin that indefinitely reserves itself. Such a certainty never had to learn that Thought would always be to come.[31]

The reduction of reduction can mistake present certainty for presence of being; then value is mistaken for knowledge, which announces a certain end or *Telos*. However, if Difference is maintained and value is not reduced to the factual, then tradition (or the procession of a forwards and backwards questioning) has the possibility of providing unique decisions in touch with the secret of the future, the "to come." He calls this a "transcendental disquietude," but later changes this to "quasi-

30. Derrida, *Margins of Philosophy*, 22.
31. Derrida, *Edmund Husserl's "Origin of Geometry*," 153.

transcendental" to emphasize that he is describing general experience and not a category of Platonism. Everything else that Derrida writes is the description of how certainty must always learn that Thought is always *to come*; the present of time is misunderstood unless it remembers itself as a decision which entails some sacrifice, which can remain only in silence, unspeakable. Disquietude characterizes this remembering of self, which remains reserved and somewhat hidden, because it is always a remembering that can only arise from double reduction. Disquietude marks a sense of one's limits; a consciousness of an impurity or memory that disseminates through all thought and all being.

Although Derrida writes on a seemingly endless list of topics where this observation applies, this paper tries to describe phenomenological reductions and questions of being. When considered together then one begins to see what Derrida means by prayer insofar as "the question of the question," its indecision, is overlapped upon the reduction of reduction. Here prayer is disquieting to any universality, the recognition that no certainty and no selfhood sustains itself. Rather such principles are better conceived as generalities, or familial dwelling places where exchanges somewhat forget themselves and are perhaps less concerned with self-preservation. Thus, disquietude is an opening of metaphysics and questioning ontologies, an insufficiency of eGodicy. In short, it is a place of prayer.

Also, it can be said that a prayer of disquietude always prays with both hands. This is what Derrida says about his writing. He describes himself as a writer, one who prays and seeks to touch the hidden unknown One who has given the gift of language—so he gives thanks—but also one who must beg for mercy. However, he is also a writer who attempts to catch himself and protect against a fall. "Everything I do, especially when I am writing, resembles a game of blind man's bluff: the one who is writing, always by hand, even when using machines, holds out his hand like a blind man seeking to touch the one who he could thank for the gift of a language, for the very words in which he declares himself ready to give thanks. And to beg for mercy as well."[32] So one hand is stretched out, either catching oneself before a fall or begging for mercy, as a blind man not knowing which is appropriate. "While the other, more prudent, hand, another blind man's hand, tries to protect against the fall,

32. Derrida, *Monolingualism of the Other or the Prosthesis of Origin*, 64.

against a headlong premature fall, in a word, against haste."[33] So even as he describes the act of writing in disquietude, with both hands on the computer, he is blind, "digitizing like a madman." While one hand gives thanks to whoever has given the language, and also begs for mercy (an equivocating hand which simultaneously says "*merci*" and begs "mercy"), his other hand always reaches out to catch himself but is always too late. This is what a Derridian opening of prayer will be like. A prayer out of brokenness, caught between both a will to go forward and an inseparable complete anxiety.

This is contrasted to sighted memory, remembrance as a cognitive discourse that always becomes the plaintiff when he writes history, even in the course of fair play. So Derrida advocates blindness insofar as no anticipation is sufficient in itself. When asked to be a guest curator at the Louvre, he chose blindness as a theme for arranging the art. Does the unconscious call one to a pure anticipation, to expect the unexpected stranger? Derrida cannot answer this definitively; if he could then there is no need to write for him, which is always both a divine discourse (thanksgiving/mercy is combined in the French, *merci*) but one that is aporetic, which calls for a faith that he does not have. Since he knows his vulnerabilities, he protects himself as well.

If one compares Derrida's description of his writing to Habermas's description of Rousseau's letter-prayer, which is vulnerable to a universal audience and thus an example of prayer, then some immediate differences become clear. Derrida's writing/prayer is always impure, tainted with an immediate need to protect himself from falling, even while giving thanks, as he says both guest and hostage to language. This performance of faith is aporetic, a prayer is undecidable in itself; it is always also a fake and a way to hedge one's bet. Prayer, writing, or any participation is language is both faith and non-faith, regardless of vulnerabilities to criticism. In fact, the more vulnerable then the more likely one is to be less faithful, more protecting of self; this is in contrast to the axiom, more vulnerable, more purity.

In contrast to the quietism of a Barthian prayer or the piety of a Habermasian one disquietude informs prayer of its own impurity and its reliance upon an already announced *Telos*. Prayers of disquietude may then begin by opening confession to confession, that the thought of the other is best unthought, decided to be undecidable as negative theology

---

33. Ibid., 64.

is aware. Then, the question of responsibility in prayer—the question "To whom am I responsible?"—central to any inter-subjectivity or discourse, is asked first for the sake of others or for the sake of the Other, rather than for the sake of a determinate identity based in knowledge.

The *Telos* or a universalizable culture of faith, pure anticipation, is available by advancing on its Origin, which is utterly broken in history as an ongoing apocalypse but which can thus have a sense of the present as alienated from its past by crisscross questioning or *Rückfrage*. In this prayer one is caught between one's response to others and to the Other; between ethics and religion; between duty and sacrifice to the paradox of faith. As Derrida concludes from reading Kierkegaard's *Fear and Trembling*—which "declines the autobiography which is always auto-justification, *eGodicy*"—there is then a justified hiddeness if response is to be more than a response, more than an action out of a duty to respond. This is true for one's relation to G*d as it is for one's relation to others, especially one's loved ones. "If I obey in my duty towards God (which is my absolute duty) *only in terms of duty*, I am not fulfilling my relation to God. In order to fulfill my relation to God I my must not act *out of duty*, by means of that form of generality that can always be mediated and communicated and that is called duty. The absolute duty that binds me to God himself, in faith, must function beyond and against any duty I have."[34]

This is a dimension of sacrifice that is monstrous and banal, but also contains the possibility of an inspiration beyond that of tragic figures. In this same essay, Derrida goes on to describe how one might speak without speaking, and what it means when one who says nothing except what is general or indeterminable, "a sacrificial passion that will lead him to death, by a society that doesn't even know why it acts the way it does."[35]

Caught between the double bind of history, prayer can be nothing else but impurity if it wishes to be a place of exchange, if it seeks responsibility rather than assurance or clean conscience, if disquietude is not reduced to an economy or ordering of itself. Prayer is an opening of discourse that cannot justify itself, either in religious silence or in ethical inter-action. Prayer then is a questioning, a questioning of the absent, the unknowable. Prayers of disquietude will not give up on the

---

34. Derrida, *The Gift of Death*, 63.
35. Ibid., 75.

possibility of a redemption of past injustices, nor will it read history as a progression or triumphal spirit.

The person of prayer is someone who is not concerned with an objective Good, a measurable result, but rather with "a gift of infinite love, a goodness that is forgetful of itself."[36] Derrida writes, "I never have been and never will be up to the level of this infinite goodness nor up to the immensity of the gift, the frameless immensity that must in general define (*in*-define) a gift as such."[37] One is never responsible enough, he writes, because there are two contradictory movements of responsibility: while one must respond as oneself, accountable for what one says and does, also one must "forget or efface the origin of what one gives." While one may be accountable to respond, and to what one says oneself, this same accountability is obtrusive, and contrary an effacement of oneself as an origin of "being good through goodness." Thus responsibility is a new mythology insofar as accountability and radical integrity is contrary to self-effacement, thus an orgiastic freedom of self-interest is not done away but is merely watched over in responsible freedom. "Although it is incorporated, disciplined, subjugated, and enslaved, the orgiastic is not annihilated. It continues to motivate subterraneously a mythology of responsible freedom that is at the same time a politics, indeed the still partly intact foundation of politics in the West."[38] This same sense of responsibility (which begins with Christianity and continues into modernity—a mondialatinization or globalization) is the topic of disquietude.

The thinking of responsibility without disquietude is like a wake without mourning, it is an ordinary vigil. A human responsibility that forgets radical evil, incorporates it subterraneously even as it believes freedom triumphs over it. "The coming of the other can only emerge as a singular event when no anticipation sees it coming, when the other and death—and radical evil—can come as a surprise at any moment. Possibilities that both open and can always interrupt history, or at least the ordinary course of history."[39] Again, by "ordinary," the allusion is to any determinate or calculable sense of being that amounts to a form of eschatology, so many apocalypses, or final closures of metaphysics. An ordinary is the ordinal, the countable, an accountability that counts death

36. Ibid., 51.
37. Ibid.
38. Ibid., 19.
39. Derrida, "Faith and Knowledge," 17.

as the end has no sense of the infinite. Such accountability becomes sovereign over death, a sovereign sense of justice which has lost touch with the indeterminable, surprising aspects of death and thus of life.

Derrida recognizes the same stigma on the present as does Habermas, but instead listens for opportunities to address it. Even though the living will continue to benefit from the murderous past, there are two brief sentences that say a lot about how pervasive a disquieting prayer is, already accentuating the responsibility to the promise that comes in advance. I might call it a prevenient grace, that life continues even though it should not. "This justice inscribes itself in advance in the promise, in the act of faith or in the appeal to faith that inhabits every act of language and every address of the other. The universalizable culture of this faith, and not of another or before all others, alone permits a 'rational' and universal discourse on the subject of religion."[40] While the first sentence points to a sense of justice that must also be original as an act of faith prior to factuality, no special knowledge can evoke it as if by magical incantation or abracadabra. This is contrary to Habermas's anticipatory act of successful communication.

Derrida's word participates in that which inhabits every act of language that then by its performance covers over the mystical by an affirmation of its own practice. Revelation and revealability are inverted here, but once the memory of the secret is lost, then religion can only start over spontaneously, "with the automaticity of a machine."[41] Then in the second section he writes of a universalizable sense of faith that "permits a 'rational' and universal discourse on the subject of religion." By ingesting the mystical, a universal discourse can be restored. This ingestion is the role of a language that does not already prescribe the access to Being. Early in his work, Derrida seeks to describe this role of language which phenomenology may access by the reduction of temporalization within intersubjectivity. "Here delay is the philosophical absolute, because the beginning of methodic reflection can only consist in the consciousness of the implication of another previous, possible, and absolute origin in general . . . Now a primordial consciousness of delay can only be a pure form of anticipation. At the same time, pure consciousness of delay can

40. Ibid., 18.
41. Ibid., 19.

be pure and legitimate, and therefore a priori, presumption, without which (once again) discourse and history would be possible."[42]

This "delay" would mark any universality that is nonetheless necessary to discourse and which retain critical perspective. What must be restored, for Derrida, is an awareness that it is not possible to "live enclosed in innocent undividednes (*indivision*) of the primordial Absolute, because the Absolute is present only in being deferred-delayed (*different*) without respite, this impotence and this impossibility are given in a primordial and pure consciousness of Difference."[43]

Isn't this the awareness presented in the first prayer? What are previously words of magical incantation, then become words of prayer once one is aware of the impossibility of innocent undividedness, or what can be called "utter brokenness." Putting words in Derrida's mouth here, prayer is possible once it is understood that existence is dividedness, either from an Absolute or that which is beyond this. In Derrida's terms, decision always divides but it also establishes a sense of memory and informs it of today's meaning, even if deferred or delayed.

My next question is whether such prayer is discovered, or maybe it discovers me in the "itterbility of the mark beyond human speech acts?"[44] The disquietude of prayer is precisely the unanswerability of this question, because if prayer entails an awareness of absence or deferment, this originary brokenness is immediately covered over by religion. A pure reflexivity of the religious mark establishes or institutes a presence that is utterly mechanical in its reflexivity and contains no salvational content. In this case, institutional religion instructs that if one prays thusly, to *this G*d*, and lives accountable to *this prayer* then integrity is regained. Religion provides an immunity of the soul as a mechanism of indemnification, it promises to bring back together what is broken or even justifies apocalypse, irreparably torn apart and broken.[45] A happy ending is already provided by identification of that which is holy, sacred, *heilig*.

42. Derrida, *Edmund Husserl's "Origin of Geometry,"* 152–53.

43. Ibid., 153.

44. Derrida, *Limited Inc.*, 134.

45. "*Indemnis*: that which has not suffered damage or prejudice, *damnum*; this latter word will have given in French '*dam*' (*au grand dam*: to the detriment or displeasure of . . .) and comes from *dap-no-m*, tied to daps, *dapis*, that is, to the sacrifice offered to the gods as ritual compensation. In this latter case, one could speak of *indemnification* and we will use this word here and there to designate both the process of compensation and the restitution, sometime sacrificial, that reconstitutes purity intact, renders integrity

Like Heideggerian ontology, words have the capacity to too quickly decide upon a unity of questioning and answering; to too quickly relate discourse and descriptions of reality inadequately suspended. In contrast Derrida refers to the disjointure (*Un-Fuge*) of time, as when Hamlet comments, "the time is out of joint." Derrida refuses to bypass or cover over this disjointure by a perspective of immune integrity or jointure (*Versammelung, Fug*). He thinks about religion as a combination of the assessments of Husserl and Heidegger, and the need to simultaneously suspend suspension by faith and crisscross knowledge, to question and listen in anticipation without a pre-determined end. "First error to avoid . . . If there is a question of religion, it ought no longer be a 'question-of-religion.' Nor simply a response to this question. We shall see *why* and *wherein* the question of religion is first of all the question of the question"[46] (italics mine).

Derrida seizes upon Heidegger's indecision and Husserl's crisscrossing double reduction so to understand why and wherein religion is first of all the question of the question. It is first of all a prayer to something beyond brokenness that remains nameless and hidden for now. It strikes me that this seizure—a symptomatic tremor of the mysterious, as he describes it—is a prayer that is not only a performance; a true communication not only a hollow publicity of prayer, which piety can contribute. It is a confrontation of apocalypse, a public exchange of eschatological ends, like an open letter. So before considering the inappropriate ends of others and their appropriations of an Other, one is responsible to consider ones own ends in light of any appropriated justification. Derrida poses the question in this long sentence: "Beyond right, and still more beyond juridicism, beyond morality and still more beyond moralism, does not justice as relation to the other suppose on the contrary the irreducible excess of disjointure or an anachrony, some *Un-Fuge*, some 'out of joint' dislocation in Being and in time itself, a disjointure that, in always risking the evil, expropriation, and injustice (*adikia*) against which there is no calculable insurance, would alone be able to do justice or to render

---

safe and sound, restores cleanliness <*propreté*> and property unimpaired. This is indeed what the word unscathed <*indemne*> says: the pure, non-contaminated, untouched, the sacred and holy before all profanation, all wound, all offense, all lesion. It has often been used to translate *heilig* (sacred, safe, sound, intact) in Heidegger." Derrida says that he associates "unscathed, indemnity, indeminification" with "immune, immunity, immunization, and above all auto-immunity." Jacques Derrida, "Faith and Knowledge," 69–70.

46. Ibid., 59.

justice to the other as other?"[47] It is when prayer is listening to the rules of being rather than questioning them there is slavery, but to question unceasingly is an enthronement of self.

If prayer neglects this aporia between quietistic slavery and pious questioning, then prayer is simply a rehearsal for an already decided end to history that has presumed to calculate the end already. Is it not the case that an indecision of being in prayer, a disquietude, is necessary if both parties are respected in the prayer—the alterity of the broken and the Other?

47. Ibid., 27.

6

Prayer as Courage

BEFORE WE ASSESS WHAT A FRAMEWORK FOR THE study of prayer might look like, let us summarize some of the issues. We have been asking how prayer can engage, and be engaged, as a critical discourse. Prayer, as the beginning and renewal of all religious life, presents a problem to anyone attempting to understand it. These issues are inseparable to the problem of its object—to *what* or *whom* is prayer directed? Even a comparative study of prayer is hard pressed to move beyond a mere reportage of prayer to some critical reflection upon how it works within modern public debates that already tend to take a political or rhetorical direction.

Especially relevant to our conversation about the study of prayer is a consideration of apocalyptic thought—its history, its ability to focus on suffering and injustice, and how it entered the twentieth century as a serious criticism of the limits of modernity and a continuing intellectual contributor to political theory. As the use of language within social structure limits communication, problems are presented to anyone reflecting critically on the use of apocalyptical prayers designed to engage suffering in a public way. My approach to the study of prayer as memory that some may see as a minimalist theology or even a non-religious one, addresses the issues and options that relates to an understanding of prayer and discourse.

All speech, as an act from within a collective memory, is challenged in two ways. As an outcome of the interplay between society and the individual, language is used to display a moral consciousness that is able to discern the distinctions between values, norms, and facts. Human beings are creatures of narrative, natural storytellers who weave together these elements. The first step toward knowledge is taken by conscientiously distinguishing when to express a personal feeling and when to assert a factual claim that all others can verify. Our finitude and consequent anxiety are constant tests of the moral courage necessary for the pursuit of truth. Prayer, as a participant in this communal project, is able to reflect on the universal applicability of norms from the perspective of both a moral imagination and the priority of the communicative freedom of all. Prayer's potential for critical insight is short-circuited by private mystifications that place the salvation of the individual above the community.

One finds that moral courage to pray must then also be tied to intellectual honesty. The person in prayer must be honest enough to recognize their own blindness with respect to the object of their prayer. Like Derrida's blind man's bluff, prayer needs to be offered with two hands, recognizing the depth of the moral consciousness that is called for as an individual of faith within community. It is in the silence of prayer that one is acquainted with the bottomless nature of being and to learn that listening is not easily learned.

Beyond Piety

As I have described a possible place for prayer within communicative action theory and a possible listening as an act of ongoing deconstruction, this next chapter reflects upon the question of memory. If there is no past perfection of language or moral discourse, nor any perfection of discursive performance that exemplifies the social project of rationalization, then what is one to say of prayer as an act of language? Considering how fallible our practice always is and how undecidable our questions about the social fluidity appropriate to discourse, can truth be pragmatically addressed from within intersubjective relations of communication. Is prayer engaged in the ongoing project of an emancipation?

This is difficult to address partly because each party desires to criticize the relative integrity between what is said and what is done, even if within the appropriate contexts. It is complicated by freedom; that it is always possible to go in opposite directions over memory and its interpretation of truth.

This brings up the incompatibility of approaches to the life-world. A reconstructed inter-subjectivity means a position is already taken, even codified, upon the mind's ability to transcend its life-world or not. This explains how it is effective to work within the same boundaries of time and space, for the sake of coming to mutual agreements apart from traditionally assumed life-worlds. Human knowledge is always limited knowledge to the extent it is and is not able to sense its origin and end. Therefore, even an inter-subjective knowledge based in the project of freedom fails to achieve the fulfillment of its promise and always remains tied to past violence.

Even philosophy that occupies the same space (relations of language in an intersubjective life-world) is capable of pointing in different directions. While Habermas describes the life-world as "uncriticizable" by definition; always at our backs so that when one turns then it becomes criticizable but no longer functions as a life-world. Derrida finds true philosophy always searching for an appropriate "criteriology" that may pass between the inner and external spaces of any life-world without doing further damage. Both Habermas and Derrida attempt to negotiate this passage that is usually colonized by the metaphysical commitments of faith, by their analysis of discourse or what passes for discourse.

Habermas criticizes both a philosophical faith in subjectivity and a negative theology designed around a need for communicative freedom. His option describes and analyzes successful acts of communication that contain a stubborn transcendence of reason; able to unify a fallible but participatory discourse. He argues for this unity of reason by a narration of the unfolding of modernity, which increasingly questions all perspectives and is thus able to contribute to the construction of a universal community based in emancipatory discourse. Within this unfinished project of the enlightenment Habermas calls for religion to be a contributor to the extent it is vulnerable to questioning and remains reflexive and involved in the rationalization of society within time.

Habermas contends that the "ideal speech community" is implicit within every act of successful communication because it performs as a mutual understanding. His pragmatic approach recommends the construction of social identities able to critique oneself with regard to the performative dimension of language and thus understand how its consistency instructs cooperative action. Because there is no exemplary model of this, Habermas is sometimes called utopian in the sense of Hegel's description of the community of spirit in the last pages of *The Philosophy of Religion*, where the subject is both an immediacy of self and a consciousness of universal idea.[1] However for Habermas, at no

---

1. Hegel writes, "The community begins with the fact that the truth is at hand; it is known, extant truth . . . the relationship of the subject to this truth, the fact that the subject, to the extent that it is related to this truth, arrives precisely at this conscious unity,

time are particular ideas of G*d, cosmic soul, or divine spirit, which are outside the constraints of time and space and therefore insufficiently public, allowed to stand without some validation from within. This means a post-metaphysical contribution by social theory and theology to understanding interaction or method. Therefore I have characterized Habermas' approach as a strict *piety* of language, where the action and consequences are determinative of validity claims.

Jacques Derrida's pragmatism runs in a different direction. He is like Habermas insofar as he also calls for pragmatic validation of enlightenment project, in the sense of living out an enlightened life, and he also is Hegelian in sense of stressing the inter-connections of community and individual life, which are in dynamic flux. For these reasons Richard Rorty once accused Derrida of "believing in happiness" and being a pragmatist at heart. Interestingly, Derrida's reply was not a denial but rather remembering that from the beginning "the question concerning the trace was linked with a certain notion of labor, of doing, and what I called then *programmatology* tried to link grammatology to pragmatism."[2] For this reason his reflections within social contexts open and expose mimetic aporias as a way to unleash an emancipatory potential as yet unfulfilled.[3] He finds within generalized concepts a placement of exchange that serves to designate an overlap of faith and knowledge, which is necessary for all regional ontologies or traditions of knowledge. Thus, metaphysical assertions are not something one may move beyond but need be exposed and opened to criticism from within. Knowledge, that reduces religion to pious action in order to make it criticizable, not only limits everyday practices of imagination but also loses a sense of inspiration necessary to the project of enlightenment, which then can only deny and delay, defer and differ.[4] Derrida characterizes language always

---

deems itself worthy of this known unity, brings this unity forth in itself, and is fulfilled by divine Spirit." Hegel, *Lectures on the Philosophy of Religion*, 473.

2. Derrida, "Remarks on Deconstruction and Pragmatism," 78.

3. "For me, the texts that are apparently more literary, and more tied to the phenomena of natural language, like *Glas* or *La Carte Postale*, are not evidence of a retreat towards the private, they are performative problematizations of the public/private distinction. There are a number of examples: in its way, the question of the family in Hegel discussed in *Glas*, of the relation of the family to civil society and state, can be seen as a performative elaboration of the private on the theoretical, philosophical and political plane; it is not a retreat to private life." Derrida, "Remarks on Deconstruction and Pragmatism," 79.

4. Derrida, *On Cosmopolitanism and Forgiveness*.

within a silence; remembering that language is a *disquietude*, character-ized by an absence of origin and therefore an undecidable future.

For these reasons, I have characterized Habermas and Derrida in terms of their respective approaches to language as *pietist* and *quiet-ist*, both of which have serious ethical intent. Both thinkers approach time as a limiting or criterion of critical perspective, allowing either a transcendence from within or a trace of *différance*. But plainly these two thinkers approach time and intersubjectivity from opposite sides of the life-world. However, I argued in chapter 5 that this does not mean they are completely incompatible even if they should remain incommensu-rable. For now I can say that a person of prayer who speaks with some sense of something beyond apocalypse but is unwilling to make this a premise in an argument, finds Habermas most helpful when thinking about practices within structures and necessities of a public society. A person of prayer who does not want to dismiss or neglect modern forms of suffering (often the silenced) or an ongoing apocalypse, will find Derrida helpful when questioning the functions of concepts and press-ing the limits of any perspective from within traditions. I propose that both are important if prayer is to remain a relevant and potent, rather than a banal, ritual. Neither of them banish G*d from consideration and both describe how language remains indebted in significant ways to a tradition of monotheism. In both, G*d remains an open question that is not explicitly addressed. However, the point of prayer is to address G*d in conversation—to question and be questioned explicitly.

Johann Baptist Metz emphasizes the importance of addressing G*d as a practical reflection or praxis. He writes, "In itself, the Christian idea of God is a practical idea."[5] So the concept of G*d, speaking of G*d, is a question of a fundamental theology, that is prior to church or dogmatic statements about G*d. He questions the possibility of a more generic ap-proach to G*d but not one of transcendental reduction of the concept of G*d. He notices that the concept is within everyday thought, not the domain of academics or theologians, regardless of which organized reli-gion one might espouse.

Metz goes on to state that, "God cannot be thought of at all unless this idea irritates and encroaches on the immediate interests of the per-son who is trying to think of it [*der ihn zu denken sucht*]."[6] For Metz, G*d

---

5. "*Der christlich Gottesgedanke ist aus sich selbst ein praktischer Gedanke.*" Metz, *Faith in History and Society*, 51.

6. Ibid.

is a practical check against pursuit of self-interests, and if not then it does not even approach the impossible conception of G*d—what is called God with certainty is an imposter. Metz describes prayer as a reflection upon both the *interests* and the *impossibilities* of knowing G*d. The relevance of Metz is that he brings together both elements—Habermasian piety and Derridean quietude—into the practice of prayer. Here, modern reason and memory are not separable but distinct aspects of a prayerful narrative. As he states, it is for the sake of practice that the "concept of God is basically narrative and memorative."[7]

It is a considerable contention of this book that within this practical vein of thought that sets about the task of an ordering of interests, prayer may serve to correct the myopia of current discourse while still intensifying the valid contributions of both communicative-action and disquietude. This cannot be done with a transcendental foundation which posits an uncriticizable univocity from within personhood. Rather, as I have used the term, an *apocalyptical* discourse admits various metaphysical ends to be considered in relation to an ongoing apocalypse or suffering. Such reasoning reserves some judgment upon encapsulated meanings like personhood, society, justice, or history. An apocalyptical discourse will suspend and question motivations and consequences of these frames of meaning, in solidarity with suffering rather than explaining or abstracting it. This is the continuing practical test for any prayer striving after both moral courage and intellectual honesty.

Memory and Suffering

The pervasive question throughout our discussion about prayer has been its ability to reflect on suffering without explaining it away. Metz is especially interesting for our inquiry of prayer because he describes memory engaged in a questioning of suffering as, *leidensfrage*. Memory is questioned fundamentally as "a category of the salvation of identity" and also "a category of resistance to the passage of time (interpreted as evolution) and, in this sense, as the *organon* of an apocalyptical consciousness."[8] These two functions orient the present between past and future; one is oriented around questions of a lost mutual integrity and another around responsibility. This characterizes an apocalyptical consciousness because where both are understood then one has a sense of bounded time that

7. Ibid.
8. Ibid., 184–85.

has an eventual end. Thus as Metz states many times, the myth of modernity is most destructive as an evolutionary or unlimited sense of time; either homogenous or empty of meaning.

The point is made that both functions inherent to an apocalyptical consciousness are important for an accountability to questions of suffering or theodicy.[9] it is an intersection between deconstructive or re-constructive pragmatics. This is not incidental that this location of remembrance, what Metz calls *anamnesis,* is also important to a sense of prayer. This raises questions for prayer that either places a transcendentalized sense of suffering within G*d or, if history is leveled, into a metanarrative of origins. Metz has explicitly criticized theologians, including his mentor and friend Karl Rahner, for depending upon argumentation and transcendental perspectives upon human possibilities for responsible relations. By developing a theory of interruption, apocalyptic reflection is stabilized enough to reflect within time and still listen to the radical questions.

For reasons relating to this intersection of past promise and future expectation, I contend that recent interpretation of Metz, which add too much to his more general meaning of *anamnesis,* intended to operate within but also broaden modernity by reconnecting procedures of decision with a deeper sense of responsibility found in prayer rather than a phenomenology of a transcendental selfhood.

It is too easy to avoid the point of interruption as it relates hermeneutics to history and spirituality. In his book *Interruptions,* Ashley outlines the development of Metz's theory from an earlier to a later period. Ashley's central thesis is that the *continuities* in Metz shed light on the *discontinuities* of his early and later development. I suggest that the discontinuity sheds more light on the continuities of his development. The continuities Ashley chooses within Metz include; 1) Karl Rahner's argumentative strategies; 2) Enlightenment subjectivity guided by the ideal of *Mundigkeit* that emerges out of Christianity, not in spite of it; and 3) Metz' own interest in spirituality. Ashley argues that the perspective of

9. One should be reminded of Walter Benjamin's call for a new "messianic" view of history which has two primary elements. The present may not be indifferent to its past, which is not closed. The future is open to the extent one commits to fulfilling the promise of the past. Habermas comments that this as reminiscent of Jewish and Protestant mysticism where humanity is made somewhat responsible for the fate of G*d, when G*d "relinquished his omnipotence in favor of human freedom." Habermas, *Philosophical Discourse of Modernity,* 14–15.

the above *transcendental* theme sheds light on the political theology of Metz. He describes then a shift away from the political theology of the 1960s. This shift is typified and developed as Metz's performance of the *Seinsfrage* (question of being and meaning) morphs into the *Leidensfrage* (questioning of suffering). Ashley argues that Metz' reflections on political reality and human suffering are derived from a deeper transcendental commitment, at least insofar "that the shifts he made derived from these deeper commitments."[10]

I believe that the relation of suffering to any conception of continuity, which Ashley underlines for us, is dubious and warrants further consideration. So for example, Ashley remarks; "that Metz's later work is still a fundamental theology in the form of a theological anthropology, and that the three categories of memory, solidarity, and narrative are an alternative set of *existentialia*, is presented in my book, *Interruptions*."[11] Here, much hangs on the word, *existentialia*, and its precise meaning may be unclear here. While Ashley notes that the parting methodological difference between Metz and Rahner was that Rahnerian spirituality proved insufficient for answering questions of human suffering.[12] The two theologians operate from different stages of a greater whole, says Ashley. "Finally, then, both had a deeply rooted intuition that their distinctive mystical-political positions, just like the weeks of the *Spiritual Exercises*, are part of a greater whole, that both are initiations into the greater breadth and length and height and depth of the love of Christ which surpasses all knowledge (including that of theological systems!)"[13]

I certainly agree that spirituality and knowledge are not reducible to one another, but I must respectfully question the claim that Metz represents a mere addition of Rahner rather than a break. Ashley's point about spirituality (that if one's spirituality changes so too do political concerns) is indicative of his own interest in a phenomenology that potentially may pre-decide issues of political justice. He offers Metz as a case study of the relation of mysticism and politics and is, to his credit, cognizant of his own phenomenological framing of Metz.[14]

10. Ibid., vii.

11. Metz, *A Passion for God*, 176.

12. Ashley, *Interruptions*, viii.

13. Ibid., 191.

14. Ashley ends his introduction to *Interruptions* by admitting, "For it may very well be objected that I have not so much explained Metz's development, including its divergence from Rahner's, as I have displaced it to the realm of spirituality and the history of

However, if one is to understand Metz as Metz then this phenomenological framing of spirituality seems less than legitimate when one
considers Metz's position that anti-semitism is not just identified by
blatant assaults but also with silence, both of which characterize a modern gnosticism found in theology.[15] I am convinced that the *existentialia*
which Ashley identifies amount to a step in the direction of Rahner and
thus toward a particular brand of hope found only in silent listening in a
way that is not true to the concerns of *non-identity*. Metz explicitly states
that this differentiates his thought from Rahner and transcendental
method, or as I have called it *quietism*. If so, then the phenomenological reduction of a relation between mysticism and politics seems to me
unfair to both Metz and Rahner; as each man stands on either side of
an unfathomable brokenness, Ashley and each reader of Metz will be
tempted to forget what is called interruption. The question stands, if
Ashley envisages an *ordo salutis* or a "genuine understanding" of suffering which corresponds to the silence or hiddeness of G*d, would this not
re-scholasticize or explain suffering in a way that is still guilty of "gnosticism"? Isn't this like the teachings that blinded Metz from desiring to
make an earlier visit to Flossenbürg?

It is sufficient to suggest for now, that the phenomenological performances may always continue to indicate a hidden and totalizing discourse, which uncovers some aspects of suffering while covering over
others. My distinction between apocalypse and apocalypticism, as an
apocalyptical prayer that remains an ongoing and daily event, is intended to help prevent this type of covering. Like the manna from G*d in the
wilderness it cannot be stored or systematized to guard against danger.
The point is that prayer is dangerous.

Our attention is called to the theological concept of an *ordo salutis*
and its impact on relations based in communication. Succinctly, if an
assumption of an ultimate "proper order" for "genuine understanding" is added to history or even the interruption of history, then Metz'
anamnesis, which he intends as an *opening* of modernity, is filled-in or

spirituality." Ibid., xii–xiii.

15. Metz tells an interviewer, "Antisemitism does not exist only as a crude racism;
in theology it hardly appears in that guise anymore. However, it is to be found in a
more refined, genteel form, that is, psychologically or metaphysically. Under this guise it
became the Tempter of Christian theology from its very beginnings. What I am primarily thinking of are gnostic motifs and notions." Schuster and Boscher-Kimmig, *Hope
Against Hope*, 16. Also see Stephen Haynes, *Reluctant Witnesses*.

covered-up. The human capacity to face our guilt in prayer is once again neglected. Rather than an orderly path to salvation, this road is always disorderly with surprising bumps and shifting accounts, but the messiness and diversity of views also feed a culture of memory; a cultivation of memory.

Questioning G*d

Questioning our concept of G*d within a transcendental frame is talking about talking with G*d. While prayer is a fragile discourse philosophically, it is the most stubborn discourse of everyday life. The language of prayer is the most elementary form of spiritual sustenance to people who pray and yet a most fleeting of commodities in a modern society, which wants everything measurable or quantified. This is the practical wisdom that comes from doing; a praxis fed by prayer where anything can be said to G*d. Metz tells an interviewer, "Ultimately one can say anything to God, even that one cannot believe in God, if only one tries to say it to God. In that sense prayer contains a great deal of wisdom concerning what is said: when it comes to G*d there is always something still open, and even in theology we must have unconditional respect for that."[16]

Prayer is spoken in confidence but also acceptance, confidence in reason that one will be understood, yet an acceptance that the outcome remains unknown. When seeking to understand and be understood without determination of the outcome that prayer is language of solidarity, or perhaps a tarrying, laboring by remaining within this double polarity, neither defeatist nor triumphal, neither masochistic nor magical; in short, responsible to question and even investigate G*d.

Metz uses the word *Leidenfrage* to describe prayer that questions G*d about suffering while accepting no final consolation, neither from a religious tradition nor a commitment to critical reasoning. This refuses the usual role prescribed to religion within modernity, that Metz believes makes excuses for G*d or explains away suffering, a sidestepping of theodicy as an apocalyptical questioning of G*d. He calls for a renewal of an apocalyptical and non-contemporary theme inherited from the biblical traditions. Succinctly, the theme that time has an abrupt and unpredictable end is unavoidable. Modernity is typified by the hermeneutic strat-

16. Schuster and Boscher-Kimmig, *Hope against Hope*, 43.

egy whereby apocalypticism and theodicy are relegated to an ancient past or mythical image of the world, but the opposite is true for Metz. This is in contrast to apocalypticism, which does not take theodicy as seriously. It mixes an imminent expectation of the kingdom of God, *parousia*, within a perception and definition of the world. Such religious believers are more willing to force a worldview on others that is far from being reduced to mythical relics. "They are not simply at the disposal of our discourse about the God of the Bible, provided we have not long ago transformed God into a nameless Platonic idea and refashioned Christianity into Platonism or more clearly into a Plotinism of the modern age, all in order to shield it from the abysses of the human history of suffering and to spare theology the downright apocalyptic uneasiness of questioning God."[17]

The point is that the question of suffering is transformed in the apocalyptical context. Rather than trying to feed reason to some immediate ends, instead all ends are suspended by the question of G*d's response. The desire for an ongoing discursive consideration of all intersubjective claims to normativity is not necessarily contradicted, but rather G*d is called to make a response in the same way any participant in discourse may be called upon. A description from within prayer is, in a sense, post-metaphysical and conducive to communicative freedom and including G*d in that freedom. This is what Metz calls *suffering unto G*d* that includes the landscape of cries throughout all history, spoken to G*d and awaiting response.[18] This praxis of prayer is described as "a poverty of spirit" in simple solidarity with a suffering humanity; G*d is not a choice but a partner with those who resist. At the center of this "poverty of spirit" is capacity of memory and narrative to resist. As an illustration of what he means, Metz mentions the example of the Ray Bradbury novel, *Fahrenheit 451*, "about men and women who, after the brutal destruction of all books and libraries, have learned to store by heart, as a wisdom that resisted oppression and manipulation."[19]

17. Metz, *A Passion for God*, 57–58.

18. The German is *leiden an Gott* which translated literally mean "suffering from G*d" which is not entirely inaccurate since G*d is necessary for this suffering to be felt. G*d becomes a nuisance where suffering is considered. "With God, risk and danger enter into, and return to religion." Metz, "Suffering unto God," 613. This is what Metz adds to the Habermasian argument for reason, given to the cynic in *Moral Consciousness and Communicative Action*, except it is not reason that compels one to speak but suffering.

19. Schuster and Boscher-Kimmig, *Hope against Hope*, 32.

Prayer that questions G*d is language as partnership with history, not only as characters within it but as authors of it. Metz describes prayer as a textuality or participation within a historical solidarity. "What do we know about the history of humanity? . . . The history of humanity seen as popular history is basically the history of religion, and religious history in the final analysis is the history of prayer. And this is not limited to the history of Christian Europe . . . Through prayer we become part of a great historical solidarity."[20]

Like recent communitarian theology, Metz links narrative and religious practice. But very importantly, unlike communitarians, he does not identify a true or authentic practice of prayer by placing it within a certain tradition or liturgical approach. He describes prayer that is both personal and communal; it is language of identity and justice simultaneously. This recognizes prayer as a healing of language itself, or as the possibility of political reconciliation in the deepest sense, in recognition that those who speak are the consequence of an ongoing violence. Without prayer there is no real hope for a healing of language, prayer may provide a vision for an impossible communication beyond self-interest; "a language of prayer which has authentically taken up into itself society's conflicts and sufferings: this language brings out clearly how much humanity would lose of its potential for expressing crises of and suffering in language, were the centuries old language of prayers to disappear from its midst."[21] This function of prayer may be seen as its potential for healing language itself but especially its potential as a broadening of political decisions and responsibility as often done in the universal history of mysticism.

Prayer is often helpful in the construction of more responsible structures of reasoning in the recognition of something beyond the brokenness of the present. Prayer is able to give birth to a non-privileging narrative when there is no suffering before G*d that cannot be articulated and no short cut to happiness. "Does this mean to sense God's absence? Absolutely! That sense of absence plays between mourning and hope . . . Mourning is not at all an attack of weak hope . . . Mourning is hope in resistance, resisting the frenetic acceleration of time . . . [H]ope resists the attempt to expel a sense of what is absent from our wisdom about

20. Metz and Rahner, *The Courage to Pray*, 13.
21. Metz, *The Emergent Church*, 100.

our lives."[22] Then one cannot ignore that prayer is given to suppressions of fear or guilt, which can "constrict our hearts and render us incapable of conceiving our own anguish or that of those around us."[23] This constriction of heart is also a worthy object of suspicion, but the traces of prayer that survive in a post-religious age are often the lamentations for self-meaning and justice.

So Metz describes an approach to prayer as a type of negative dialectic. He writes, "I mean here the powerless rebellion against overwhelming meaninglessness, the lament and elegy which manage to survive in spite of the suppression of sadness and melancholy in contemporary society, and the cry for justice for the unexpiated suffering."[24] This powerless rebellion is prayer that has become evident as a shift of responsibility, both social and political. A revolution of interests happens when, "Prayer demands that we love our fellow humans; we have no choice. It can make prayer extremely dangerous . . ."[25] The relation to G*d is not an ideology but rather a form of communication that is dangerous precisely because it is an ultimate vulnerability; an opening of all ideology; a recognition again of the stigma that is on the present. In such a dangerous-solidarity, a deconstructive practice of prayer informs relations without privilege either to self or any other metanarrative of presence.

Metz describes a revolution of thought that occurs when all conceptions of time are accepted only as useful ideas rather than limits on metaphysical reality. In this sense Metz widens Habermas' post-metaphysical confidence in communication; the saving grace is not just a moral consciousness of reason but also of G*d. This is what Metz calls revolution as *interruption*; the powerless rebellion that comes from a hope of something different. This is Metz's short definition of religion, *interruption*, which means that religion must be about G*d if it truly has the capacity to interrupt, otherwise there is only an evolution within time and all that there can be is the triumph of the victors within history. This understanding, as we will see, is at the center of the problem of interpreting Metz, even for his admirers. Key to the nature of *interruption* is its relation to life's decisions and responsibilities, which are never formulaic if they work from within a broken capacity to grasp reality. Relation to the G*d who interrupts is given through an ongoing repre-

22. Metz, *A Passion for God*, 160.

23. Metz and Rahner, *The Courage to Pray*, 16.

24. Ibid., 18.

25. Morrill, "Book Review of Interruptions," *Theological Studies* 60.4 (1999) 19.

sentation and formation of the memory of suffering that is shared with the sacred (*memoria passionis*). The point is not so much a Christian apologetic, although this should not be ignored either. The intent is to share suffering in some form of partnership with G*d by a solidarity with all others, such that enables one to keep from pre-deciding the correct interpretation of history. *Passion* is understood in a sense of suffering humanity that does not encompass or encapsulate memory because the question of G*d is not only about sin and guilt but the suffering in which men and women find themselves once liberated from "revelation positivism" and free enough to enter into discourse with others.[26] Out of such remembrance and meditation, prayer in the world can be both critical and practical.

Gnostic closures of how prayer should be finally and forever offered are ineffective because they refuse to admit the possibility that G*d is not anything we know. By this he means that every divine attribute carries an eschatological stamp and therefore necessitates a negative theology, "which is the most widespread way of talking about God, particularly if we take the language of prayer into account."[27] So when Metz says that "Suffering leads into a void unless it be a suffering unto God," he means that the reality of suffering often presents us with a false choice between explanation or justification. One is too often led to explain how G*d must allow suffering in the world to enable human freedom, or to justify suffering for the sake of an ultimate outcome. By accepting the fact that G*d suffers with us and that there can be no redemption without justice, G*d's fate is intertwined with our own. One opens the discourse on messianicity, the future of the future, whereby theories of ultimate salvation need be questionable in the present.

Talk about G*d begins by a description of an everyday experience of suffering for the sake of bringing redemption and suffering into immediate relation. So he succinctly describes his work as a soteriology insofar as G*d's name is *soter* (salvation), speaking to questions of justice as well as redemption.[28] Everyday prayer questions G*d (*soter*) without becoming argumentative to the extent one forgets that it is narrative. Prayer is organic, a soteriology as he defines it: "My thesis is that a soteriology must neither condition nor suspend the event of redemption

26. Metz, *A Passion for God*, 62.
27. Schuster and Boscher-Kimmig, *Hope against Hope*, 48.
28. Metz, *A Passion for God*, 69.

nor can it ignore or dialectally bypass the non-identity of the history of suffering. A purely argumentative soteriology cannot avoid these dangers. It must be made explicit in narrative. It is a fundamentally memorative and narrative soteriology."[29] He observes in a footnote here that von Balthasar and Moltmann are encoded forms of narrative theology rather than the pure argumentative theology for which they are interpreted. Aside from the accuracy of this statement, this serves to help us understand what Metz means by narrative and argument, which will be further described below. For now it is important to understand that Metz interprets his work as a soteriology that is not reliant upon argument nor dialectical evasions, but an ongoing narrative as a journey through time to an eventual outcome. The biblical dowry is a G*d that draws Abraham onto the path without showing G*dself, also true for the exodus. To Moltmann, who wrote *The Coming God*, Metz replies, "God *is* in coming. This coming, which can neither be extrapolated nor anticipated, constitutes the primal stratum of the imaginative perception of reality in late Jewish and New testament thought . . . What is at issue here is not just an historical time contained in the cosmos transcending that time, but the temporalization of the cosmos itself within the horizon of bounded time"[30] Toward this end, Metz denies any final economy of meaning which neglects or forgets a questioning of G*d (*Rückfrage an Gott*). Even in Paul's Christology, for example, "the apocalyptic sting has not been drawn from this eschatology."[31] His point is that G*d must not be separated from religious practice because this amounts to a cessation of questioning. Religion that limits or legitimates certain questions is reduced to a "praxis of contingency management," as Metz quotes Hermann Lübbe.[32] However, it is risk and danger that G*d contributes to any religious discourse. The admittance of this risk is a key to a future that is different than a repetition of the past or present. Most succinctly stated, Metz's theme is *no G*d, no interruption*.

So the issue remains "how one can speak of God at all in the face of an abysmal history of suffering in the world, in *His* world."[33] Notice how this is the practical underside of the similar situation which Karl Barth articulated concerning the dilemma of theologians who are confronted

29. Metz, *Faith in History and Society*, 133.
30. Metz, *A Passion for God*, 82–83.
31. Ibid., 83.
32. Metz, "Suffering Unto God," 613.
33. Ibid., 612.

by the freedom of G*d. Metz answers that if one can speak of G*d it is either as a question of theodicy or as a partner in questioning which never forgets suffering.

When there is an inclusion of G*d in a discourse of memory, when G*d is questioned, then there is a twofold effect. The first is that the question of theodicy continues to be unavoidable and important; it is the eschatological question.[34] The second is that all answers to theodicy are mythical attempts to avoid or cover-up guilt, rather than leaving the question of evil open in an apocalyptical consciousness. Without both theology becomes a lip service and religion is no longer inclusive of G*d—it no longer asks G*d for G*d; it no longer needs to pray. Metz states that there is "no theological foothold in the crevices" of a dialectical history, rather G*d must be taken more seriously than any pre-mature compromise between G*d and humanity allows. This is evident in his discussion of modern society and conceptions of G*d that might be summarized by his rejection of a well-known formula often attributed to Jürgen Moltmann.[35] Metz states, "Emancipation is not simply the immanence of redemption, nor is redemption just the transcendence of emancipation."[36] There is no simple identification of modern conceptions of freedom with redemption, although this relation remains an unavoidable question.

As already noticed, this fundamental approach to G*d parallels Barth's apocalyptic understanding of G*d's freedom outside human conception until G*d decides otherwise, but for Metz the condition of human suffering indicates human inability for knowing G*d; negative theology will not allow him to draw conclusions about G*d, even G*d's freedom. Metz is no less apocalyptic than the early Barth, maybe more so because there is a fundamental barrier between G*d and humanity where human knowledge is concerned, that he articulates in terms of a fundamental double questioning, a *Rückfrage*. Humans *cannot* speak of G*d but nonetheless *must* speak of G*d, so G*d is spoken about only insofar as G*d is spoken with, which means in the sense of a negative

34. Metz, *A Passion for God*, 56.

35. In a footnote Metz cites Jürgen Moltmann, *Perspectiven der Theologie,* 207. However, in the same note he adds, "That Moltmann himself understands the relation between redemption and emancipation in a more differentiated manner than this formula would aver can be seen in his later work, *The Crucified God.*" Metz, *Faith in History and Society*, 134.

36. Metz, *Faith in History and Society*, 122.

theology; with the G*d who is still to come.[37] From a non-religious perspective it is not knowable what this will mean or how this will happen. One can thus see how prayer is indispensable in the fundamental method of both Barth and Metz, but for the later it is the actual everyday life of human suffering, rather than only suffering G*d's freedom that marks an apocalyptic origin of prayer. It is the freedom of G*d that is meaningful when it is especially helpful to not forgetting the everyday suffering of billions.

This everyday life of suffering cannot be limited or in any way systematized nor abstracted, but remains irreducible in the face of G*d. Neither is this then an exclusively Christian experience or history that decides nothing finally about G*d, but it may be nonetheless "a medium" for a particular tradition.[38] From his earliest work in *Poverty of Spirit* where he writes, "Poverty can never be isolated from the roots of existence and laid hold of,"[39] the importance of this starting point of an apocalyptical memory is consistently held by Metz throughout his career. So he is concerned that human suffering is addressed but always in a way that does not reduce the complexities of life.

> The non-identity of the history of suffering cannot be canceled out in a dialectical process of the trinitarian history of salvation in such a way that it preserves its historical character. This is because this non-identity is not the same as the negativity of the dialectical process . . . A purely conceptual reconciliation between the history of salvation, as an expression of the history of redemption accomplished in Jesus Christ, and the history of man's suffering is, in my opinion, not possible because it can lead either to a dualistic gnostic perpetuation of suffering in God or to a reduction of suffering in the level of a concept.[40]

Theology then finds itself in a dilemma between competing conceptions of reality. One which either separates G*d from the world or one which reduces G*d to worldly purposes; generally speaking between gnosticism or ideology. Theodicy, or the questioning of suffering, is not

37. "For ultimately all talk about God stems from talking with God. This is what marks out the domain proper to theological language, particularly for a semantically disciplined theology." Ekhard Schuster, and Reinhold Boscher-Kimmig, *Hope against Hope*, 31.

38. Metz, *Faith in History and Society*, 123.

39. Metz, *Poverty of Spirit*, 31.

40. Metz, *Why Narrative? Readings in Narrative Theology*, 258.

adequately addressed in either case but rather continues to be the appropriate ultimate question to ask of any worldview. The G*d that is Wholly Other cannot be addressed while the G*d that is reduced to phenomenal categories can only confuse by a reductionism. Prayer that addresses the condition of human suffering from within religious traditions must be capable of working discursively within these two opposites and question both. It is this courageous discourse in which Metz enlists narrative and memory.

He speaks of a solidarity then in terms of a discourse, or a questioning of G*d from where humanity resides. This is not limited to one particular religious tradition. "Discourse about God either speaks in a vision and promise of a comprehensive justice, which even touches this suffering of the past, or it is empty and without promise, even for those now living . . . In my eyes this is 'the' question of theology; it may not be eliminated or left unanswered. It is 'the' eschatological question, the question in response to which theology responds not with answers that reconcile everything but rather with an incessant requestioning of God [*Rückfrage an Gott*].⁴¹" This notion of *a Rückfrage* will be explored in the next two sections, where its affinities with Derrida's description of a double suspension will be explained. The term refers to an exploration of the origin of various hermeneutical concepts, an ongoing analysis helps one avoid pre-determining interpretations and outcomes. This is what is meant by a hermeneutics of danger. There are some questions of origin that are always left unanswered and therefore any conceptions of reality is incomplete. Time is better understood as a temporalization of selfhood, a formation of one's subjectivity.

Questioning Memory

Before focusing on Johann Baptist Metz' notion of *memoria passionis*, let us briefly describe what is meant by the term "memory." It should be clear that memory is a relation of past, present, and future. Without some memory then there is no capacity for knowledge, because memory has a capacity to do two things simultaneously: memory both attests to something particular and also something general and more universal. A simple claim, "I have a lamp on my desk," is made only by the use of memory, which connects the present to some past experiences. And if I

41. Metz, "Suffering unto God," 613.

say, "I like the lamp on my desk." then this implies some desirable experience of a presence of the lamp. Thus both past and future are related within memory when attention is paid to the lamp.

There are at least three competing notions found in the history of philosophy of memory. Plato called memory *anamnesis*. It is the basis of rational knowledge because one must remember first in order to test knowledge at all. It therefore is capable of giving a sense of moving toward truth. This has led to the metaphor of memory as a storehouse, which influenced Augustine to write of the "great cave of memory" in his *Confessions*.

A second notion of memory is typified in Søren Kierkegaard when he reflects upon his trip to Berlin for a second time. He notes how his actions cannot be repeated identically, even while the action as a whole is repeated, therefore the repetition of an act contains distinctions and potentially gives a person a sense of moving forward in time. One may return to a vacation spot, or return to one's boyhood home, but the return to the same is always different. This is associated with a naïve realism, which holds that memory corresponds to knowledge, the strict sense that some things don't change; they are what they are for evermore.

A third position reflects on both of these practical understandings of memory. It is argued that a combination of these notions of memory, platonic anamnesis, and distinctions in repetition, are found in Hegel. More recently Pierre Nora opens an entire field of memory studies based on an observation that historicity and historiography come together in modern sites of memory. Museums, festivals, cemeteries, archives, monuments, and others locations mark a breaking-in of the past into the present. "[T]hese are the boundary stones of another age, illusions of eternity. It is the nostalgic dimension of these devotional institutions that makes them seem beleaguered and cold—they mark the rituals of a society without ritual."[42] Within a secular age there is a rift between memory lived (as with a living tradition) and history that can be separated from the present, a marker of the past overcome.

Hegel's philosophical work as a whole demonstrates, perhaps more fully than that of any other modern thinker, his concern with memory in which the previously known (that is *a priori*) truth of classical metaphysics is mediated with the history of freedom of the human spirit. This memory, according to Hegel's intention, is opposed to any purely

42. Nora, "Between Memory and History," 12.

representational attitude towards history in the historical consciousness. It is, however, taken out of the grip of Plato's anamnesis. In it, what is particular to history does not become a pure example or a mere case of a general phenomenon that is previously known. It does not recall truth as an abstraction from historical relationships.[43]

The significance of Hegel and Nora to someone like Metz, and the study of prayer, is that for thought to refrain from both gnosticism and ideology then memory must incorporate within itself, both "metaphysics and history, archaeology and eschatology."[44] This is important if a questioning of a tradition's idea of G*d is to be true to both the past and the future, and not become either an ideology or some utopian dream. If one side of memory is neglected, then that which is called G*d becomes a hideout from the really hurtful questions to oneself and also an obstacle to a new selfhood. Memory is a re-occurrence of something past, an action where remembering is also an embodiment of what is forgotten and how it was temporarily lost.[45]

One can immediately see how Metz occupies a notion of memory similar to the deconstruction of Derrida and Nora. He proposes memory as a *mimesis* that desires not to differ nor defer justice, and for this reason commits itself to a *Rückfrage*, a double suspension able to reflect forwards and backwards and capable of reading the trajectory of knowledge as it moves out of a past and into a future. For both Metz and Derrida the forward and backward movement within memory is capable of posing the question of the messianic, as an action that looks for a *new* day that comes to take place in the most real sense. Also similar to Derrida, Metz understands an "apocalyptic tone" of a "deconstruction already underway" within the emancipatory processes of modernity, insofar as

43. Metz, *Faith in History and Society*, 189.

44. Ibid.

45. I find some a similarity with Norman Malcolm's notion of memory as "coming to remember." The issue that this philosopher of language raises is that memory with how the senses enable knowledge. The past is not accessible by memory the same way the senses are a source for knowledge about the present surrounding. The act of memory here is a matter of retention more than acquisition, and is thus is dependent upon public techniques like literature. Malcolm, *Knowledge and Certainty*, 230. One may also be reminded of Ludwig Wittgenstein who writes, "The words with which I express my memory are my memory-reaction." Wittgenstein, *Philosophical Investigations*, 110.

emancipatory claims remain hollow and the questions of justice remain unasked let alone unanswered.[46]

A political theology of the subject—for which memory, as a definite memory, is fundamental (this definite memory being that of humanity's process of becoming subjects in the presence of G*d)—is bound to criticize the usual theological idea of man and the subject, especially when it becomes increasingly clear that this idea only acts as a camouflage for one definite subject (the central European) or when the idea of the modern subject in theology has the obvious aim of avoiding all the problems that have arisen in the last two hundred years.[47]

The criticism here is of an Enlightenment society that looses its messianic hope, its expectation of something still to come. Religion itself becomes bourgeois in the sense that the status quo and an insular privatization of faith is prized over any radical risk or expectation acted upon. Although Metz does not deny that a "change of heart" as an "inward process" is a first step, this cannot be reduced to an ideology "with which we yet again conceal from ourselves our failure and refusal to change."[48] Although historical identities of the self are indispensable to naming who we are and possible reconciliations, they are nonetheless limited to "our preconceived bourgeois future."[49] Rather Metz believes that for hope to be real hope, it must have expectations of something *completely new*; the future is not prolonged in evolution, neither completed nor transfigured, but instead our notions of the future are always able to be disrupted in themselves.

One may understand what Metz means by this type of "apocalyptical tension" if one recalls his criticism of Martin Heidegger's degradation of "all history into mere anthropophany, in which the human appears to itself eternally and without salvation."[50] This was written in 1961 when existential theology was all the rage. Metz agrees with Heidegger's denial of any non-historical viewpoint from which to understand ourselves—existence calls for an authentic being. But unlike Heidegger, Metz will not countenance history that is spoken and heard as an abstraction of his-

---

46. "These violent deconstructions are under way, it is happening, it doesn't wait for someone to complete the philosophico-theoretical analysis of everything I just evoked in a word." Derrida, *Points . . . Interviews, 1974–1994*, 356.

47. Metz, *Faith in History and Society*, 67.

48. Metz, *Faith and the Future*, 19.

49. Ibid., 18.

50. Johann Baptist Metz, "Theologische und metaphysische Ordnung," 7.

tory, an essentialization, thus an identification of authenticity by gnostic myth. Thus Metz will not identify memory with any one view of history, whether it culminates in an authenticity [*Dasein*] or any transcendental embrace of human meaning. Rather history is not reducible to any one temporal viewpoint or perspective.

Metz does not move completely opposite of Heidegger, like Karl Rahner who offers the different perspective on human authenticity discovered in a transcendental relation to G*d rather than time itself. Although Metz can agree with the assessment of liminality, which is historically embedded, he would disagree with any prescription of courage or parenesis, whether understood in the form of action or thought. So one sees in a critique of Heidegger's authenticity and Rahner's parenesis that a dynamic of memory that questions incessantly is affirmed. He refuses to close Being (*Dasein*) to Heidegger's *existenze* or Rahner's transcendental path. To choose one or the other is to either dismiss or excuse G*d; it is a cessation of a questioning of one's present memory. While one abstracts authenticity the other forgets history, thus both cease to question and contribute to a loss of hope.

If there is a fork in the road where Heidegger and Rahner chose different directions, Metz refuses to choose definitively one over the other. The relation of G*d to history remains open to the extent that memory cannot be limited to either "no God without being" or "no being without God"; memory provides no map by which to move from lament to prayer, or back.[51] For Metz, this open question of the relation of G*d to history means that one must *question incessantly* because this fundamental question cannot be avoided or answered. An eschatological hope means that one continue to question in solidarity with an ongoing suffering, an apocalypse which has not ended. One questions in expectation of an answer but without the answer predetermined. The questioning of G*d about suffering is close to what I have already characterized as apocalyptical, neither swallowed up in apocalypse, nor assured of the response. Thus, there is no *ordo salutis* here between suffering and hope, and memory is always between these two. Memory is a courageous discourse.

---

51. One remembers the fictional example of Sethe in *Beloved*, who laments that she was never given a map to know how to find herself. Her lack is true for all of us, once one recognizes the problematic nature of cultural systems that promise a completed identity.

However, a resurrection is the other side of the passion, as Metz allows for an apocalyptical tension within memory to be lived as an opening of all canons, a fundamental questioning without ceasing. There is a praxis of solidarity that prescribes no formula for renewal or process for hope; no equation of forgetting and forgiving. However, this suspension within history and memory permits an opening of each metaphysic to a narrative criticism from within, it thus is discovered by a supplement to each performance of communicative action. Modern gnostic impulses to understand or explain a broken and untrustworthy world in an attempt to retrieve truth from it are only one form of narrative among many.

Metz connects this disruption of memory to a sense of G*d, something Derrida is not willing to do. The questioning of memory enables one to take suffering seriously, neither closing G*d out nor defining G*d as the ongoing resistance to any institutionalized hatred. So the name of G*d is not secret where political community is concerned.

> When there is opposition (based on memory) to the refusal to allow man to be a subject, this opposition is not merely to feudalism or capitalism, it is also to any form of suppression or institutionalized hatred. In this process, the God of this dangerous memory does not secretly become a political utopia of universal liberation. The name of God stands rather for the fact that the utopia of the liberation of all human subjects is not a pure projection, which is what that utopia would be if there were only utopia and no God.[52]

When the questioning of memory and theodicy are intertwined, then a fundamental resistance characterizes our personhood; one becomes a prayer. This is a radical reflexivity in everyday exchanges that not only asks about how the present can be implemented in the future, but also why it should be so. One asks not only what all present have to say and do, but also what the past and future have to say to those present. In this way, G*d is made a practical partner in discourse to the extent it may call for a conversion, a truly new future that has not forgotten.

So a *memoria passionis* discourages amnesia from within any theological discourse, and in this way bring old bones to life. Communicative reason is thus grounded in "anamnestic reason" as he puts it.[53] This is an approach to language that resists any predication of memory without

---

52. Metz, *Faith in History and Society,* 67.

53. Metz, "Suffering unto God," 615.

recognition that all such predication itself is already forgetting. The important potential of this suspension is that it may also put one in-touch with the other. Apocalyptical reflections may freshly begin remembrances of catastrophe or the unexplainable; it is an encountering of history as a risky venture. I have contended that without apocalyptical reflection explanation becomes self-satisfied, history becomes consoling myth, and canons harden. Thus, apocalyptical reflection may be understood as a humbled and fragmented participation in history as itself an apocalypse. It refuses any final consolation or realized eschatology. It refuses any escape from human history as anything more than brokenness, even our own. This is similar to what Derrida is referring to when he uses the word *différance*, as both differing and deferring.[54]

Questioning Narrative

A narrative is a representation of memory. Like memory, it relates a beginning, middle, and end. The continuity and discontinuity of these relations is the story itself. Consider a children's story, for example, Humpty Dumpty who sat on a wall and then had a great fall. The narrative does something by moving from a start to a middle and then an end, and in this case it seems to be a warning about sitting on high walls.

The questioning of G*d or soteriology is, performatively, a questioning narrative. As discussed in the previous section, memory moves forwards and backwards in time and is an experience of some repetition and some irreducibility of each event. It is possible to question at all because of these capacities of memory, or remembering. Narrative builds on memory and adds a performative dimension to this experience of memory. Narrative does stuff, that's intended. Walter Benjamin famously describes the performative aspect of narrative. "Most born storytellers pursue a practical interest . . . [T]his is indicative of the distinctive nature of all true stories, all of which have an overt or hidden use—a moral, a practical instruction, a rule of life. In every case, the storyteller is a man who knows what to do with the listener . . . His stories are based on experience, either his own or other people's, which he transforms into the experience of those who listen to the stories."[55] It is also a connection of performance to a practice, capable of a questioning of G*d and memory as already described.

54. Metz, "Productive Noncontemporeneity," 21.

55. Interestingly, Benjamin also writes of the storyteller, "With these words, soul,

A good or bad story is usually measured by how successful the storyteller is in pursuing their practical interest and in becoming an intersubjective conduit between a past and many possible presents. Therefore narrative has two remarkable characteristics, as it is a place of exchanging these experiences. First, it "is not ideologically unconscious," or, in other words, the narrative presents its interests in the story that is told, or is chosen to tell.[56] This is most apparent in histories; it is almost impossible for a historian not to be asked why they tell this particular story and in this particular way, their ideology is out there in the story. Second, narrative contains a transcendence from within, there is a "sacramental" aspect to an effective story.[57] The constellation of the words and actions within the story form a type of composite meaning which in turn can be reflexively read back into the story again. Different stories are aided by this universal sense of unity and diversity of narrative. Metz makes the point that all theology and understanding of the relation of life to death, involves narrative of irreducible experiences.

All this is disclosed in narrative. The world created from nothing, man made from dust, the new kingdom proclaimed, the new man, even resurrection as a passage through death to life, the end as a new beginning, the life of future glory—all these show that reasoning is not the original form of theological expression, which is above all that of narrative. The logos of theology, so long as it conceals its own narrative form, is as embarrassed by them as reason is by questions concerning the beginning and the end and the destiny of what is new and has never yet been.[58]

Metz goes on in the same paragraph to state that "Kant was aware of this when he spoke of the 'rhapsodic beginning of thought' which was not open to argumentative thought." If reason limits itself to argumentative logic then it will inevitably lose touch with why it argues, or for what purpose it reasons, which Metz observes in late modern society. In *Meditations*, Metz names some of the modern economies that are limited and enfeebled by a loss of their own narrative: "It is not only the growth of our economic potentiality which is limited, as people insist to us, the potentiality of our thinking seems also to be limited, and it is as

eye, and hand are brought into connection. Interacting with one another, they determine a practice." Benjamin, *Illuminations*, 108.

56. Metz, *Faith in History and Society*, 208.

57. Ibid.

58. Ibid., 206.

if our reserves were dwindling, as if there were the danger that the big words with which we made our own history—'freedom,' 'emancipation,' 'justice,' 'happiness'—in the end will have no sense which has not been exhausted and dispersed."[59] Narrative is thus so important for suffering to be addressed, for any redemption to take place. Without narrative, then suffering either becomes ignored or accepted as part of the natural order of things. "The category of narrative memory prevents salvation and redemption from becoming paradoxically unhistorical and does not subordinate them to the logical identity of argumentation."[60] Again, there are two avenues to banality, an unhistorical salvation and/or a triumphal logic.

Narrative has a capacity that does not overstretch history nor discount it. Like Ernst Bloch's future proletariat, who Metz cites here, a narrative of salvation does not necessarily confuse the history of suffering with a theology or soteriology. Nonetheless, this narrative must still be careful not to make G*d "the dialectical key" which solves the problems of history.

Yet narrative is inescapable for anyone who desires a sense of history's redemption. Metz makes this point especially to theologians who attempt to address a history of suffering with a history of salvation. Therefore as Metz states, "The introduction of narrative memory (*erzählenden Erinnerung*, telling remembrance) and the accentuation of its cognitive primacy in theology is therefore not an *ad hoc* construction."[61] It is indispensable to making present the mediation of salvation and suffering. Even in projects that rely on the de-mythology of narratives, it is forgotten that critical argument is inherently narrative-shaped as it portends a redemptive movement of criticism.

I am reminded of Jürgen Habermas at this point, who narrates the unfolding of an emancipatory reason as the discourse of modernity, remembering that his narrative is about inappropriate or false mediations for the construction of a community of communication. The question reoccurs whether such narrative can depend upon a continuity of history; is there a rationality inherent to these events or is it inferred by the narrative of them?

59. Metz and Moltmann, *Meditations on the Passion,* 29.

60. Metz, *Faith in History and Society,* 211.

61. Ibid., 212.

The debates on the question of narrative and rationality, described in previous chapters, revolve around two foci; either a continuing project of the rationalization of an enlightened society or, alternately, a space of subjectivity and alterity; one moving irrevocably forward while the other questions this progress as that of a machine, and as irresponsible. One may see the entire project of modernity as a reduction of religious narrative to either a privatization of faith, in danger of losing social significance, or its rationalization, a renunciation of religions symbolism and myth.[62]

Theorists like Jürgen Habermas respond to religion reduced to privatistic reductions. He prizes a rational continuity indicated by non-coercive communicative action. While theorists like Derrida and Levinas, who prize an ethics of alterity, respond to religion too often reduced by cognitive pressures of modern sciences. Metz characterizes the first as the "post-Marxist Frankfurters," while the second is represented by advocates of a social risk and proponents of "existential-political decisionism."[63]

The narrative remedy for the current impasse between pragmatic and transcendental reductions of religion is a pragmatics of communication. Metz calls this a "broadening of reason" or one might say to enlighten the Enlightenment on affairs of religion.[64] This is why it is important to ask along with Habermas and those wishing to preserve the enlightenment project, "What would a non-divided reason be?"[65] But Metz also asks, along with Derrida and so called postmoderns, whether rational discourse "imposes a privileging of contemporaneity on the readiness of reason to recognize the Other."[66] In other words, discourse can be both fair to all present participants and also the absent, if it refuses any abstraction of human suffering or consolation by myth as a disguised attempt to forget and move beyond our past or remove memory from reason.

Metz indicts present society for continuing the same genocide, or what can be called pneumacide or murder of spirit. This issue comes into stark relief when one considers Auschwitz and what it represents.

62. Metz and Moltmann, *Faith and the Future,* 32.
63. Ashley, *Interruptions,* 193.
64. Ibid., 142.
65. Metz, *The Emergent Church,* 193.
66. Ibid., 191.

But whether it be the murder of Jews at Auschwitz or the lynching of African-Americans in New York City, these events live in the present when we forget to remember the past as our past, confronted by a continuing stigma. Today's reasoning does not do justice to the past when it is not anamnestic in its fundamental constitution, and this is why theology books attach a chapter on eschatology at the end. This is one more symptom of today's memory or one can say cultural amnesia that is either compensatory or a temporary consolation. "Memory, which keeps track of this forgetting, is split off from historical reason and reduced to a compensatory category removed from history and pregnant with myth; it becomes the museum piece of traditionalism and of counter-enlightenment—or it drifts off into postmodern fictionalization of history."[67] Memory *qua* remembrance is not a compensatory category, nor one in which memories may be exchanged for others or even painlessly warehoused.

Metz welcomes reason's fundamental liminality as a performance within narrative. Human being is thoroughly historicized. Even more than in the thought of Heidegger. The view of humanity is also historical in the sense that the present is inseparable from its past, as Nora discusses. Past and present share a common horizon of meaning and perception.[68] It is this second aspect, a solidarity within meditative thought (*Angedenken*) and remembrance (*Eingedenken*) is rediscovered as a discourse between narratives as they question themselves with respect to others.[69]

He argues that these biblical manners of reflection which begin with the other or the neighbor, are irreconcilable to Platonic anamnesis when it exempts itself from time and history and in so doing also loses a sense of purpose for its own sense of freedom. Although Christianity and European culture are presented as a synthesis of Hebrew and Greek intellect, others reject Hellenization as a certain wrong turn or self-alienation. Metz does not underestimate or refute a Greek influence on Christianity but rather wishes to understand the distinction because it is relevant to the present day crisis of the *Geisteswissenshaften*, which

67. Ibid.

68. Ibid., 192.

69. Ibid., 190. This neo-logism is used first in 1976 by Metz, which is the year the sermons contained in *Courage to Pray* were preached. In this small book co-authored with Karl Rahner, as Ashley points out, the phrases *Rückfrage an Gott* and *Leiden an Gott* are also first used by him and become key concepts for Metz throughout all subsequent works. This occurs shortly after his visit to Central America.

has lost a particular capacity of reflection in the service of freedom. This is a "recognition of the capacity for guilt as a dignity for freedom."[70] Metz supports this discovery of a biblical reason by citing contemporary Jewish philosophy, noting diverse thinkers such as Walter Benjamin, Franz Rosenzweig, Hans Jonas, Emmanuel Levinas, and Ernst Bloch, "who despite all their differences seem to agree that thinking is remembrance and that undivided reason has an anamnestic deep structure."[71]

In this way joy and suffering are not mutually exclusive, but rather are seen to propel each other, making both proponents for honest forgiveness and justice; neither of which can be separated from each other. Exteriority is the ground, the place of induction, from which interiority is born, by which G*d knows us. G*d sees and knows us in a way that is affective for us, to be known by G*d is all the transformation which we could hope for, could withstand. Our narratives are read not just to see truth, but also to be seen *by it*, to be humbled but also reborn in an exchange of experiences. In a performative mode, narrative is capable of fashioning all metaphysical statements and ideas of G*d, and capable of questioning and being questioned by them. Reality is opened within this happy exchange.

Prayer as *Anamnestic* Discourse

How prayer operates in connection with modern discourse is illuminated by an anecdote of an exchange between Johann Baptist Metz and the great critic of Enlightenment, Max Horkheimer. Metz retells it; "As we were parting from a train station, Horkheimer said to me, "Do you see how cruel a train is, Herr Metz, how it moves off so quickly and separates people from one another?" This was probably meant as a practical critique of the excesses of instrumental reason. I only remember responding, "But after all, Herr Horkheimer, it does not just draw people apart, it also brings people together."[72] Metz is misunderstood if his theory of prayer is interpreted as a rejection of modern reason, or a too easy affirmation. Prayer, in all it negative dialectics, is able to broaden and compliment projects of the Enlightenment, especially as they relate to discourse.

70. Metz, "Anamnestic Reason," 190.

71. Ibid., 194.

72. Schuster and Boscher-Kimmig, *Hope against Hope*, 23.

I have argued that prayer is describable, and can be studied comparatively, in light of its capacity for remembering the past, and remembering the forgotten. He describes a prayer that desires to give voice to the voiceless. This is language as partnership with history, not only as authors of it but as characters within it. Thus, Metz describes prayer as a textuality or participation within a historical solidarity. "What do we know about the history of humanity? . . . The history of humanity seen as popular history is basically the history of religion, and religious history in the final analysis is the history of prayer. And this is not limited to the history of Christian Europe . . . Through prayer we become part of a great historical solidarity."[73]

Like some recent communitarian theology, Metz links narrative and religious practice but unlike communitarians he does not identify a true or authentic practice of prayer by placing it within a certain tradition.

But prayer is not linked to any one community. It is found through many languages and many traditions. In all, prayer becomes the words for the healing of language by adjusting proximities to the other; "a language of prayer which has authentically taken up into itself society's conflicts and sufferings: this language brings out clearly how much humanity would lose of its potential for expressing crises of and suffering in language, were the centuries old language of prayers to disappear from its midst."[74] Thus, the function of prayer is described as its potential as a broadening of political decisions by more responsible rationalities. Which means deepening pious words by thoughtful reflection, and moving beyond disquietude to action. This potential of prayer is born of a non-privileging narrative in which there is no inarticulable suffering before G*d but also no short cut through a technique of language to happiness. This does not negate that prayer is given to suppressions of fear or guilt, which can "constrict our hearts and render us incapable of conceiving our own anguish or that of those around us."[75] As said already, constrictions are also worthy objects of suspicion, but prayer remains, even in a post-religious age, as the lamentation for self-meaning and justice.

Everyday millions cry out in anguish and millions more ignore their cries unless it is in their interests. Prayer in its simplest form is a cry that calls a divided world to task for the sake of the unheard. It is a call

73. Metz and Rahner, *The Courage to Pray*, 5.
74. Johann Baptist Metz, *The Emergent Church*, 100.
75. Metz and Rahner, *The Courage to Pray*, 18.

for solidarity with the forgotten. The trace of prayer becomes evident as a shift of responsibility, both social and political. "Prayer demands that we love our fellow humans; we have no choice. It can make prayer extremely dangerous."[76] This dangerous solidarity of prayer does not permit privilege either to self or any other metanarrative of presence. It is capable of being a discourse centered around an apocalyptical time, discourse that accepts uncritically neither "dramatically accelerated progress, nor as aggressively heightened evolution, but rather as a rebellion against the fact that everything keeps going on as before. This would be revolution as interruption."[77]

Discourse takes on a different dimension when it is complimented by *interruption*. In short, one is able through the course of a lifetime to learn different positions regarding how one listens or is attune to the truth. Every person, everyday is being thus temporalized, learning to act as author and character within their various narratives. In this situation, the opposite of responsibility is not irresponsibility, so much as it is banality, the loss of questioning itself. A banality that characterizes some of the worst crimes against humanity during the last century.

The incessant questioning of a relation between deconstructive practices and re-constructive pragmatics is the location of the answer to the question, "What may one hope for?"

There is a subtle contrast between a theology of interruption, that welcomes a narrative of brokenness as simply that and without hidden meaning, and a theology based on chosen suffering exposed by phenomenological observation. This contrast may be seen when suffering is explained or described for a purpose, or a more real and genuine understanding; for Metz this is the same as suggesting a "happy fall" or some other universal explanation for brokenness. For this reason, theodicy serves in an inverse way and never allows a silence of the questioning that questions all questions. This is also the reason why Metz most basic statement of memory as *memory passionis* and his negotiations never advance beyond or cover over this.

The real everyday suffering of actual persons cannot be decided upon as hopeful signs or anticipations. Nor can an *ordo salutis* or an "in order to" provide any determined or genuine understanding of this suffering which continues. This subtle but crucial distinction between phenomenology and interruption is vital to a performance of prayer,

76. Ibid., 19.
77. Ibid., 13.

because a belief in a repeatable liberation from suffering, even in democracy, fails to correct a myopia of modernity that permits and then glorifies a "history of the victors."[78] "For the *remembrance*[79] of someone else's suffering is by nature no passive observation; against its horizon resistance to suffering is unconditionally commanded, a resistance that is not guided by the myth of complete freedom from suffering, of course, but rather has a sober recognition that there will always be situations that create suffering among men and women."[80]

This has great relevance for a modernity that relates political and theological discourse insofar as its spirit depends upon its own triumph. Prayer is such a reconsideration of our relation to all others who are forgotten by this modern spirit. More specifically the substance of an apocalyptical prayer is a morally suspended narrative of a broken memory that offers itself in repentance for the sake of a new or just future. Such a practice of discourse within narrative would refuse any covering up of guilt, either individual or cultural memory.

This performative practice can be neither indebted to a particular tradition nor tied to a universal syncretism. If this prayer successfully avoids these forms of banality or ideology, then it is itself a criterion both inside and outside religious practices. It is a participation in a wider family of religious persuasions, while accepting each one's differences as a beginning of a new day. Thus, prayer can be a narrative of memory intensely caught up in the world as it is now, not as it should be someday, or any conditional formula for coordination of various participants. Rather, prayer allows for a deepening of the present by an unconditional participation in conversation. Prayer then is speaking in faith, not only that others will understand, but that G*d answers.

What can be the purpose or function of this prayer? Why pray if not for emancipation, justice, or happiness? One would then have to say this prayer is given as its own end of meaning; as representation fragmentation within. Prayer meditates upon an end that is an exhaustion of

---

78. Ashley, *Interruptions*, 144–45 "Biblical monotheism is really a pathic monotheism, . . . a monotheism constitutionally broken by the theodicy question, a question that can as little be answered as it can be forgotten. It is a monotheism for which history is not simply the history of the victors, but above all a history of suffering." Ibid., 145.

79. Remembrance is translated from *eingedenken*—more literally, *the remembering*. As best I can tell this neo-logism, which is close to a word used by Walter Bejamin *eindenken*, and is again used first in 1976 by Metz.

80. Metz, *A Passion for God*, 145.

all historical meanings, limited action and limited thinking tired to the point of having nothing left, at an end of all ends. This can be a prayer that is apocalyptical. Again, this is like some communitarian theologians who unalterably link historical narrative and a practice of prayer, but he does not identify Christian prayer as the true prayer. Prayer itself is like a bottomless placement of exchange, where memory and narrative act on one another. Thus, prayer is a conversation between the person and their G*d. This conversation is not for any other purpose than its own end. It is not to be reduced to an idea nor a strategy, but also its meaning is not passively received as if no eschatological reserve remained. Thus prayer may take part in the end as it is its own end, non-reducible.

If prayer narrates from a memory of suffering, this means a continual questioning of both humanity and G*d. Criteria begin to emerge for the study of prayers that may represent in various ways and degrees an apocalyptic consciousness that does not forget. In other words, a prayerful approach to cultural memory would listen to all suffering, so to guard against fatalism or triumphalism. If prayer goes on to narrate a *memoria passionis* of humanity then this can mean neither a modern demythology nor a surrendering to fate and a drying up of autonomy. Such prayer sets about the task of what Paul Ricoeur called a parallel history to success. "We need therefore, a kind of parallel history of, let us say, victimization, which would counter the history of success and victory. To memorize the victims of history—the sufferers, the humiliated, the forgotten—should be a task for all of us at the end (of this century.)"[81]

To memorize the victims of history, sufferers and the humiliated, this is difficult enough, but to memorize the forgotten? What is it to memorize the forgotten? I don't think it is the same as keeping track of forgetting. Keeping track of forgetting is one more anxious act of memory, continuing to count and keep score for the forgotten. But to memorize, to commit to memory the forgotten, is "a task for all of us at the end . . ." Ricoeur completes the sentence "at the end of this century" as if the numbering of a millennium had something to do with remembering the forgotten. Rather, I think Metz's description of religion as interruption, is the end of prayer, an end where prayer is heard and answered in each unheard cry of anguish in history. As if their prayers are what make our prayers even possible.

81. Ricoeur, "Memory and Forgetting," 10.

7

Prayer in Discourse

DISCOURSE IS REASON IN ACTION. BY VIEWING IT AS A PERFORMANCE, it is opened, incomplete, unfinished, included already within a traditioning process. There is an acknowledgement of fallibility in the discursive moment. I argue that discourse needs prayer, or something like it, in order to engage both a moral consciousness and a responsible representation of suffering. Toward this end it is also my project to develop a critical framework for the comparative study of prayer engaged in discourse able to take place within many religious traditions. It has been my endeavor to describe the function of prayer to speak from utter brokenness, an experience of apocalypse to something beyond. Prayer is capable of a critical discourse where it is recognized that G*d is questioned; prayer in its simplest form is a questioning of G*d; the sacred.

The Challenge

The most comprehensive description of discourse is *The Theory of Communicative Action*, by Jürgen Habermas. He identifies the performance of discourse with the unfinished project of enlightenment that seeks to establish critical discussion of social norms. "For a norm to be valid, the consequences and side effects of its general observance for the satisfaction of each person's particular interests must be acceptable to all."[1] I have described the principle of universalization as a procedure of public discourse, permitting a method of ethics that is based in description. A theory designed to allow for a maximum variety of understandings of rightness that do not detract from an intersubjectively shared life-world that, in turn, allows for individualization.

1. Habermas, *Moral Consciousness and Communicative Action*, 197.

Habermas says that this is his version of John Rawls' original position of justice. Rawls and Habermas share a common desire for justice and screen out coercion and uncriticizable social habits from argumentation and decision. Both theorize the best conditions for an impartiality of moral judgment that wins the day only by the "unforced force of the better argument."[2] However, Habermas critiques Rawls original position as fictitious and idealized. Rather, he argues that the rules of discourse be grounded in the world *as it is*, not in some ideal. His alternative then is to describe consensus-oriented discourse that is always already present in each address or assertion. He refrains from reliance on principle by pointing again and again to concrete examples and performing as an example for us. Discourse is not only an idea; it is a performance. "Discourse can play this role because its idealized, partly counterfactual presuppositions are precisely those that participants in argumentation do in fact make."[3] Habermas describes communicative action as inherently reflexive and thus criticizable in terms of its value, norm, or fact.

There is much to unpack here; indeed Habermas represents the most sophisticated social philosophy of modernity. The great contribution of this theory is that it allows for a critical dialogue between philosophy and the social sciences that does not automatically privilege one discipline or the other. Where previously "actor-world relations" differentiated types of action which then subverted rationality to standards of strategic accomplishment, Habermas marks an enlightenment which tries to make all action criticizable from a universal criterion. Actor-world relations are increasingly distinguished today by a socialization process that contributes simultaneously to both individual identity and interdependence. Thus modern reasoning either contributes to a consensus seeking discourse or it tends to polarize individuals and further fragment society, contributing to the need for reification. People who need rationalization more and more, tend to be more susceptible to ideology that helps them find an easy narrative in which to live their lives. This approach to the dynamics of modernity has informed our questioning of prayer throughout this book.

So in our times prayer is challenged to be increasingly either private or universal. In a fragmented society prayer may find it more and more difficult to contribute to both individuality and interdependence,

2. Ibid.
3. Ibid.

contributing to a process of critical consensus. Prayer may be more likely to cover over these distinctions in order to enforce its own traditional narrative, reasoning like a parasite that keeps the host alive for its own version of the past and future.

My response is to assert that prayer is a critical discourse. There are many possible perspectives on the question of the interaction of prayer, including a secular rejection of religious traditions. While one person may question whether the cultural or religious practice of prayer is particularly (in)separable from salvation or redemptive outcomes resulting from prayer, another questions whether all prayer is equally valuable or contributive to knowledge. Still another questions whether prayer changes anything; does it contribute anything new or is it simply another economy of exchange? I have tried to include all these approaches within a framework for the study of prayer.

For a study of prayer to remain epistemologically valid, then the methods of social science and critical theory remain engaged with a multi-disciplinary paradigm that contains shifting categorizations of truth and a fluid memory. One discovers that a concern for prayer cannot exclude a concern for social justice that may be rationalized in between descriptive and prescriptive assertions. However, because prayer is language intentionally directed to G*d, or what is called sacred. Infinite, creator, unspeakable in multitudinous traditions, it does not permit its own verification as other language directed to the world-as-it-is.

So one has two competing forms of phenomenology that arise here, one typified by the turn toward reason and one by the turn toward memory. The latter is more familial to Husserl's earliest *epoche* or a bracketing within time; the former is of another family that brackets the present. When prayer listens to the unheard it cannot permit description of the world-as-it-is or descriptions of G*d to be irreducible to each other. Prayer that amounts to determinable reductions of the relation between the world and G*d may still permit various perspectives on the world as-it-is. Because when prayer is performed within the overlap of these non-reductions then it also sets itself about a different task, one open to a final unknown judgment but one spoken in solidarity. However, when past and future are closed off then this amounts to a rigidity of prayer. This rigidity is more prone to ideology rather than a discursive reconnaissance. It is more an ultimate perspective on the world than a dialogue.

So a further study of prayer will be a test of this theoretical framing. I will suggest some hypotheses that arise from this frame that may
direct comparative studies of prayer to test whether it may be an open
and conscientious prayer performed in a plural world with solidarity and
integrity of life.

Habermas allows for a practical discourse about G*d if it is able to
refrain from secularization and mystification. Rejecting any transcendental perspective made possible by religion, remembering his interpretation of Theunnisen in this way. He quotes Metz' description of a
culture that depends upon its sensitivity to truth to balance positions
of universalism and relativism, salvation is an "invitation." This must be
continually and practically tested. But he also sees that Metz affirms "a
rational conception of law which has been hermeneutically sensitized to
its eurocentric limitations."[4] Acknowledging that the polycentric world
church remains one of many communities of interpretation that articulates a conception of salvation, it must internalize outsider perspectives
while at the same time entering into a contest between religious and
metaphysical worldviews. Habermas notices that this situation is different from the one in which Catholic Christianity is historically familiar,
because there is no common basis of human rights or the common good.

By contrast, in the case of the dialogical contest between religious
and metaphysical worldviews, a common conception of the good which
could play the same role as this shared legal and moral basis is lacking. This means that this contest has to be played out with a reflexive
awareness that all concerned move in the same universe of discourse,
and respect each other as collaborative participants in the search for
ethical-existential truth. To make this possible, a culture of recognition
is required that takes its principles from the secularized world of moral
and rational-legal universalism.[5]

What is necessary for cooperative action between persons is a sphere
of "non-coercive exchange." A sphere of discourse centered around normative validity claims that are submitted for testing. Habermas makes
the point that a majority culture must subordinate itself to the shared
political culture for the sake of minorities, and in his view this happens
only by "uncoupling" political and religious levels of the integration of
life-world and social systems.

4. Habermas, *Religion and Rationality*, 136.
5. Ibid., 137.

On the other side of this question is Derrida who denies that any such "uncoupling" is possible. A modern cosmopolitanism is no less reliant upon a line between hidden and visible, between faith and reason, especially when normative claims are being tested. Language and communication is pragmatic, but it rests upon the unsayable or that which is the end of all ends. Along these lines he recommends the words of Angelus Selesius. "But an arrow is only an arrow; it is never an end in itself. Selesius says this well when he speaks precisely of the possibility of the most impossible or of more than the most impossible (*'Das überunmöglichste ist möglich'*). It specifies you recall: 'With your arrow you can not reach the sun, with mine I can sweep under my fire the eternal sun.'"[6] Every communication is a sign of a relation that is not exemplary in itself, but only insofar as it moves as a possible consciousness of the impossible, in the Heideggerian frame of Dasein "open to being as being through the possibility of going beyond the present of what is."[7]

The challenge then is to continue to think about prayer that is uniquely qualified to keep both approaches toward prayer within a comparative study of its performative mode. The validity of prayer may be seen as it relates to both cultural practices, even in argumentative modes of reason, and also universal concerns that probe the impossible encountered in the present through an unfinished theodicy that orients questioning. If either end of prayer is ignored or surrendered, it then may fall into banal ideology and obsessions that radicalize its own pursuits rather than contributing to mutual recognitions of what a final justice might look like. Thus, prayer may be studied as a fundamental discourse between narratives and between memories. It may be challenged within modern times to perform itself legitimately as questioning or opening of metaphysical ideals and cultural practices so that suffering may be more justly represented in language and addressed with practical action.

Hypotheses for Comparative Studies of Prayer

While recognizing that so much comparativism refrains from actual comparison, this study has questioned previous theory about the nature of prayer's communication and its status as a discourse. This leads to

---

6. Derrida, "Post-Scriptum: Aporias, Ways and Voices," 304.
7. Ibid., 306.

eight hypotheses here that direct future investigations of the variety of prayer.

Let us consider prayer as speech to a party that is perceived to have an advantage of knowing us better than we know ourselves, regardless of any mask. It is not difficult to imagine such a communication partner if we remember times when a mother or father show such knowledge of a child. In response to this asymmetry, prayer needs an honest tension between descriptive and prescriptive assertions. When prayer is performed without this *apocalyptical* understanding, then it ceases to be a discourse and contributes more to an ideology. Sometimes there is too much proximity; there must be both the capacity to mask and to reveal if prayer is more than pretension.

This especially relates to traditions that point to a final salvation or redemption that is beyond the supplicants ability to achieve. Prayer functions within a discursive structure of eschatology, as recently described by Martin S. Jaffee. He states that a self-disclosure of G*d enables action to be understood within an onto-social understanding that is discursively implemented within human community by a rationalization of eschatology. As Jaffee writes; "Each form of elective monotheism is a distinct parole, a historical mobilization of the discursive structure of elective monotheism in a unique symbolic vocabulary, whose distinctive parameters and possibilities of expression are worked out in the context of historical tradition."[8] Jaffee goes on to describe how each monotheism inevitably uses eschatology to explain the limited nature of its community established by an all-powerful universal G*d. Because the eschaton is the time which G*d, selfhood, and community are finally bound together in a universalist moral community, history is the time of struggle with the communal other. Jaffee seems to indicate historical inevitability of violence by any monotheism; this may or may not be the case.

One possible caveat is that prayer functions within this discursive structure of eschatology. At issue is the moment when one considers the world as it is, irreconcilable with G*d; in this moment is there an alternative approach to history other than impatience with the future, that contributes to immediate plans of eschatological fulfillment? In these cases, the hypothesis is well warranted that prayer functions within a discursive structure of eschatology that justifies violence by it metaphys-

8. Jaffee, "One God, One Revelation, One People: On the Symbolic Structure of Elective Monotheism," 774.

ics, yet prayer's performative language is able to open it from within the structure, or *parole*.

This relates to a second hypothesis; that prayer is able to differentiate the world as it is from the world as it ought to be. What is the capability of prayer at opening its own metaphysical assertions? The person in prayer is often mindful of G*d's freedom, mostly because of the suffering all around. Religious devotees experience the deconstruction of their theological concepts everyday if they are looking around. A study of prayer cannot begin by pretending to know whether this possibility is the case or not. In fact, to not know the answer of G*d's ultimate end is constitutive of prayer; it is fundamentally language of risk born in a suffering finitude.

A third hypothesis is that prayer represents an experience of the negative in memory, an *apocalypse* that is used as a narrative. Questions continue to arise about this strategy of religious thought that goes back to Darius. What if prayer attempts to economize or work through a knowledge or faith of G*d's ultimate end?

A fourth hypothesis is that prayer functions as a criticism of religious language, and this is often conducive to a public mode of reasoning. It may be discovered through careful and detailed anthropological study that prayer goes hand in hand with labors of love that respond to the suffering of others without contributing to it by way of explanation or eschatology that contains hidden theodicy, and therefore prayer includes the forgotten and/or our constant reliance upon a discursive inter-subjectivity for the renewal of memory. Such prayer then is an *apocalyptical* discourse open to be validated by a continual questioning of normative action. Historians might question whether the gift of a new age is born in prayer that is engaged in the opening of social discourse.

A fifth hypothesis centers on a political dynamic. A society faced with a plethora of moralities and the everyday incommensurability of narratives is able to thrive with plurality and the ensuing norms. Is this related to the recognition of the false choice between self-referential or cultural perspectives discovered in prayer? When prayer is an expression of brokenness then it may contribute to an awareness of a false choice between self-referential or cultural rationalizations between life-world and society. This connects with Habermas' point that the normative sphere of discourse should not be reduced to an affirmation of an assumed life-world and a criticizable system must be open to all questions. Also

Derrida's point that any inter-subjective procedures will be grounded in violent and incomplete origins, and therefore prone to continual shifting of norms. It may be found that prayer contributes to cultural norms by questioning their origins. Prayer in conversation with G*d therefore questions one's own practical conceptions of G*d first, if prayer is to be more than a function of it's own political interests.

Sixth, prayer remembers the past in relation to an open future. A prayerful understanding of history informs a practice of hermeneutical sensitivity and aesthetic imagination that may inform relations within and between traditions. When the point of prayer is both to interrupt an unending march of time as more of the same that bleeds the present dry of meaning, and also to work with others in a mutual understanding of meaning, then history must be a teacher. The incommensurability of traditions or otherness is not to be confused with their incompatibility, when prayer seeks to find new ways to relate to the previously unrelatable by questioning one's own memory of suffering.

Another well warranted hypothesis is that tradition or religious narrative does not hold practitioners of prayer captive but sometimes can inform a freedom to question. Prayer, among other things, is the possibility of exchanging experiences within a narrativity of meaning; it is the hope to understand otherness. Prayer then should criticize traditional understandings, not blindly reinforce them as if this is the nature of faith. This means there are examples of religious practitioners that are able to pray with their eyes open, often becoming leaders of reform.

Eighth, there are prayerful persons and communities that avoid false essentialism, uncriticizable metaphysics, or hidden politics, which always distort or oversimplify incommensurable narratives. The procedures of discourse theory and deconstruction can be brought into relation when reciprocating criticisms in dialogue—meant to build structures of cooperation—also mean a questioning of G*d from the perspective of an incomplete theodicy or eschatology. Prayer in its broadest sense is the end of all ends in perspective of an unknown end of time, or, as I have described an apocalyptical sense, of the end in the meantime; between brokenness and its beyond.

Through a comparative study of prayer, and the testing of all of the above hypotheses, it may be someday concluded that the discourse of prayer entails a responsibility that arises when one realizes the plurality of incommensurable traditions of prayer. The origin of prayer is not any particular religious tradition but instead a universal form of solidarity. Far from being other worldly, prayer entails an engagement with an active and questionable discourse, so as to understand the other and be understood, and thus work together for more just structures of discourse.

This may be especially important to an American audience charged with negotiating modern plurality that permits spiritual considerations. Prayer can be an important form of questioning all onto-theology and it's entwinement of knowledge and power that is a source of violence and also the possibility of a coming justice.

As one who will not cease the project of unraveling unjust entwinements of knowledge and power, this is motivated by a search for peace. I keep questioning if there is an onto-theology that has a possibility for peace and not violence. As a child I was taught that the ministry of John Wesley and subsequent movements of the "Great Awakening" contributed to England's avoidance of a French Revolution, while it is often proposed that enlightenment reason contributed to subsequent spirals of terror and oppressions of the French Revolution. Yet the spiraling of violence within the closure of onto-theology also seems an everyday occurrence. Like Michel Foucault, I see that one example of unjust closure is the Cartesian impulse to subject knowledge to certainty. This metaphysically enthrones the person and thus devises an economy of domination; religious fundamentalism can also be a variant of this same spiral. This "logic" of mastery subverts identity and internalizes aggression, spiraling fear into absolute terror. So Derrida and others can see the furnaces of the Holocaust and other holocausts as the consequence of a partial nihilism that asserts self by negating other. Prayer permits another possibility. Each death, and all its related contingencies, identify each of us and thus call each of us. When modern knowledge denies or turns its back on any death (either speculative or a particular) then it is also a denial of an aspect of memory.

Prayer's form, although it includes the apophatic, begins in brokenness and is originally formed and fundamentally an apocalyptical act of speech in solidarity with the prayers of all untold sufferers. I am making the point that the most common experience of G*d in prayer is a questioning, dare I say a deconstruction already underway. While apophasis relies on the negation of some positivity, apocalyptic is simple negation with no prior experience of the object. We discussed this earlier in Toni Morrison's *Beloved*, and Walter Benjamin mentions this experience in

Proust: "when time turns into something we have lost." This loss happens to us—it is not by our own design; it is a violent end of time. Doesn't one experience this every time one speaks? Derrida's point is relevant as well, that every time an exchange or interaction happens, it is inadequate to its purpose, and one arrives too late to know this.

If, as a North American white male, I wish not only to notice the crucified peoples of the world but to also help remove them from the cross, then theories of communicative action give assistance in devising mutual and pedagogical praxis. If quietist approaches help us recognize an inescapable responsibility, then piety may help a performance of this responsibility. As one who unavoidably profits from systemic and past injustice, it is necessary for me to be vulnerable to a real critical standard. The stigma of the past continually reforms the performance of non-contradiction as a sustainable standard for mutual coordination of action for peace and justice.

This is similar to what is called the "prior substance" of thought and action, to use Ricoeur's words. He writes, "I still see an incessant coop-eration in life as the essence of the pastoral act, as he writes; I can be open to the story, the history of others, each of whom is in question as a self. Then the question arises of my participation in the stories and histories of others, which themselves are open/closed stories/histories. Is not this kind of mutual exchange and mutual aid in the dialectic of openness and closure the essence of the pastoral act?"[9] Ricoeur points out that we are caught up in the sameness of others, characters within a larger narrative, while at the same time I may be still an author of my own plot. I have done little more than point out that this is true for prayer in everyday life as well. This "pastoral act" makes itself and G*d accountable to each other, questionable, responsible. Religion and prayer are no exception to the tension of *ipse* and *idem*, and may be the best example of how beings are caught within this tension. Prayer engages a tension within cultural memory that is available to constant criticism; also an attention to oneself as another without succumbing to a leveling or mystification of the communicative act.

Multiculturalism is addressed today by diverse sources; from critics like Neil Postman, who write that a larger narrative and shared purpose is lost by the hyphenation of identities, to sociologist Jeffrey Alexander, who also criticizes this hyphenation of identity but for the reason that

9. Ricoeur, *Figuring the Sacred*, 314.

one side is often seen as more legitimate, more of an insider, than the other side of the hyphen. The language of the old-world is spoken at home while the language of the new-world is adopted in the marketplace. Along these same lines, I have theorized how changing times and violent events can cause one side of a hyphenated language to fall out of grace in the larger society. The worst genocides of recent history result from unstable hyphenations of cultural identity that turn to forced assimilation and worse, but also the act of communication is similarly unstable and always potentially coercive.

The distinctions between multiculturalism and the other two forms of social incorporation, hyphenation and assimilation, are most often worked out in prayer. Arguably, multiculturalism is a moral preference. It resists a choice about the status of human identity. The role of multiculturalism is that it "dramatically expands the range of imagined life-experience for core-group members."[10] This expansion of the imagination that contributes to understanding of others is a capability of prayer. This aesthetic education of a cultural memory may have its origins in an apocalyptical prayer made out of human brokenness, prayers that begin within and continue to listen to all the possible articulations of brokenness.

10. Jeffrey Alexander, *The Civil Sphere*, 452.

Bibliography

Alexander, Jeffrey. *The Civil Sphere*. Oxford: Oxford University Press, 2006.

Apel, Karl-Otto. *Towards a Transcendental Semiotics*. Edited and translated by Eduardo Mendieta. New Jersey: Humanities, 1994.

Ashley, James Matthew. *Interruptions: Mysticism, Politics, and Theology in the Work of Johann Baptist Metz*. Notre Dame, IN: Notre Dame University Press, 1998.

Assmann, Jan. *Religion and Cultural Memory*. Translated by Rodney Livingstone. Stanford, CA: Stanford University Press, 2006.

Augé, Marc. *Oblivion*. Translated by Marjolijn de Jager. Minneapolis: University of Minnesota Press, 2004.

Augustine. *Confessions*. Translated by Henry Chadwick. Oxford World's Classics. Oxford: Oxford University Press, 1992.

———. *On Free Choice of the Will*. Translated by Thomas Williams. Indianapolis, IN: Hackett, 1993.

Barth, Karl. *Anselm: Fides Quaerens Intellectum*. Translated by Ian W. Robertson. London: SCM, 1960.

———. *Church Dogmatics*. 14 volumes. Edited by G. W.Bromiley and T. F. Torrance. Translated by G. T. Thomson and Harold Knight. Edinburgh: T. & T. Clark, 1936–77.

———. *The Epistle to the Romans*. 6th ed. Translated by Edwyn C. Hoskyns. London: Oxford University Press, 1968.

———. *Evangelical Theology: An Introduction*. Translated by Grover Foley. New York: Holt, Rinehart and Winston, 1963.

———. *The Holy Spirit and the Christian Life: The Theological Basis of Ethics*. Translated by R. Birch. Louisville, KY: Westminster John Knox, 1993.

———. *The Humanity of God*. Translated by John Newton Thomas and Thomas Wieser. Atlanta: John Knox, 1960.

———. *Prayer*. Translated by Sara F. Terrien. Philadelphia: Westminster, 1949.

———. *The Word of God and the Word of Man*. Translated by Douglas Horton. Gloucester, MA: Smith, 1922.

Benjamin, Walter, and Theodor W. Adorno. *The Complete Correspondence 1928–1940*. Translated by Nicholas Walker. Edited by Henri Lonitz.. Cambridge, MA: Harvard University Press, 1999.

Benjamin, Walter. *Illuminations*. Translated by Harry Zohn. Edited by Hannah Arendt. New York: Schocken, 1968.

Blundell, Boyd. *Paul Ricoeur Between Theology and Philosophy: Detour and Reason*. Bloomington, IN: Indiana University Press, 2010.

Bolt, Robert. *A Man for All Seasons*. New York: Vintage, 1990.

Borradori, Giovanna. *Philosophy in a Time of Terror: Dialogues with Jürgen Habermas and Jacques Derrida*. Chicago: University of Chicago Press, 2003.

Browning, Don, and Francis Schüssler Fiorenza. *Habermas, Modernity, and Public Theology*. New York: Crossroad, 1992.

Caputo, John D. *Deconstruction in a Nutshell*. New York: Fordham University Press, 1997.

Castelli, Elizabeth A. *Martyrdom and Memory: Early Christian Culture Making*. New York: Columbia University Press. 2004.

Critchley, Simon. *The Faith of the Faithless: Experiments in Political Theology*. London: Verso. 2012.

Critchley, Simon, Jacques Derrida, Ernesto Laclau, and Richard Rorty. *Deconstruction and Pragmatism*. Edited by Chantal Mouffe. New York: Routledge, 1996.

Crossan, John Dominic. *The Greatest Prayer: Rediscovering the Revolutionary Message of the Lord's Prayer*. New York: HarperCollins, 2010.

Derrida, Jacques. *Deconstruction and the Possibility of Justice*. Translated by Drucilla Cornell. New York: Routledge, 1992.

―――. *Edmund Husserl's Origin of Geometry: An Introduction*. Translated by John P. Leavey Jr. Lincoln, NE: University of Nebraska Press, 1989.

―――. "Faith and Knowledge." In *Religion*, translated by Samuel Weber, 1–78. Stanford, CA: Stanford University Press, 1998.

―――. *The Gift of Death*. Translated by David Wills. Chicago: University of Chicago Press, 1995.

―――. *Limited Inc*. Translated by Alan Bass. Evanston, IL: Northwestern University Press, 1988.

―――. *Margins of Philosophy*. Translated by Alan Bass. Chicago: University of Chicago Press, 1982.

―――. *Monolingualism of the Other or the Prosthesis of Origin*. Translated by Patrick Mensah. Stanford, CA: Stanford University Press, 1998.

―――. *Of Grammatology*. Translated by G. C. Spivak. Baltimore, MD: Johns Hopkins University Press, 1976.

―――. *Of Spirit*. Translated by Geoffrey Bennington. Chicago: University of Chicago Press, 1987.

―――. *On Cosmopolitanism and Forgiveness*. Translated by Mark Dooley and Michael Hughes. London: Routledge, 2001.

―――. *On the Name*. Translated by David Wood, John Leavey Jr., and Ian McLeod. Stanford, CA: Stanford University Press, 1995.

―――. *Points. Interviews, 1974–1994*. Translated by Peggy Kamuf. Stanford, CA: Stanford University Press, 1995.

―――. "Post-Scriptum: Aporias, Ways and Voices." In *Derrida and Negative Theology*, translated by John Leavey, edited by Harold Coward and Toby Foshay, 283–323. Albany, NY: SUNY, 1992.

―――. "Remarks on Deconstruction and Pragmatism." In *Deconstruction and Pragmatism*, edited by Chantal Mouffe, 77–88. London: Routledge, 1996.

―――. *Spectres of Marx: The State of the Debt, the Work of Mourning, and the New International*. Translated by Peggy Kamuf. New York: Routledge, 1994.

Dodds, E. R. "The Parmenides of Plato and the Origins of the Neo-Platonic One." *Classical Quarterly* 22 (1922) 129–43.

Dosse, Francois. *History of Structuralism: The Rising Sign, 1945–1966*. Translated by Deborah Glassman. Minneapolis, MN: University of Minnesota Press, 1997.

Ebeling, Gerhard. *The Lord's Prayer*. Philadelphia: Fortress, 1966.

————. *Word and Faith.* Philadelphia: Fortress, 1963.

Feuerbach, Ludwig. *The Essence of Christianity.* Translated by George Eliot, with an introduction by Karl Barth. New York: Harper and Row, 1957.

Frege, Gotlob. *Logical Investigations.* Translated by P. T. Geach and R. H. Stoothoff. New Haven, CN: Yale University Press, 1977.

Fricker, Miranda. *Epistemic Injustice: Power and the Ethics of Knowing.* Oxford: Oxford University Press, 2010.

Garver, Newton, and Seung-Chong Lee. *Derrida and Wittgenstein.* Philadelphia: Temple University Press, 1994.

Gibbs, Robert. *Suffering Religion.* New York: Routledge, 2002.

Habermas, Jürgen. *Between Facts and Norms: Contributions to a Theory of Law and Democracy,* translated by William Rehg. Cambridge: MIT, 1996.

————. *Communication and the Evolution of Society.* Translated by Thomas McCarthy. Boston: Beacon, 1979.

————. "Communicative Freedom and Negative Theology." In *Kierkegaard and Post/Modernity,* edited by Martin J. Matustik and Merold Westphal, 182–98. Bloomington, IN: Indiana University Press, 1995.

————. "The Conflict of Beliefs: Karl Jaspers and the Clash of Cultures." In *The Liberating Power of Symbols: Philosophical Essays,* translated by Peter Dews, 330–44. Cambridge: MIT, 2001.

————. *The Inclusion of the Other: Studies in Political Theory.* Translated by Ciaran Cronin. Cambridge: MIT, 1998.

————. *Justification and Application: Remarks on Discourse Ethics.* Translated by Ciaran P. Cronin. Cambridge: MIT, 1993.

————. *Moral Consciousness and Communicative Action.* Translated by Christian Lenhardt. Cambridge: MIT, 1990.

————. *On the Pragmatics of Communication.* Translated by Thomas McCarthy. Cambridge: MIT, 1998.

————. *Philosophical Discourse of Modernity.* Translated by Frederick G. Lawrence. Cambridge: MIT, 1987.

————. *Postmetaphysical Thinking.* Translated by William Mark Hohengarten. Cambridge: MIT, 1992.

————. *Religion and Rationality.* Edited and translated by Eduardo Mendieta. Cambridge: MIT, 2002.

————. "Remarks on Hegel's Jena Philosophy of Mind." In *Theory and Practice,* edited by John Viertel, 142–69. Boston: Beacon, 1974.

————. "A Reply to My Critics." In *Habermas: Critical Debates,* edited by John B. Thompson and David Held, 219–83. London: Macmillan, 1982.

————. *Theory of Communicative Action.* Translated by Thomas McCarthy. Boston: Beacon, 1984.

————. "Transcendence from Within, Transcendence In This World." In *Habermas, Modernity, and Public Theology,* edited by Francis Schussler-Fiorenza, 226–50. New York: Crossroad, 1992.

Hardin, Garrett. "The Tragedy of the Commons." *Science* 162 (December 13, 1968) 1243–48.

Hegel, G. W. F. *Lectures on the Philosophy of Religion.* Peter C. Hodgson. Berkeley, CA: University of California Press, 1988.

Heidegger, Martin. *On the Way to Language.* Translated by D. Hertz. New York: Harper and Row, 1972.

Jaffee, Martin S. "One God, One Revelation, One People: On the Symbolic Structure of Elective Monotheism." *Journal of the American Academy of Religion* 69.4 (2001) 753–75.

Janicaud, Dominique. *Phenomenology and the "Theological Turn."* Translated by Jeffrey L. Kosky. New York: Fordam University Press. 2000.

Jaspers, Karl. *Der Philosophische Glaube Angesichts der Offenbarung.* Munich: Piper, 1984.

———. *Von der Wahrheit.* Munich: Piper, 1991.

Jüngel, Eberhard. *Karl Barth: A Theological Legacy.* Translated by Garrett E. Paul. Philadelphia: Westminster, 1986.

Kant, Immanuel. "What is Enlightenment?" In *The Enlightenment,* edited by Frank E. Manuel, 34–41. Englewood Cliffs, NJ: Prentice Hall, 1965.

Keller, Catherine. *Apocalypse Now and Then: A Feminist Guide to the End of the World.* Boston: Beacon, 1996.

Lincoln, Bruce. "Apocalyptic Temporality and Politics in the Ancient World." In *The Encyclopedia of Apocalypticism,* edited by John J. Collins, 457–74. New York: Continuum, 2000.

Lowe, Walter. *Theology and Difference: The Wound of Reason.* Bloomington, IN: Indiana University Press, 1993.

Luther, Martin. *Commentary on Romans.* Translated by J. Theodore Mueller. Grand Rapids: Zondervan, 1954.

———. *Luther's Works.* General editor, Helmut Lehmann. Philadelphia: Fortress, 1958.

Malcolm, Norman. *Knowledge and Certainty.* Englewood Cliffs, NJ: Prentice Hall, 1963.

Margalit, Avishai. *The Ethics of Memory.* Cambridge, MA: Harvard University Press, 2002.

McCormack, Bruce L. *Karl Barth's Critically Realistic Dialectical Theology.* Oxford: Clarendon, 1995.

McFague, Sallie. *The Body of God.* Minneapolis: Fortress, 1993.

McGinn, Bernard. *The Encyclopedia of Apocalypticism Vol.II.* New York: Continuum, 2000.

———. *The Foundations of Mysticism: Origins to the Fifth Century.* The Presence of God: A History of Western Christian Mysticism. New York: Crossroad, 1995.

Medieta, Eduardo. "A Conversation about God and the World." In *Religion and Rationality: Essays on Reason, God, and Modernity,* 147–68. Cambridge: MIT, 2002.

Metz, Johann Baptist, and Jürgen Moltmann. *Faith and the Future: Essays on Theology, Solidarity, and Modernity.* Maryknoll, NY: Orbis, 1995.

———. *Meditations on the Passion.* New York: Paulist, 1979.

Metz, Johann Baptist, and Karl Rahner. *The Courage to Pray.* Translated by Sarah O'Brien. New York: Crossroad, 1981.

Metz, Johann Baptist. "Anamnestic Reason: A Theologian's Remarks on the Crisis of the Geisteswissenshaften." In *Cultural-Political Interventions in the Unfinished Project of the Enlightenment,* edited by Axel Honneth et al., 189–96. Cambridge: MIT, 1992.

————. *The Emergent Church*. Translated by Peter Mann. New York: Crossroad, 1981.

————. *Faith in History and Society: Toward a Practical Fundamental Theology*. Translated by David Smith. New York: Seabury, 1980.

————. "Messianic or 'Bourgeois' Religion?" In *Faith and the Future: Essays on Theology, Solidarity, and Modernity*, 17–29. Maryknoll, NY: Orbis, 1995.

————. *A Passion for God: The Political-Mystical Dimension of Christianity*. Translated by J. Matthew Ashley. New York: Paulist, 1998.

————. *Poverty of Spirit*. Translated by John Drury. New York: Paulist, 1968.

————. "Productive Noncontemporeneity." In *The Spiritual Situation of the Age*, edited by Jürgen Habermas, 169–77. Cambridge: MIT, 1985.

————. "A Short Apology for Narrative." In *Why Narrative? Readings in Narrative Theology*, edited by Stanley Hauerwas and L. Gregory Jones, 251–62. Grand Rapids: Eerdmanns, 1989.

————. "Suffering Unto God." *Critical Theory* 20.4 (1994) 611–22.

————. "Theology as Theodicy?" In *A Passion for God*, edited by J. Matthew Ashley, 54–71. New York: Paulist, 1998.

Morrill, Bruce T. "Book Review of Interruptions." *Theological Studies* 60.4 (1999) 776–77.

Morrison, Toni. *Beloved*. New York: Plume, 1988.

Murphy. Frederick J. *Introduction to Apocalyptic Literature*. The New Interpreter's Bible. Nashville, TN: Abingdon, 1996.

Nouwen, Henri J. M. *With Open Hands*. Notre Dame: Ave Maria, 1995.

Nora, Pierre. "Between Memory and History: *les Lieux de Memoire*." Representations 26 (1989) 7–24.

Obermann, Heiko. "Luther and Mysticism." In *The Dawn of the Reformation*, edited by Richard Kearney and Mark Dooley, 5–17. Grand Rapids: Eerdmans, 1992.

————. *Luther: Man between God and the Devil*. Translated by Eileen Walliser-Schwarzbart. New York: Doubleday, 1990.

Peirce, Charles Sanders. *Writings of Charles Sanders Peirce: A Chronological Edition*. Bloomington, IN: University of Indiana Press, 1986.

Peukert, Helmut. *Science, Action, and Fundamental Theology: Toward a Theology of Communicative Action*. Translated by James Bohman. Cambridge: MIT, 1984.

Rahner, Karl. *Foundations of the Christian Faith: An Introduction to the Idea of Christianity*. Translated by William V. Dych. New York: Crossroad, 1978.

————. *Hearer of the Word: Laying the Foundation for a Philosophy of Religion*. Translated by Joseph Donceel. New York: Continuum, 1994.

Ricoeur, Paul. *Figuring the Sacred: Religion, Narrative, and Imagination*. Translated by David Pellauer. Minneapolis, MN: Fortress, 1995.

————. "Memory and Forgetting." In *Questioning Ethics: Contemporary Debates in Philosophy*, edited by Richard Kearney and Mark Dooley, 5–17. London: Routledge, 1999.

————. *Memory, History, Forgetting*. Translated by Kathleen Blamey and David Pellauer. Chicago: University of Chicago Press, 2006.

Robinson, James M., and John B. Cobb. *The Later Heidegger and Theology*. New Frontiers in Theology. New York: Harper and Row, 1963.

Roth, Michael S. *Memory, Trauma, History: Essays on Living With the Past*. New York: Columbia University Press, 2012.

Rothberg, Michael. *Multidirectional Memory: Remembering the Holocaust in and Age of Decolonization.* Stanford, CA: Stanford University Press, 2009.

Schuster, Ekhard, and Reinhold Boscher-Kimmig. *Hope against Hope: Johann Baptist Metz and Elie Wiesel Speak Out on the Holocaust.* Translated by J. Matthew Ashley. New York: Paulist, 1999.

Schwarz, Hans. *Eschatology.* Grand Rapids: Eerdmanns, 2000.

Thucydides. *The Landmark Thucydides: A Comprehensive Guide to the Peloponnesian War.* Translated by Richard Crawley. New York: Touchstone, 1998.

Tracy, David. "Charity, Obscurity, Clarity: Augustine's Search for Rhetoric and Hermeneutics." In *Rhetoric and Hermeneutics in Our Time*, edited by Michael J. Hyde, 255–74. New Haven, CN: Yale University Press, 1997.

———. *Dialogue with the Other: The Inter-Religious Dialogue.* Grand Rapids: Eerdmans, 1990.

———. "Form and Fragment: The Recovery of the Hidden and Incomprehensible God." Palmer Lecture. Center for Theological Inquiry, 1999. Online: http://www.ctinquiry.org/publications/tracy.htm.

———. "The Hidden God: The Divine Other of Liberation." *Cross Currents* 46.1 (1996) 5–15.

———. "Theology and the Many Faces of Post-Modernity." *Theology Today* 51.1 (April 1994) 104–15.

Wittgenstein, Ludwig. *Philosophical Investigations.* 3rd ed. Translated by G. E. M. Anscombe. Englewood Cliffs, NJ: Prentice Hall, 1958.

Zaleski, Philip, and Carol Zaleski. *Prayer: A History.* New York: Houghton Mifflen Company, 2004.

Zizek, Slavoj, and Boris Gunevic. *God in Pain: Inversions of the Apocalypse.* Translated by Ellen Elias-Bursac. New York: Seven Stories Press, 2012.

Index

198   *Index*

Durkheim, Emile, 40

Ebeling, Gerhard, 26, 31, 116–17
Emerson, Ralph Waldo, 25
Eschatology, 29, 39, 47–50, 52, 76,
    79, 141, 165, 172, 186

Feuerbach, Ludwig, 34, 54, 55, 57,
    80, 104
Fiorenza, Elizabeth Shüssler, 47
Freud, Sigmund, 16, 22, 34
Forgetting, 16, 19–20, 42, 123, 132,
    162, 167, 168, 178
Foucault, Michel, 16, 187
Fricker, Miranda, 20

Gadamer, Hans-Georg, 13, 92
Girard, Renee, 23

Habermas, Jürgen, 7, 17, 43, 51, 65,
    85–120, 122, 123, 126, 131,
    134, 136, 142, 148–51, 158,
    171–72, 179–82
Hanson, Paul, 30, 47
Hardin, Garrett, 21–24,
Hauerwas, Stanley, 32
Hegel, G. W. F., 61, 87, 101, 148,
    149, 164, 165
Heidegger, Martin, 93, 98, 107,
    128–30, 135, 144, 166–67
Herbert, George, 35–36
Heschel, Abraham, 35
Historiography, 15, 26, 37, 53, 66,
    72, 79, 82, 164
Hobbes, Thomas, 23
Horkheimer, Max, 102, 119, 120,
    174
Husserl, Edmund, 106, 124–26, 128,
    137, 144, 181

idem and *ipse*, 8, 188
Inter-religious Discourse 19, 92,
    95, 115
investigare 28, 69, 78

Jaffe, Martin, 48–51, 82, 184
Jaspers, Karl, 90–96, 102, 103, 106,
    109
James, William, 34
Job, 44–45, 54
Jonas, Hans, 173
Judaism, 33–34
Jüngel, Eberhard, 57, 60, 62, 73

Kafka, Franz, 6
Kant, Immanuel, 60–61, 65, 80, 85,
    87, 93, 101, 112–13, 170
Käsemann, Ernst, 31
Keller, Catherine, 45, 47, 50, 57, 59,
    122
Kierkegaard, Søren, 34, 98–100,
    101, 104, 140, 164
Koran, 19

Lamentation, 34, 116, 158
Levinas, Emmanuel, 13, 122, 172
Lewis, C. S., 23
Lowe, Walter, 60
Liberation theology, 9
Lincoln, Bruce, 9
Listening, 5, 8, 10, 18, 32, 77, 93,
    106, 118, 129, 144, 147, 154
Lübbe, Hermann, 43

McAffee-Brown, Robert, 36–38
McCormack, Bruce, 63, 65, 72, 73,
    79–81
McFague, Sally, 67
McGinn, Bernard, 47
Marion, Jean-Luc, 13
Memory
    cultural, 21, 50, 177, 178, 188,
        189
    collective, 6, 16–18, 53, 76, 86,
        146
    remembering the Holocaust, 17,
        31, 91, 187
Merleau-Ponty, Maurice, 13